RESOLVING DISPUTES ABOUT EDUCATIONAL PROVISION

Resolving Disputes about Educational Provision

A Comparative Perspective on Special Educational Needs

NEVILLE HARRIS
University of Manchester, UK

SHEILA RIDDELL
University of Edinburgh, UK

With Allan Osborne, Charles Russo, Emily Smith, Elisabet Weedon and Paul Zoontjens

Routledge
Taylor & Francis Group
LONDON AND NEW YORK

First published 2011 by Ashgate Publishing

Published 2016 by Routledge
2 Park Square, Milton Park, Abingdon, Oxfordshire OX14 4RN
711 Third Avenue, New York, NY 10017, USA

First issued in paperback 2016

Routledge is an imprint of the Taylor & Francis Group, an informa business

British Library Cataloguing in Publication Data
Harris, Neville S., 1954–
Resolving disputes about educational provision : a comparative perspective on special educational needs.
1. Special education – Law and legislation – England. 2. Special education – Law and legislation – Scotland. 3. Special education – Law and legislation – Netherlands. 4. Special education – Law and legislation – United States.
5. Mediation – England. 6. Mediation – Scotland. 7. Mediation – Netherlands.
8. Mediation – United States. I. Title II. Riddell, Sheila, 1953–
344'.0791–dc22

Library of Congress Cataloging-in-Publication Data
Harris, Neville S., 1954–
Resolving disputes about educational provision : a comparative perspective on special educational needs / by Neville Harris and Sheila Riddell.
p. cm.
Includes index.
ISBN 978–1–4094–1925–9 (hardback : alk. paper)
1. Special education – Law and legislation – Great Britain. 2. Dispute resolution (Law) – Great Britain. I. Riddell, Sheila, 1953– II. Title.
KD3663.H37 2011
344'.0791–dc22 2011011355

ISBN 13: 978-1-138-27109-8 (pbk)
ISBN 13: 978-1-4094-1925-9 (hbk)

Contents

List of Figures

List of Tables

List of Contributors

Neville Harris is Professor of Law at the University of Manchester and is currently the Director of Research in the School of Law. He has a special interest in education law and social security law, has conducted a wide range of research projects in these and related fields, and is the author of a number of books, including *Special Educational Needs and Access to Justice*; *Challenging School Exclusion*; *Social Security Law in Context*; and *Education, Law and Diversity*. He is the general editor of the *Education Law Journal* and the *Journal of Social Security Law*.

Allan G. Osborne, Jr. is the retired Principal of the Snug Harbor Community School in Quincy, MA. During his 34 years in education he has been a teacher and administrator and also served as an adjunct professor of school law. He is a past president of the Education Law Association and the 2008 recipient of the McGheghy Award for lifetime service. He received his doctorate in educational leadership from Boston College and a master's in special education from Fitchburg State College.

Sheila Riddell is Director of the Centre for Research in Education Inclusion and Diversity, University of Edinburgh, and was previously Director of the Strathclyde Centre for Disability Research, University of Glasgow. After seven years teaching English in a Dorset secondary school, she undertook a PhD at the University of Bristol on the topic of gender and subject option choice. She moved to Scotland in 1988 and has researched and written extensively in the fields of education, employment and social care, disability studies and gender and education. Sheila has served on a number of government committees and was a member of the National Equality Panel which reported in January 2010.

Charles J. Russo is the Joseph Panzer Chair in Education in the School of Education and Allied Professions and Adjunct Professor in the School of Law at the University of Dayton. The 1998–1999 President of the Education Law Association, and the 2002 recipient of its McGhehey Award, he has authored or co-authored numerous publications including more than 200 articles in peer-reviewed journals; and nearly 40 books as author, co-author, or editor. Dr Russo has spoken extensively internationally on education law.

Emily Smith is a doctoral student in the School of Law, University of Manchester, researching the experiences of young fathers in custody and on return to the community. She has previously worked as a Research Assistant in the School on a number of projects, including prison based research on Black Minority Ethnic

Offenders in prison; training provision for young offenders; and, as assistant to Neville Harris for the Economic and Social Research Council project on special educational needs dispute resolution in England.

Elisabet Weedon is Deputy Director in the Centre for Research in Education Inclusion and Diversity (CREID) at the University of Edinburgh. Her main research interests are in the area of lifelong learning and social justice. She has been involved in research into the experiences of disabled students in higher education, the use of restorative practices in education and dispute resolution in the area of additional support needs. Current projects include an investigation of the experiences and outcomes for Muslim pupils, research into lifelong learning in Europe and learning in the workplace.

Paul Zoontjens is Professor of Education Law and Senior Lecturer and Researcher in Constitutional and Administrative Law at Tilburg University. He has written about a wide variety of issues concerning education law. His main focus is on problems of higher education, international and comparative education law and special education. He is a member of the National Education Council of the Netherlands.

Preface

The education of children with disabilities and or learning difficulties was, until relatively recently, a neglected area. In many developed countries, including England and Scotland, it was not until the 1970s that a duty was placed on local authorities to educate all children; before this, some children were termed 'uneducable and untrainable'. It is still the case that, in poorer countries, the majority of children receive no education at all. According to UNESCO, an estimated 98 per cent of children with disabilities in developing countries do not attend school.[1] The principle of including such children in education has now been reinforced by the UN Convention on the Rights of Persons with Disabilities (2006) and various other initiatives. Since the 1970s, developed countries have placed much more emphasis on the delivery of high quality education to all children with special educational needs, using inclusive settings if at all possible. Alongside the growing focus on inclusive education, since the 1980s, governments in many countries have sought to encourage choice in education as a means of driving up standards. School choice policies have been justified partly as a means of encouraging the active engagement of individuals and communities, and partly as a means of creating quasi-markets within the public sector. In the field of special educational needs, it has also been part of a wider ideological commitment to parental engagement as a means of ensuring a partnership approach to identifying and meeting children's needs. In order to secure such active engagement, and to ensure that parental rights are capable of enforcement and are thus meaningful, it is necessary to devise systems of redress and dispute resolution to deal with disagreements when these arise. This inevitably leads to debates about how formal such systems should be, and whether parents' and children's rights are best protected by judicial or non-judicial systems. It is particularly important at a time when parents' willingness to challenge decisions about their children's special education, particularly over its content and the setting in which it is to take place, has made this field one of the most dispute-laden areas of education.

This book explores the nature of the disputes that arise in the arena of special educational needs and the different methods adopted for the resolution of these disputes. The analysis covers four countries, the US, England, Scotland and the Netherlands. Each of these countries varies in relation to the proportion of the school population identified as having special educational needs, the extent to which these children are educated in mainstream schools and the type of redress mechanisms which are used. The US appears to have the most litigious system,

1 http://www.unesco.org/education/efa/know_sharing/flagship_initiatives/disability_last_version.shtml [accessed 28 January 2011].

with large numbers of parents seeking to have special educational needs disputes resolved through court proceedings or via due process hearings. England, strongly influenced by the US system, established a tribunal in the mid-1990s to hear appeals relating to special educational needs disputes. Over recent years, however, much greater emphasis has been placed on mediation as the best means of resolving disputes. A decade after the English tribunal was established, Scotland set up its own tribunal to adjudicate on cases involving children with additional support needs, but has also emphasised the use of mediation. Very strict conditions for accessing the tribunal in Scotland meant that it is used far less than the English tribunal or the court system in the US. Finally, the education system in the Netherlands operates within a very different historical and cultural context. The system is academically selective at all levels, with a large special sector, although recently there have been moves towards the development of more inclusive systems. Parents are able to use the courts to adjudicate on disagreements over special education provision, but few have done so due to cost and access issues.

By examining the approach taken in four countries to the resolution of disputes in this field, this book is able to address the following major questions:

- What kinds of disagreements and disputes arise in the field of special educational needs?
- What use is made of different systems of redress in different countries, in the light of their different educational and legal traditions?
- What are the upsides and downsides of judicial and non-judicial approaches to dispute resolution?
- Are parents' and children's rights equally well served by different types of dispute resolution operating in different countries?
- How effective are the various approaches in safeguarding citizens' rights in this field, and what are the lessons for dispute resolution more broadly?

The two lead authors have recently completed a major study[2], funded by the Economic and Social Research Council, into dispute resolution, including the use of mediation, in these cases. The findings are incorporated into this book and, we hope, will be of interest not only to people concerned with education issues, but also to those who are interested in the role of mediation as a dispute resolution mechanism more generally. We wish to express our gratitude to the many parents and professionals in England and Scotland who, by agreeing to be interviewed or by completing and returning our questionnaires, contributed so much to the evidence we were able to gather on the experience and perceptions of dispute resolution in this field.

The structure of the book is as follows: chapter 1 provides an overview of the nature of disputes and the framework of rights governing the relationship between

2 Dispute Resolution and Avoidance in Education: A Study of SEN and ASN in England and Scotland, ESRC grant RES-062-23-0803.

parents, children and state agencies such as schools and education authorities. In chapter 2, the different types of dispute resolution methods, as well as their respective advantages and disadvantages, are discussed, set in the theoretical context of administrative justice. Subsequently, chapters 3, 4, 5 and 6 explore the approaches to special educational needs policy and practice which have developed in particular national contexts, and their associated dispute resolution mechanisms. Finally, in chapter 7 we return to the questions outlined above in drawing some wider conclusions in relation to disputes over provision for children with special educational needs.

At the time of writing, as a consequence of the economic recession, there has been a retrenchment of the state in many developed countries, with a growing emphasis on privatised solutions to social problems. We believe that, to achieve justice for children with special educational needs and their families, it is vital to maintain a range of strong judicial and non-judicial dispute resolution mechanisms. Without these safeguards, there is a strong chance that the rights of vulnerable children and their families will be neglected, as public bodies struggle to balance the books. As to whether the increased opportunities for settlement of disputes in this field through non-judicial means, such as mediation, bring overall benefits, is open to debate. It could be seen as acknowledging and building on a tradition of negotiated settlement to disputes about children's special educational needs and it is clearly consistent with the increasing policy preference for proportionate methods of dispute resolution more generally. Yet there is an argument that it involves privately negotiated solutions to disputes which can present risks to social justice through the resource allocations that occur. We hope that the book adds new perspectives to this debate and provides a useful case study of the experience of using mediation and other mechanisms, including tribunals and courts, for resolving disputes. We also hope that in doing so it may offer lessons for dispute resolution in other contexts where citizens disagree with administrative authorities over key decisions affecting them.

NEVILLE HARRIS AND SHEILA RIDDELL

Abbreviations

ACTB	Advisory Commission on Admission and Guidance (*Adviescommissie Toelating en Begeleiding*)
ADB	Anti Discrimination Bureaux
ADHD	Attention deficit hyperactivity disorder
ADR	Alternative Dispute Resolution
AJTC	Administrative Justice and Tribunals Council
ASN	Additional support needs
ASNTS	Additional Support Needs Tribunals for Scotland
CADRE	Consortium for Appropriate Dispute Resolution in Special Education
CECSR	UN Committee on Economic, Cultural and Social Rights
CRC	Committee on the Rights of the Child
CRPD	Convention on the Rights of Persons with Disabilities
CSP	Co-ordinated support plan
DCA	Department for Constitutional Affairs
DCSF	Department for Children, Schools and Families
DES	Department of Education and Science
DfE	Department for Education
DfEE	Department for Education and Employment
DfES	Department of Education and Skills
ECHR	European Convention on Human Rights
ESRC	Economic and Social Research Council
ETC	Equal Treatment Commission
FAPE	Free appropriate public education
FTT	First-tier Tribunal
GALA	General Administrative Law Act
HCESAC	House of Commons, Education Science and the Arts Committee
HCESC	House of Commons Education and Skills Committee
HCWPC	House of Commons Work and Pensions Committee
HESC	Health, Education and Social Care
HLSCC	House of Lords Select Committee on the Constitution
ICCPR	International Covenant on Civil and Political Rights
IDEA	Individuals with Disabilities Education Act
IEP	Individual education plan (or individualised education program [US])
IPS	Independent Parent Supporter
IPSEA	Independent Panel for Special Education Advice
ISEA	Independent Special Education Advice
ISOVSO	(Temporary) Act on Special Education (Netherlands)

LA	Local authority
LEA	Local education authority
LGO	Local Government Ombudsman
LRE	Least restrictive environment
NAO	National Audit Office
NASDSE	National Association of State Directors of Special Education
Ofsted	Office for Standards in Education, Children's Services and Skills
PHSO	Parliamentary and Health Service Ombudsman
PPS	Parent partnership services
SAO	Senior assessment officer
SEED	Scottish Executive Education Department
SEN	Special educational needs
SENCO	Special educational needs co-ordinator
SENDA	Special Educational Needs and Disability Act
SENDIST	Special Educational Needs and Disability Tribunal
SENT	Special Educational Needs Tribunal
UNCRC	UN Convention on the Rights of the Child
UT	Upper Tribunal
VO	Voluntary organisation

Chapter 1
Grievances, Disputes and Education Rights

Neville Harris

Introduction: The right to education and the right to redress

Hugely important issues may be at stake when decisions concerning the education of children with special educational needs (SEN) are taken.[1] That there can and will be disagreement over such decisions is undeniable. That disputes will require effective and fair resolution is widely accepted. But questions arise as to the processes that are needed and how they should operate. In part the issue of how disputes should be resolved can only be answered with reference to the legal frameworks governing the education processes and associated administrative practices relevant to the decisions that are being challenged, which are explored in chapters 3–6 covering the different national systems. But there is also a need to reflect on the nature of disputes themselves and the framework of rights that help to determine the relationships between parents, children and state agencies such as schools and education authorities.

The fact that education is in itself the subject of a discrete fundamental right underlines its inherent importance. The recognition given under international law, not only to the right to education per se[2] but also with regard to the individual's right of preference concerning how and where education is provided,[3] reinforces and recognises the interests of each citizen in education. The perceived influence of education on the individual's social, cultural, mental and psychological development, as well as his or her future career prospects and social participation

---

1 The term 'special educational needs' is used here in a general sense to refer to all children who face significant barriers to learning due to a disability or other inherent cause of difficulty. There are variations in how such children are identified and how their needs are defined under national education legislation and systems, as discussed in later chapters.

2 UN Declaration on Human Rights (1948), Article 26; European Convention for the Protection of Human Rights and Fundamental Freedoms (ECHR) (1950), Article 2 of Protocol 1; European Social Charter (1961, revised 1996), Arts. 15, 17 and 30; International Covenant on Economic, Social and Cultural Rights (ICESCR) (1966), Articles 13 and 14; UN Convention on the Rights of the Child (UNCRC) (1990), Articles 28 and 29; Charter of Fundamental Rights of the European Union (CFREU) (2000), Article 14(1).

3 See, for example, the European Convention on Human Rights 1950, Article 2 of the First Protocol below and Article 26(3) of the UN Declaration on Human Rights 1948, Article 26(3): 'Parents have a prior right to choose the kind of education that shall be given to their children'.

more generally, means that the right to education may be regarded, in the words of the UN Committee on Economic, Cultural and Social Rights, as an 'empowerment right' (CECSR 1999, para. 1). As has been widely observed, it holds the key to the enjoyment of other rights of citizenship, notably political and civil rights (Coomans 2007, pp. 185–186; Fabre 2000, pp. 125–126; Meredith 2001, p. 207). The importance of the right to education itself is underlined by the principle that it is to be enjoyed on the basis of equality[4] and the way that it should recognise the socialisation and developmental functions of education. Those functions are reflected, in particular, in the obligation on States Parties under the UN Convention on the Rights of the Child (UNCRC), in recognising the child's right to education, to ensure that education is directed towards, inter alia: 'the development of the child's personality, talents and mental and physical abilities', 'the preparation of the child for a responsible life in a free society' and the 'development of respect for the … national values of the country in which the child is living … and for civilizations different from his or her own'.[5] Also recognised is the need for special protection for the rights of children with disabilities, including a requirement on states to ensure effective access to education and freedom from discrimination on the grounds of disability more generally.[6] According to the Committee on the Rights of the Child (CRC) (CRC 2007, para. 66), education for disabled children should be premised on the goal of inclusion.[7] This is now reinforced by the UN Convention on the Rights of Persons with Disabilities, which the UK has ratified and to which the Netherlands and the U.S. are signatories. It includes a requirement on States Parties to recognise the right of people with disabilities to education.[8] In realising this right, without discrimination and on the basis of equality, States Parties must 'ensure an inclusive education system at all levels and lifelong learning' directed to various specified matters including the 'full development of human potential and sense of dignity and self-worth'; respect for human rights and human diversity; 'the development by persons with disabilities of their personality, talents and creativity, as well as their mental and physical abilities, to their fullest

4 Equality may be provided for expressly in this context, as in Article 28 of the UN Convention on the Rights of the Child or by virtue of general non-discrimination requirements which may be applied to education rights, as in Article 14 of the ECHR.

5 UN Convention on the Rights of the Child 1990, Art. 29.1. See also the International Covenant on Cultural, Economic and Social Rights (1966), Art. 13.

6 Articles 2 and 23. See also the Salamanca Statement and Framework for Action on Special Needs Education adopted by the World Conference on Special Needs Education: Access and Quality, Salamanca, Spain, 7–10 June 1994 (UNESCO and Ministry of Education and Science of Spain).

7 The Committee (2007, para. 7) adopts the definition of disabilities in the then draft Convention on the Rights of Persons with Disabilities: 'Persons with disabilities include those who have long-term physical, mental, intellectual, or sensory impairments which in interaction with various barriers may hinder their full and effective participation in society on an equal basis with others.'

8 UN Convention on the Rights of Persons with Disabilities, Article 24.1.

potential'; and effective participation by disabled people in a 'free society'.[9] The Convention also calls on States Parties to ensure that '[e]ffective individualised support measures are provided in environments that maximise academic and social development, consistent with the goal of full inclusion'.[10]

Obligations of this kind have tended to operate more as declarations of fundamental values rather than enforceable rights, although the Optional Protocol to the Convention on the Rights of Persons with Disabilities, which the UK has also ratified, does provide for a right of individual complaint. With regard to the ECHR's right to education under Article 2 of the First Protocol (A2P1) (in effect incorporated into domestic law in the UK as a result of the Human Rights Act 1998), this right to has tended to offer few guarantees for parents and their children, especially with regard to choice over educational provision, other than in the most extreme cases where the right is limited 'to such an extent as to impair its very essence and deprive it of its effectiveness',[11] or where individual freedoms or equalities are violated, especially if other fundamental rights (such as those concerned with religious freedom) are involved. This has been the case both internationally and in cases before the UK courts (Harris 2007, ch. 2). A2P1 not only requires states not to deny anyone the right to education, but also requires the state when exercising its functions relating to education and teaching, to 'respect the right of parents to ensure such education and teaching in conformity with their own religious and philosophical convictions'. The limited effect of this obligation, in the light of the case law under the Convention, was summarised by Lord Bingham in *Ali*, an important judgment by the UK House of Lords (now the UK Supreme Court) in 2006:

> 'The underlying premise of the article was that all existing member states of the Council of Europe had, and all future member states would have, an established system of state education. It was intended to guarantee fair and non-discriminatory access to that system by those within the jurisdiction of the respective states. The fundamental importance of education in a modern democratic state was recognised to require no less. But the guarantee is, in comparison with most other Convention guarantees, a weak one, and deliberately so. There is no right to education of a particular kind or quality, other than that prevailing in the state. There is no Convention guarantee of compliance with domestic law. There is no Convention guarantee of education at or by a particular institution. There is no Convention objection to the expulsion of a pupil from an educational institution on disciplinary grounds, unless (in the ordinary way) there is no alternative source of state education open to the pupil …'[12]

9 Ibid.

10 Ibid., Article 24.2.

11 *Leyla Şahin v Turkey* (2005) 44 EHRR 99, at para. 154.

12 *Ali v Headteacher and Governors of Lord Grey School School* [2006] UKHL 14, [2006] ELR 223, para. 24.

The limitations of the right to education extend to children with special needs and disabilities, as illustrated by a recent case in England, *A v Essex County Council.*[13] It concerned a child, A, with severe learning difficulties resulting from autism, epilepsy, communication problems and challenging behaviour. When the boy's behaviour deteriorated badly, as he approached the age of 12, his parents were asked to keep him away from school for health and safety reasons. Some provision was made for A at home but no tutor was available. Meanwhile his medical and psychiatric needs were assessed, but this took eight months and thereafter there was difficulty in finding a placement for him. After 18 months away from school the boy was placed at a residential special school where he was to receive 24-hour provision at a cost to the local authority of over £200,000 per year. A claim was brought under the Human Rights Act 1998, seeking damages for the violation of A's right to education during that 18-month period in which there was a delay in getting his educational arrangements resolved through an appropriate placement. The court accepted that what had happened had been the result of the lack of resources available to carry out the medical assessment combined with the fact that a school place to meet the child's needs was not readily available. The court further held that in principle a failure to make sufficient provision for A while he was away from school could give rise to a violation of his right. However, the test would be whether the very essence of the boy's right to education under A2P1 had been violated. The court accepted that if significantly more educational assistance had been provided to him while out of school it would have mitigated the failure that occurred. However, the majority of the court considered that the parents should not at such a late stage in the case be allowed to pursue this alternative cause of action since it could not lead to any significant award of damages. Lord Philips said that 'A2P1 does not impose a positive obligation on contracting states to provide effective education for children who have special educational needs' and that:

> 'Insofar as a state's system of education makes provision for children with special needs, [A2P1] guarantees fair and non-discriminatory access for those children to the special facilities that are available. But if the facilities are limited, so that immediate access cannot be provided, the right of access must have regard to that limitation. Thus the right of access to education conferred on A by A2P1 had to have regard to the limited resources actually available to deal with his special needs. These caused the delay in catering for his special needs. In these circumstances that delay did not constitute a denial of his right to education.'[14]

This case, therefore, reaffirms the inherent weakness of the right to education under the ECHR. It means that regardless of the requirements of domestic law, the fact that a child with SEN does not receive the provision he or she requires will not persuade a court to intervene on behalf of the parents simply on the basis that 'there is not

13 [2010] UKSC 33.

14 Paras 81 and 86.

currently available in the system the special educational facilities that their child needs'.[15] The case illustrates the latitude accorded by the courts to governmental resource allocation constraints and policy prioritisation.[16] It builds on an established position in which, provided the action taken by the state avoids an unjustified interference with basic individual freedoms such as a freedom from indoctrination, individual parental wishes, even if based on a philosophical belief as to how a child should be educated, are unlikely to prevail.[17]

Thus we have the rather contradictory position in which education is recognised as a fundamental human right, but is a right that is very difficult to enforce. Part of the reason for this is the absence of firm international standards with regard to educational provision and entitlement, which are matters left largely to the autonomy of individual states.[18] This means that it is domestic law that dictates most of the education rights and obligations which underlie educational provision in the UK and other states. Moreover, even the ECHR does not seem to be greatly interested in the mechanisms by which education rights can be enforced. It provides, in Article 13, for everyone to have 'an effective remedy before a national authority' if their 'Convention rights and freedoms have been violated', but it has been unable to guarantee fully the right under Article 6 for a determination of a civil right via 'a fair and public hearing within a reasonable time by an independent and impartial tribunal established by law', because the courts have been reluctant to class education rights as civil rights due to their essentially public law character.[19] However, judges in the UK have recently advised caution in applying that restriction and, significantly, the European Court of Human Rights has now held that education rights *are* rights of a civil nature, as in any event are rights that are enforceable via a judicial remedy.[20] It

---

15 Ibid., at para. 92.

16 See also *Simpson v United Kingdom* (1989).

17 See in particular, *Belgian Linguistics* (No 2) (1979–1980) 1 EHRR 252; *Kjeldsen, Busk Madsen and Pedersen v Denmark* (1979–1980) 1 EHRR 711; *Valsamis v Greece* (1997) 24 EHRR 294; [1998] ELR 430; *Folgerø v Norway* appln no.15472/02 [2007] ELR 557. Often a factor is the right of parents to educate their children privately (*Kjeldsen*) or to instil their religious or philosophical values at home (*Valsamis*). In *CB*, Sullivan J noted that the parents could make alternative arrangements, albeit at their own cost, if they did not want their child to attend the prescribed boarding school: *CB v London Borough of Merton and SENT* [2002] ELR 441. Sullivan J held that although an order requiring a child with SEN to attend a boarding institution was prime facie an interference with family life for the purposes of ECHR Article 8 (the right to privacy and family life), it was justified (within the terms of Article 8(2), which permits interference in some circumstances) if the tribunal considered that the school put forward by the local authority, and no other mentioned, would meet the child's needs, which arose from bilateral sensory hearing loss.

18 See in particular *Belgian Lingustics*.

19 Applying *Simpson v United Kingdom* (1989) 64 DR 188.

20 *R (LG) v The Independent Appeal Panel for Tom Hood School and The Secretary of State for Children, Schools and Families* [2010] ELR 291, CA; *Oršuš v Croatia* appln no.15766/03 [2010] ELR 445 (Grand Chamber).

could mean that an attempt, via a human rights challenge, to resist erosion of rights to redress in this field might now face less difficulty. For example, the UK Coalition Government's current Education Bill seeks to give effect to the Conservatives' pre-general election commitment to abolish the independent appeal panels that hear school exclusion appeals and replace them with 'review panels' with lesser powers. The joint committee on Human Rights has concluded that this reform effectively reducing a right of redress would not be compatible with the ECHR notwithstanding the assertion by the government (DfE 2010c, para. 3.29), that the panels will be independent (Joint Committe on Human Rights 2011, paras. 1.35–1.43).[21] The Committee's view is that even though complainants could ultimately seek redress in the courts via judicial review, that process would not give an opportunity for factual findings to be challenged and that a proper independent appellate process is required. In practice, however, disputes within the modern education system vary so widely in nature that an array of different dispute resolution mechanisms, not merely appeal bodies which issue binding decisions, is accepted to be needed.

That education has a propensity to generate disputes may seem in itself unsurprising. It is a sphere in which a large number and wide range of decisions are made and disparate interactions between providers and users or recipients of the education services occur. Enormous tensions can be generated by their direct impact on the interests of individual recipients of education or their families, whose wishes may be in conflict with the resource and wider policy driven concerns of the providers and decision makers. This is particularly so in the case of decisions concerning SEN, as discussed in later chapters. Many of these decisions have significant legal consequences. Outside the above framework of international law obligations concerning the right to education, public educational provision is grounded at the national level in extensive legislative powers and duties on the part of administrative authorities, schools and professionals. The operation of the most highly contested of administrative procedures in respect of education are in this category, namely those relating to the determination of admission to a school, or a permanent exclusion from a school, or the arrangements for provision to meet a child's SEN; these are all areas of decision making which are subject to a right of appeal under statutory appeal procedures. Administrative action and decision making also operate under general legislative powers or through the exercise of professional practice. In some cases they bear on individual cases, as for example in the case of the imposition of disciplinary sanctions short of exclusion, the enforcement of school uniform requirements, the assignment of a child to a particular class or group, or the award or denial of free school transport. Those decisions with a more general and collective impact include school closures, the introduction of a new

21 Under the Bill, as drafted, the review panels would not be able to quash a decision to exclude a child and direct his or her reinstatement, but would only be able to recommend or in some cases order the reconsideration of the exclusion decision: Education Bill, clause 4, inserting the Education Act 2002, s. 51A. The constitution of review panels is to be determined by regulations.

school admission policy in an area, or the arrangements for a particular form of collective worship or religious education at a school. Conflict may also arise from the general behaviour of professionals and officials in their management of pupils in general or their treatment of individuals. Professional or administrative action that, for example, involves poor communication, discourteous treatment, delayed action or administrative incompetence may generate considerable dissatisfaction among those affected by it, even if it is arguably less fundamental to a child's welfare and development than the examples cited earlier.

Education decisions are thus viewable, both objectively and subjectively, as very important to those affected by them regardless of the degree of legal weight that may be attachable to them. Due to the fact that many parents are likely to be conscious of the risks arising from disadvantageous decisions or treatment, education decisions are particularly liable to be contested. Even though the evidence in the UK suggests that among those who rely on them there is in general broad satisfaction with schools and universities (Ivens 2008; HEFCE 2010), it is highly likely that at some point during a child's many years in the education system or a student's three or more years at university a grievance will arise, given the fact that even those who are broadly satisfied with provision made can 'easily' identify faults (Ofsted 2007, Annex para. 1). In the 1970s and 1980s, the emergence of a rights culture in many states, whether grounded in constitutional law or, as is the case in the UK, through the introduction of a quasi-market in schooling and an attempt to transform the balance of power over education by moving power away from local authorities and teachers and towards parents as 'consumers', increased the importance of redress. There was a growing awareness of the possibility of challenging education decisions. It was accompanied by the introduction of new mechanisms, including some of the appeal process discussed in this book, a process which has continued. Many local authority respondents to the ESRC research in England thought that the availability of these mechanisms may in fact play a role in generating disputes about SEN in the first place, because their existence may encourage parents to challenge decisions with which they disagree. In summary, greater parental sensitivity to education decisions, closer parental engagement with aspects of their children's education, and the conferment of important new procedural rights seem to have precipitated a greater willingness to challenge decisions and actions perceived to threaten what were perceived as legitimate interests. The place of rights of redress as a facet of consumerism is discussed further in chapter 2.

Today, as discussed in later chapters, there are large numbers of cases involving the use of complaints, appeals or other mechanisms such as court action arising in connection with education. Nevertheless, they may merely represent the tip of the iceberg. Research has clearly indicated that for a whole variety of reasons some people with a grievance against a public authority do not invoke the processes for securing redress that are open to them (e.g. Adler et al. 2006, p. 11; see also Genn 1999; Harris et al. 2000; Adler and Gulland 2003; Genn et al. 2006). Cowan and Halliday (2003, p. 203) declare that 'understanding individual micro decisions about whether to engage in a dispute is a complex business'. Factors such as the advice people receive and the quality of their relations with the public authority in question may be influential, as discussed in chapter 3. In the field of education parents may adopt an alternative strategy such as to withdraw a child from a school whose provision they are unhappy with rather than bring a challenge (Ofsted 2007). Parental reluctance to bring a challenge may also be borne out of a concern not to damage their continuing relationship with their child's school and to avoid any repercussions for their child (Goriely and Williams 1997, p. 32). Even if grievances are raised they will often be resolved without invoking formal redress processes. For example, the UK's DCSF (as it then was) noted that '[m]ost parental concerns about their child's school are quickly and effectively settled informally by school staff' and '[c]omparatively few complaints reach the formal stage of being considered by the [school's] governing body and the majority of these are resolved satisfactorily' (DCSF 2008, paras 8 and 9). Moreover, as noted in chapters 3 and 4, many individual grievances concerning SEN or ASN are resolved through negotiation between parents (often aided by a third party such as parent partnership services or voluntary services) and local authorities.

The nature of grievances and disputes

Even in a single field such as SEN the subject matter of disagreements can vary widely, but the notion of a 'dispute' is a unifying concept for describing the conflict between the respective parties. In basic terms, disputes, whether between private individuals or, as in most education cases, between citizen and state, arise out of grievances which in turn stem from perceived threats to the parties' interests (Lewis and Birkenshaw 1993, p. 16). But what precisely is meant by the term 'disputes' when applied in such a context?

A sequential model has been developed by Felstiner et al. (1981), which is cited in Genn's (1999) study of how citizens seek resolutions to their justiciable problems[22] and in Adler et al.'s (2006) developmental study exploring ways of characterising administrative grievances. This model asserts that an 'unsatisfactory experience' may be identified ('naming') as a problem caused by another, attracting blame ('blaming'). The problem may become a 'grievance' which may lead to a claim ('claiming') (Felstiner et al. 1981, pp. 635–636). If contested, the claim gives rise to a 'dispute'. Thus the more rapidly and conclusively grievances can be resolved the less likely that a dispute will arise. However, Genn (1999, p. 10) urges caution, because Felstiner et al.'s model is not applicable to every situation in which the individual experiences a problem: for example, '[t]hose who claim may not blame and those who blame may not claim'. Moreover, not everyone is interested in the

22 Genn (1999, p. 12) refers to cases where a dispute gives rise to a 'justifiable event'. Such an event will arise from a matter which raises legal issues regardless of whether or not it is perceived by the claimant as so doing and whether or not any potential action to remedy it would involve any part of the justice system. Genn's study focused on private law cases; but this definition is capable of broader application.

pursuit of a legal remedy, although Genn acknowledges in her conclusions (p. 254) that people are often keen to press claims which they believe are based on law and rights, it is just that they are often unwilling for various reasons to pursue legal redress in the courts. A similar critique was prompted by Kritzer's (1991) analysis of resort to litigation in tort cases, based around his 'developmental theory of litigation'. This involves a similar linear progression from injurious experience via perceived injury through to attribution of blame, grievance and claim and eventually to litigation itself (although most claims are settled). However, Lloyd-Bostock, who carried out a study of personal injury claims, found that Kritzer's staged progression is often not in evidence, with people entering the process at different stages and skipping some altogether (Lloyd-Bostock 1991, p. 430).

Either way, grievances are clearly pivotal issues, since the claims that may trigger a dispute will arise out of them. Grievances could be classified under a basic hierarchy that derives from the jurisdictional limits of the various appeal and complaints bodies in this field and their powers of redress. One may assume that if the seriousness of the grievance is judged with reference to its amenability to resolution under a particular defined process, such as a statutory appeal process, it would be placed towards the upper end. In exploring the possibility of working out a typology of administrative grievances Adler et al. (2006) consider that their amenability to individual redress is one basis for classifying them under a 'top-down' approach. This approach is based on distinctions made in the academic literature – for example, between grievances involving law and the exercise of discretion, or between those relating to outcomes (what people claim in terms of entitlement) and processes (how people are treated). But such an approach is problematic because it 'does not mesh well with the ways in which people define and describe the problems they have had' (Adler et al. 2006, pp. 17–18). The alternative approach, involving a typology based on individual citizens' perceptions of their grievance, described as a 'bottom-up' approach, is particularly subjective, but Adler et al. also find this to be the case with the top-down typology, since it is based on the perceptions of experts. Adler et al. broadly favour the top-down approach, albeit with modifications to reflect public perceptions of grievances.[23] This means that grievances are defined with reference to their identifiable characteristics – as, for example, being concerned with a decision considered 'wrong' or 'unreasonable' or a decision limiting access due to a lack of resources. However, Adler has acknowledged, when discussing this work, that '[s]ince grievances are often complex and can raise many issues, a given grievance may have several characteristics', and so 'the typologies are clearly not mutually exclusive' (Adler 2005, p. 294).

The perceived seriousness of the grievance, in the mind of the person concerned, is identified as a particularly significant factor in determining whether a grievance is

23 For example, the 'top-down' categories of grievances based on 'error of law', 'error of fact' and 'abuse/misuse of discretion/discrimination' equate with the 'bottom-up' category of 'unjust decisions and actions' and are modified to 'decision wrong or unreasonable' in the final, composite category: Adler et al. 2006, pp. 60–62.

acted upon and thus is transformed via a claim into a dispute. It may be judged slightly differently from the perspectives of the different parties. For example, it may hinge on the perceived potential consequences for the party concerned if it is unresolved. Equally, there will be a risk that if it is resolved in favour of one party it may set a precedent for other such cases. This is likely to be of particular concern to a public authority, but also perhaps of interest to the wider public, particularly if it is a well-publicised case which is perceived as a test case. It seems fairly clear that the more direct the impact on the claimant and his or her family the greater the likelihood of a challenge. Thus, for example, Genn (1999, p. 250) found that among the grievances to which people were most likely to take action were those related to children. Adler et al. (2006, p. 44) similarly found that perceptions of seriousness would hinge on the effect of the problem on the individual and their family as well as the scale and immediacy of the consequences. For the individual one of the most important factors in that perception is that there 'had been or was likely to be detrimental impact on what were seen as fundamental issues: health and wellbeing, education, housing and finances' (Adler et al. 2006, p. 44). Similarly, an Ofsted survey of parental complaints concluded that making an official complaint was 'not in the forefront of most parents' minds or likely to happen, unless it was a serious issue affecting a child's well-being' (Ofsted 2007, Annex para. 2). Several areas of education were specifically identified by Adler et al.'s focus groups as serious matters: the quality of mainstream and specialist education, safety (bullying issues) and welfare while at school. Their perceived seriousness stemmed from the way that they touched upon the individuals' personal wellbeing and affected someone close to them and vulnerable – their children (Adler et al. 2006, p. 45). This research therefore confirms the importance likely to be attached by parents to decisions and general treatment of both themselves and their children in the context of education. However, it does not point to ways of determining how particular forms of grievance should be dealt with, particularly in a case where more than one type of grievance might feature in the particular dispute.

A further issue that warrants consideration in relation to both the willingness to pursue a complaint and the choice of dispute resolution mechanism is whether the perceived seriousness of the unresolved grievance stems from its impact on the individual in question or on others and whether the claimant is motivated by the need to redress the former or the latter or a combination of the two. Genn (1999) found that the objective to attempts to secure redress in respect of a justiciable dispute tended to be that of securing an outcome directly beneficial to the claimant rather than to produce a wider social benefit. Similarly, research into school exclusion appeals found that among parents there were diverse reasons for pursuing an appeal, but the motivation was almost always instrumental, aimed at securing direct benefit: to achieve a particular outcome for themselves or the child, such as to convince the appeal panel that the child's exclusion was unnecessary, to clear the child's name or to ensure that any underlying mitigating factors in the child's behaviour at school were properly aired (Harris et al. 2000, pp. 136–137). However, other research, focussed on complaints against public sector health providers, found that claimants often had an altruistic motive, namely 'to ensure that what happened to them will not happen to others' (Wallace and Mulcahy 1999, para. 5.1). This approach aims to force the authority in question to learn lessons and respond accordingly rather than merely to offer the complainant a remedy to his or her grievance (see Lloyd-Bostock and Mulcahy 1994). However, often those seeking redress will be motivated by both personal *and* wider social objectives. Cowan and Halliday, looking at people seeking internal review in respect of homeless persons decisions by local authorities, found them obviously to be concerned with securing housing or more suitable housing; but for some who found their treatment 'undignifying or offensive' the motive was 'to expose this poor treatment and to call the bureaucracy to account' (Cowan and Halliday 2003, pp. 153–156). A right in England to make a complaint to Ofsted about the quality of educational provision or management at a school,[24] seems to be aimed at harnessing, or at least catering for, the more public-spirited motivations of some people who are willing to pursue redress. However, the fact that few parents have used this process is perhaps down to pessimism that a complaint may be a catalyst for change. In Ofsted's survey of parents there was 'little faith that a complaint from an individual could change policy or provoke any significant cultural shift in a school' (Ofsted 2007, Annex, sect. 2).

How far the perceived seriousness of the matter at the heart of the grievance influences not only the propensity to challenge the decision or action in question but also the choice of resolution mechanism as the dispute is established is another question to be asked. Cowan and Halliday (2003, p. 153), for example, found that internal review, as opposed to the complaints process, was the selected mechanism for redress among those motivated by their poor treatment, since it enabled the problem to be 'exposed'. It may reasonably be assumed that to a parent with a serious objection to a decision about the educational arrangements for their child the possibility of a binding ruling which may be capable of enforcement in cases of default, albeit via a separate court action, would be more attractive than an unenforceable mediated settlement. If one takes Adler et al.'s combined approach, one would see that such a decision would be in a similar place in the hierarchy of grievances whether judged via the top-down or bottom-up approach. However, the choice of redress mechanism in relation to it is influenced by a range of factors, and often guided by subjective perceptions, for example as to whether representation is necessary, as to the speed with which a resolution may occur or whether the process seems fair. Social and cultural factors, such as the influence of social networks, can also play an important part in choice of dispute resolution mechanism (Gomez 2007). Genn (1999, p. 252) refers to the 'complexity of the factors that influence choices about whether to take action, what kind of action to take, how much to persevere and when to give up'. Later chapters will examine the evidence on the choice of dispute resolution mechanism to resolve disputes about SEN and the factors influencing it.

24 This is discussed in chapter 3.

Disputes: The voice of the child

All of the disputes on which this book is focused concern children's education. The extent to which the centrality of the child's interests is either recognised or reflected in the arrangements for dispute resolution needs to be addressed. Over the years there has been within the UK a significant incongruity between the emphasis placed, on the one hand, within education law on the rights of parents rather than the independent rights of children; and, on the other, within the law relating to children more generally, which places children's interests to the fore and makes their 'best interests' the focus of decision-making forums, including courts.[25] One area that has been highlighted in this regard has been the right of the parent of a child with SEN in England to express a preference concerning the child's placement (O'Mahoney 2008); if a placement is named by the parent, the grounds on which it may be denied place an emphasis on educational and resource efficiency rather than the best interests principle. The underlying rationale to the subjugation of children's right to parental autonomy over education matters, namely that there may be assumed to be a unity of interests between parent and child and that children lack the competence to make decisions and must be protected from damaging their long term interests through inappropriate choices, has increasingly been found less than adequate. For example, it has failed to acknowledge the potential for conflict between the wishes and feelings of parent and older children, in particular, and evidence that parental choices concerning their children may not necessarily be appropriate. Moreover, it is acknowledged that more effective decisions may be made if they take account of children's wishes. The SEN Code of Practice, for example states that '[c]hildren and young people with special educational needs have a unique knowledge of their own needs and circumstances and their own views about what sort of help they would like to help them make the most of their education' (DfES 2001, para. 3.2.).

The UK has received significant criticism over the years from the Committee on the Rights of the Child and the UN Rapporteur on the Right to Education for its failure to accord sufficient recognition to children's independent education rights (see Harris 2007, pp. 48–66). Much of this has focused on the lack of guarantees for participation in the decisions and processes that affect their education. Strong arguments have been advanced by researchers with regard to the educational, social and psychological benefits of according pupils an effective 'voice', and various levels and means of participation have been identified (Shier 2001; Whitty and Wisby 2007). There has been a concern to ensure that participation accords

25 Article 3.1 of the CRC provides that 'In all actions concerning children, whether undertaken by public or private social welfare institutions, courts of law, administrative bodies or legislative bodies, the best interests of the child shall be a primary consideration'. Under s.1 (1) of the Children Act 1989, in England and Wales, when a court is determines any question relating to, inter alia, the upbringing of a child 'the child's welfare shall be the court's paramount consideration'.

with the state's rather broad obligations under Article 12 of the UNCRC (Lundy 2007). Under Article 12.1 States Parties must 'assure to the child who is capable of forming his or her own views the right to express those views freely in all matters affecting the child', those views to be 'given due weight in accordance with the age and maturity of the child'. The reference to age and maturity incorporates the idea of children's 'evolving capacities' – that children's normative acquisition of increased autonomy will be reflected in the gradual accrual of independent rights as their competence increases with age and understanding (see Landsdown 2005).

Under the law in the UK, participation and redress rights in respect of decisions about children's education have rested almost exclusively with parents and there has been little recognition of the 'evolving capacities' of children. The position in the UK has improved over the past decade, however (Fortin 2009; Harris 2009), in particular to give effect to Article 12. The opportunities for children to participate in complaints processes in England have increased, for example, as discussed in chapter 3. It may be seen as part of a more general trend in which a moral case has been developed for children's participation (Parkinson and Cashmore 2008, p. 9), based not only on children's rights but also recognition of the need for active and inclusive citizenship to extend to children (even if its official recognition is premised in part as a means towards the 'responsibilisation' of young people: Bessant 2003). As Fortin (2009, p. 315) argues, an approach to judicial decision making which failed to give serious weight to the wishes of children 'would be difficult to justify … to children who are being brought up in a society which constantly urges them to develop their powers of critical awareness and to act responsibly and independently'. Significant progress has been made in the area of ASN/SEN dispute resolution in England and Scotland, as discussed in chapters 3 and 4. In England, for example, the child currently is not a party to an appeal[26] but may attend and be permitted to give evidence to the tribunal.[27] As noted in chapter 3, however, the government appears finally to have accepted the case for change and in a very welcome development plans to pilot a right of appeal for children, and a right to bring a complaint of disability discrimination in their own right, in two or three local authorities with a view to a possible roll-out across England, having found the previous government's consultees on this matter to be 'overwhelmingly in favour' of such an independent right (DfE 2011, p. 56 paras 2.67–2.68). In Scotland, young people have various rights to refer matters concerned with a co-ordinated support plan to the Additional Support Needs Tribunal; an independent right to initiate a procedure known as 'independent adjudication'; and a right to access mediation arrangements.[28] The ESRC research in England and Scotland

26 *S v Special Educational Needs Tribunal and the City of Westminster* [1996] ELR 228, CA.

27 First-tier Tribunal (Health, Education and Social Care Chamber Rules) 2008 (SI 2008/2699), rule 24.

28 Education (Additional Support for Learning) (Scotland) Act 2004, ss. 15, 16 and 18 and the Additional Support for Learning Dispute Resolution (Scotland) Regulations

found considerable support for ascertainment and consideration of the views of children in SEN/ASN disputes, but it also confirmed that, in practice, children's participation in dispute resolution is currently uneven and rarely direct.

Progress in recognising children's right to be heard in relation to other processes concerning education include, in England, the introduction of a duty on school inspectors to give regard to pupil views.[29] Moreover, in England and Wales school governing bodies must invite pupils to provide their views on various matters and must have regard to them when carrying out their functions[30] and pupils over the age of 16 may now withdraw themselves from statutory acts of collective worship at the school.[31] In Scotland, development plans formulated by schools must include details of the arrangements for consulting with pupils and involving them in decisions about the school[32] and a pupil's views must now be taken into account (unless the pupil is judged to lack the capacity to express a view) in decisions concerning additional support needs or the making of a co-ordinated support plan.[33] Also in Scotland, education authorities have a general duty to have due regard to the views of a child or young person in decisions that 'significantly affect' him or her, taking account of his or her age and maturity.[34] This last duty, which is tied to the duty to ensure that education is directed to the goal of aiding the development of the child's personality, talents and mental ability 'to their fullest potential', gives effect to Article 12 of the UNCRC although it has been found to not be properly implemented by most education authorities (Her Majesty's Inspectorate of Education 2007).

Although the Article 12.1 requirement is meant to be applicable to *all* children, there is now also a parallel provision in the UN Convention on the Rights of Persons with Disabilities. Article 7.3 requires States Parties to:

> 'ensure that children with disabilities have the right to express their views freely on all matters affecting them, their views being given due weight in accordance with their age and maturity, on an equal basis with other children, and to be provided with disability and age-appropriate assistance to realise that right.'

2005 (SI 2005/501). Amendments were made by the Education (Additional Support for Learning) (Scotland) Act 2009 and the Additional Support for Learning Dispute Resolution (Scotland) Regulations 2010 (SI 2010/144) (as themselves amended by SI 2010/275).

29 Education Act 2005, s. 7.

30 Education Act 2002, s. 29B inserted by the Education and Skills Act 2008, s. 157.

31 School Standards and Framework Act 1998, s. 71(1C), as inserted by the Education and Inspections Act 2006, s. 55. In force in England from September 2007 and Wales from February 2009.

32 Standards in Scotland's Schools Act 200, s. 6(1)–(3).

33 Education (Additional Support for Learning) (Scotland) Act 2004, s.14.

34 Standards in Scotland's Schools Act 2000, s.2.

Although in some respects merely reinforcing an existing obligation under Article 12 UNCRC, by underlining the application of the principle within it to a group arguably at greater risk of denial of the right, this requirement goes further by imposing a positive obligation which seeks to ensure that disabled children are provided with sufficient help to be able to exercise this right on an equal basis to other children.

Article 12.2 of the UNCRC further requires that, for the purpose of the requirement under Article 12.1 to ensure children have a chance to express their views and be heard, the child must be provided with an opportunity to be heard in any judicial or administrative proceedings affecting him or her, either directly or through a representative or appropriate body 'in a manner consistent with the procedural rules of national law'. That does not, of course, go so far as to require the child to have party status in relation to any such proceedings. In the field of education, that status has under domestic law generally resided with parents, not only on the basis that most education rights are conferred on them but also because, as noted earlier, they are presumed to be able to act on behalf of the child and with the child's best interests at heart. Children's participation in the process of redress, where it is facilitated, is regarded not as a matter of the right of the child but rather as an important part of the evidence gathering process or as a means of ascertaining the likely effectiveness of a particular outcome, for example on the basis that a child's strong dislike for attending a particular school might increase the risk that it would not be an appropriate long-term solution to a dispute over school placement. This view is mirrored in the field of family justice, where, according to Parkinson and Cashmore (2008, p. 8), it is accepted in some quarters that 'decisions that people seek to make about children's futures … cannot be made without an awareness of how children themselves will respond to those decisions'.

There is considerable literature on children's involvement in family proceedings, including mediation (see in particular Parkinson and Cashmore 2008, chs 4 and 5, and Roberts 2008 ch. 10, for discussion of the literature). From the family research we know that, for example, children and parents generally favour children's involvement in decisions in order to have the child's interests acknowledged and because it may be conducive to better decisions, although some parents perceive possible risks that children may be manipulated, or be overly compliant with a parent's view. Professionals also consider that the child's view should be taken into account, but not all favour active participation in the litigation or mediation processes. In part this is for protective reasons to do with concern for the child's welfare if he or she is exposed to greater conflict or parental pressure. This is mirrored in the field of SEN, where there is a 'tension … between participation and protectiveness' in that while the benefit of the child's involvement is recognised there is a wish to insulate him or her from the stress of participation and to minimise the risk of the child suffering lost self-esteem (Frederickson and Cline 2009, p. 16). In the field of care proceedings, there has been found to be a tendency in the representation of children to be 'largely based on shielding them from the process rather than assisting them to participate' (Masson and Oakley 1999, p. 144). Also, there are doubts about the capacity of some children to make consistent or sound judgments. The issue of competence is seen by lawyers and judges as a critical factor in determining how much weight to attach to the child's view. Parkinson and Cashmore (2008, p. 120) note that lawyers' and judges' dominant view is that this matter would depend on the capacity of the child to make 'rational choices free from the influence of their parents'.

Similar arguments seem to apply specifically to mediation. However, Roberts (2008) identifies shifting professional perspectives on children's direct involvement in the mediation process. In the 1980s there was a belief that the disadvantages (such as extra stress for children, the inability of children – particularly at a time of crisis – to judge what was in their best interests, the potential undermining of parents' decision-making authority, and the difficulty confronting the mediator in balancing everyone's interests) outweighed the advantages (such as ensuring that the needs and interests of the child were focused upon). While these perspectives have continued, emphasis has come to be placed on consultation with children rather than their direct involvement. Part of this emphasis was on parents themselves consulting with children in order to be able to adopt more informed positions. Nevertheless, evidence has emerged that children find participation in mediation a positive experience (Parkinson 2006). This therefore suggests that a flexible approach to children's involvement is needed, as is encouraged by the policy developed by the UK College of Family Mediators on this issue (see Roberts 2008, pp. 204–205).

A similar view is held in relation to children's participation in mediation in special educational needs cases, which is discussed further in later chapters. As parents' perceptions of their child's wishes are not always accurate (Soar et al. 2006, p. 154) there is a case for hearing directly from the child, particularly since it is helpful for the parents to understand their child's point of view. But professionals also believe that it can have a negative impact on the child for the same reasons identified in the family mediation research (e.g. stresses on the child); and some believe the children may not always have an appropriate view of what is best for them (Soar et al. 2005). Hearing from the child, even indirectly, as part of the process of mediation in SEN cases is, however, regarded as important to ensure that the needs of the child are at the forefront of the discussion (Hall 1999, p. 37). The fact that the child in question will have SEN means that, in some cases at least, the child's competence to participate meaningfully may be even more in question. That competence, based also on the child's age and maturity, will have a bearing on the weight that is placed on the child's view. A further factor, according to a small survey of professionals, seems to be a perception that 'at the end of the day, it is the parents who have the dispute with the school' and they are responsible for the child; therefore, they should 'have the final say' (Soar et al. 2005, p. 39).

This raises an important question about the status of children in disputes about matters affecting them, such as education. The highly paternalistic position that education law has taken as regards children's legal capacity for self-determination in connection with choices and other decisions (see Meredith 2001, p. 206) has carried through into the mechanisms for dispute resolution. Although children are regarded as having an interest in such matters, they are forced to adopt the role of subject rather than actor in any conflict that arises over education rights. Theoretical concerns that children's inability to enforce their rights means that it may be incorrect to perceive them as holders of rights have been successfully challenged. There is indeed widespread acceptance among theorists that children are rights-holders. Nevertheless, there is an argument that parental autonomy over education decisions should prevail because 'respect for a child's future autonomy as an adult means preventing his free choice now' (see Fortin 2009, pp. 13–21). It is certainly the case that the UNCRC recognises (in Article 5) the rights and responsibilities of parents to provide guidance to the child in exercising his or her rights under the Convention and that in any event Article 12 (above) merely gives the child a right to be heard and to have his or her views given due weight but does not specifically confer a right to pursue redress. On the other hand, the Committee on the Rights of the Child has in the past criticised the incapacity of older children to bring an appeal against their exclusion from school or decisions concerning special educational needs and provision in their own right (Committee on the Rights of the Child 1995, para. 216; 2008, para. 67); and the rationale for the introduction of an independent appeal right for children in relation to SEN and disability appeals in Wales has included a specific reference to compliance with Article 12 (Welsh Assembly Government 2008).[35] Furthermore, children are entitled to bring complaints under the ECHR on their own behalf (Kilkelly 1999, p. 123). Also, there is a dominant opinion that any rights that parents enjoy in connection with their children are intended to enable the child's interests to be protected, as in Lord Scarman's view in *Gillick* that such rights exist 'primarily to enable the parent to discharge his duty of maintenance, protection and education until he reaches such an age as to be able to look after himself and make his own decisions'[36] (although age would not be the only means of judging such capacity). The child's interests would be the paramount consideration in the event of a conflict between them and the right of the parent, at least in relation to matters concerned with privacy and family life.[37]

---

35 Indeed, the Welsh Assembly Government has recently proposed a Rights of Children and Young Persons Measure which would require Welsh ministers to have regard to the Convention obligations when making policy decisions.

36 *Gillick v West Norfolk and Wisbech Area Health Authority* [1986] AC 112 and 185E.

37 This is the right in Article 8 of the ECHR. See *R (Axon) v Secretary of State for Health and the Family Planning Association* [2006] EWHC Admin 37.

This potential conflict between the child's and the parent's right, and thus, potentially, their respective interests, could be highly problematic in the context of dispute resolution. Take, for example, the position in Wales, where, in relation to the right of appeal and complaint in SEN/disability cases respectively, the child *and* the parent have each been accorded independent rights (Welsh Assembly Government 2009). The legislation provides that 'The child's rights are exercisable concurrently with the parent's rights'.[38] Children will also have a separate right of access to dispute resolution services provided by the local authority[39] and to independent advocacy services to assist them in exercising these rights.[40] Although it seems to be envisaged that children might need to exercise these rights only where their parent chooses not to do so or is incapable of exercising them (Welsh Assembly Government 2009a, para. 3.11), the legislation imposes no such condition. There is no competency test or condition, such as was mooted at the time this extension of children's rights was first proposed, but a child's claim can be brought by a 'case friend' if the child is not 'confident' enough to bring it him/herself (Welsh Assembly Government 2009a, para. 3.10).[41] These rights of the child in Wales obviously go much further than the situation in England or Scotland. It is clear that in Wales the realisation of the child's redress rights will not, in theory, be dependent on the parent's willingness or capacity to exercise their own rights of redress. The potential conflict between the parent's and child's rights is a disadvantage that is clearly seen as outweighed by the need to accord some recognition to the child's autonomy interests. However, it remains to be seen whether in practice many children would exercise their independent appeal right. In the responses to the consultation paper on this reform many respondents 'thought the complex nature of many of the issues would mean that it would be difficult for children and young people with SEN to have clear views on these matters and be able to express them' (Welsh Assembly Government 2009b, p. 6). It is therefore unlikely that many would initiate action, but another person (e.g. teacher or grandparent) might do so as a 'case friend'.[42] If the parent disagrees with such action that could make for a three way conflict.

---

38 Education Act 1996, s. 332ZA(3), as inserted by the Education (Wales) Measure 2009, s. 1(2).

39 Education Act 1996, s. 332BA, as inserted by the Education (Wales) Measure 2009, s. 5(3).

40 Education Act 1996, s. 332BB, as inserted by the Education (Wales) Measure 2009, s. 6(2).

41 Education Act 1996, s. 332ZC, as inserted by the Education (Wales) Measure 2009, s. 3(2).

42 The Explanatory Memorandum states that a 'case friend' 'could be, for example, a parent, sibling, advocate, teacher, or, in the case of Looked After Children (where the Local Authority has parental responsibility for the child), a foster carer or social worker' (Welsh Assembly Government 2009a, para. 3.29).

One of the strongest arguments for according independent redress rights to children that has emerged, and one that was highlighted by the CRC in calling for such a right (CRC 2008, para. 67), concerns the possibility that there will be no-one to seek redress if the child is in the care of the local authority – as, what is termed in England and Wales, a 'looked-after' child.[43] This is because the local authority is classed as the child's parent under education law and although the birth parents may retain parental responsibility they may be prevented from exercising it. There are approximately 60,000 looked after children in England (Ofsted et al. 2008, p. 35), of whom at least one-fifth (on the basis of the national average: see chapter 3) will have SEN. The merging of social care and education administrations of local authorities in recent years reinforces the argument that there will be no-one with sufficient independence from the local authority to bring an appeal on a looked-after child's behalf (DfES 2007, para. 4.4.5; NICCY 2008), thereby rendering the right of appeal ineffective, even though local authorities are, according to a government minister, 'expected to act as champions for the children in their care and as advocates for their needs in exactly the same way as a parent'.[44]

Conclusion

As we have seen, there is recognition in international law of both the right to education and the right of children with SEN and disabilities to receive provision that is inclusive and of equal value to that available to others. This recognition, while based on rights that are to some extent more symbolic than substantive given their relative unenforceability (except, to an extent, insofar as adopted in domestic law), both acknowledges and reinforces the importance of education to the future life of such children. The stakes in many decisions about children's education may be high and parents are liable to attach considerable importance to them. As a result, disagreement or dissatisfaction with such decisions is particularly likely, if it persists, to undergo transformation into a dispute. The rights that protect people's interests in education include rights of redress, which have burgeoned over the past three decades and which may have consumerist and/or constitutional underpinnings. They have a critical importance in a field with enormous potential for disagreement between provider and recipient of education services, where grievances are liable to be intense because they concern issues which strike at the heart of families' and especially children's interests. As the discussion in later chapters will show, however, the use of formal mechanisms is only one way in which education disputes are resolved.

Parental involvement and participation in their children's education has been encouraged and facilitated through national legislation, as discussion in later chapters will show. The right to pursue redress is a logical adjunct to these participatory

43 Per the Children Act 1989, s. 22.

44 Hansard, House of Lords Debs, col. 974, 23 May 2002, per Baroness Ashton of Upholland.

rights. However, the emphasis on parental rights and the far inferior position of children's rights in this context could be seen as problematic. The critical issue where children's participation in disputes is concerned will be whether their interests are properly protected. There is a broad consensus that the involvement of the child may be essential if that aim is to be realised. Moreover, the nature of the needs that the education that is the subject of the dispute has to provide for is such that without the child's involvement any decision may, as has been suggested, be less effective. The effective participation of children with disabilities and/or special educational needs may be more difficult to achieve than in the case of other children but is no less important. It is in the interests of equality that any barriers are sought to be overcome with a view to trying to ensure that, so far as possible, the former children will at least have the same possibility of participation as other children.

References

Adler, M. (2005), 'Constructing a Typology of Administrative Grievances: Reconciling the Irreconcilable', in Banakar, R. and Travers, M. (eds), *Theory and Method in Socio-Legal Research* (Oxford: Hart), 283–299.

Adler, M. and Gulland, J. (2003), *Tribunal Users' Experiences, Perceptions and Expectations: A Literature Review* (London: Council on Tribunals).

Adler, M., Farrell, C., Finch, S., Lewis, J., Morris, S. and Philo, D. (2006), *Administrative Grievances: A Developmental Study*, London: National Centre for Social Research.

Bessant, J. (2003), 'Youth Participation: A New Mode of Government', *Policy Studies*, 24, 2/3, 87–100.

Committee on the Rights of the Child (1995), Eighth Session. Concluding observations of the Committee on the Rights of the Child: United Kingdom of Great Britain and Northern Ireland (New York: United Nations).

Coomans, F. (2007), 'Content and Scope of the Right to education as a Human Right and Obstacles to Its Realization', in Donders, Y. and Volodin, V. (eds), Human Rights in Education, Science and Culture (Paris/Aldershot: UNESCO/Ashgate), pp. 183–229.

Cowan, D. and Halliday, S. (2003), The Appeal of Internal Review (Oxford: Hart).

CRC (Committee on the Rights of the Child) (2007), General Comment No.9 (2006), The rights of children with disabilities, CRC/C/GC/9 (Geneva: UN/CRC).

CRC (2008), Concluding Observations: United Kingdom of Great Britain and Northern Ireland, CRC/C/GBR/CO/4 (Geneva: Centre for Human Rights).

DCSF (Department for Children, Schools and Families) (2008), *A New Way of Handling Parents' Complaints about School Issues* (London: DCSF).

DfE (Department for Education) (2010a), *Statistical first release. Admission appeals for maintained primary and secondary schools in England 2008/09*, SFR 15/2010, London: DfE.

DfE (2010b), *Permanent and fixed period exclusions from schools and exclusion appeals in England, 2008/09*, SFR 22/2010, London, DfE.

DfE (2010c), *The Importance of Teaching: Schools White Paper 2010*, Cm 7980 (London: The Stationery Office)

DfE (2011), *Support and Aspiration: A new approach to special educational needs and disability. A consultation*, Cm 8207 (Norwich: TSO).

DfES (2001), *Special Educational Needs Code of Practice* (London: DfES).

DfES (2007), *Care Matters: Time for Change*, Cm 7137 (London: DfES).

Fabre, C. (2000), *Social Rights Under the Constitution. Government and the Decent Life* (Oxford: Clarendon Press).

Felstiner, W.L.F., Abel, R.L. and Sarat, A. (1981), 'The Emergence and Transformation of Disputes: Naming, Blaming and Claiming…', *Law and Society Review*, 15(3–4), 631–654.

Fortin, J. (2009), *Children's Rights and the Developing Law* (3rd edn) (Cambridge: CUP).

Frederickson, N. and Cline, T. (2009), *Special Educational Needs, Inclusion and Diversity* (2nd edn) (Maidenhead: Open University Press).

Genn, H. (1999), *Paths to Justice. What people think and do about going to law* (Oxford: Hart).

Genn, H., Lever, B. and Gray, L with Balmer, N. (2006) *Tribunals for Diverse Users* (London: Department for Constitutional Affairs).

Gillie, C. and Hubble, S. (2009), *Apprenticeships, Skills, Children and Learning Bill: provisions for children, education and learners*, Research Paper 09/15 (London: House of Commons Library).

Gomez, M.A. (2007), *All in the family: the influence of social networks on dispute processing* Stanford University PhD thesis (2007) published online at http://sls-stage.stanford.edu/publications/dissertations_theses/diss/MAGomez-dft07.pdf [accessed 18 October 2010].

Goriely, T. and Williams, T. (1997), *Resolving Civil Disputes: Choosing between Out-of Court Schemes and Litigation. A review of the literature* (London: Lord Chancellor's Department).

Hall, J. (1999), *Resolving Disputes Between Parents, Schools and LEAs: Some Examples of Best Practice* (London: DfEE).

Harris, N. (1993), 'Local Complaints Procedures under the Education Reform Act 1988' *Journal of Social Welfare and Family Law*, vol. 15, no. 1, 19–39.

Harris, N. (1999), 'The developing role and structure of the education appeal system', in M. Partington and M. Harris (eds) *Administrative Justice in the 21st Century* (Hart: 1999), 296–325.

Harris, N. (2005), 'Empowerment and State Education: Rights of Choice and Participation', *Modern Law Rev.*, 68(6), 925–957.

Harris, N. (2007), *Education, Law and Diversity* (Oxford: Hart).

Harris, N. (2009), 'Playing Catch-up in the Schoolyard? Children and Young People's "Voice" and Education Rights in the United Kingdom' (2009) *International Journal of Law, Policy and the Family*, 23(3), 331–366.

Harris, N. and Eden, K., with Blair, A. (2000), *Challenges to School Exclusion* (London: Routledge Falmer).

Harris, N. and van Bijsterveld, S. (1993) 'Parents as "Consumers" of Education in England and Wales and the Netherlands: A Comparative Analysis' (1993) *International Journal of Law and the Family*, 178–204.

HEFCE (Higher Education Funding Council for England) (2010), *2010 Student Survey results for students in England* http://www.hefce.ac.uk/news/hefce/2010/nssresult.htm [accessed 14 September 2010].

Henry, J. (2009) 'Hundreds of complaints from parents about schools – but less than 2% investigated' (21 February), http://www.telegraph.co.uk

Her Majesty's Inspectorate of Education (HMIe) (2007), *Report on the Implementation of the Education (Additional Support for Learning) (Scotland) Act 2004* (Livingston: HMIe).

Ivens, C. (2008), *Survey of Parents in England 2008*, Research Report DCSF-RW041, London, DCSF.

Joint Committee on Human Rights (2011), *Thirteenth Report Session 2010–2011, Legislative Scrutiny: Education Bill and Other Bills*, HL Paper 154, HC Paper 1140 (London: The Stationary Office).

Kilkelly, U. (1999), *The Child and the European Convention on Human Rights* (Aldershot: Dartmouth/Ashgate).

Kritzer, H.M. (1991), 'Propensity to Sue in England and the United States of America: Blaming and Claiming in Tort Cases', *Journal of Law and Society*, 18(4), 400–427.

Landsdown, G. (2005), *The Evolving Capacities of the Child* (Florence: UNICEF).

Lewis, N. and Birkenshaw, P. (1993), *When Citizens Complain. Reforming Justice and Administration* (Buckingham: Open University Press).

Lloyd-Bostock, S. (1991), 'Propensity to Sue in England and the United States of America: The Role of Attribution Processes. A Comment on Kritzer', *Journal of Law and Society*, 18(4), 428–430.

Lloyd-Bostock, S. and Mulcahy, L. (1994), 'The Social Psychology of making and Responding to Hospital Complaints: An Account of the Complaint Process', *Law and Policy*, 16, 123–300.

Lundy, L. (2007), '"Voice" is not enough: conceptualizing Article 12 of the United Nations Convention on the Rights of the Child', *British Educational Research Journal*, 33(6), 927–942.

Masson, J. and Oakley, M.W. (1999), *Out of Hearing. Representing Children in Care Proceedings* (Chichester: Wiley).

Meredith, P. (2001), 'Children's rights in education', in J. Fionda (ed.), *Legal Concepts of Childhood* (Oxford, Hart, 2001), pp. 203–222.

NICCY (2008), *Who Speaks for Us? Review of Advocacy Arrangements for Disabled Children and Young People with Complex Needs* (Belfast: NICCY).

Ofsted (2007), *Parental complaints: report on the consultation responses*, ref 070166 (London: Ofsted).

Ofsted (2008), *Safeguarding Children. The third joint chief inspectors' report on safeguarding children* (London: Ofsted).

O'Mahoney, C. (2008), 'Special educational needs: balancing the interests of children and parents in the statementing process', *C.F.L.Q.*, 20(2), 199–218.

Parkinson, P. and Cashmore, J. (2008), *The Voice of a Child in Family Disputes* (Oxford: OUP).

Parkinson, L. (2006) 'In practice: ADR professional – child inclusive family mediation', *Family Law,* 36, 483–488.

Roberts, M. (2008), *Mediation in Family Disputes. Principles of Practice* (3rd edn) (Aldershot: Ashgate).

Shier, H. (2001), 'Pathways to participation: openings, opportunities and obligations – a new model for enhancing children's participation in decision-making', *Children and Society,* 15, 107–117.

Soar, K., Burke, K., Herbst, K. and Gersch, I. (2005), 'Pupil involvement in special educational needs disagreement resolution: some perceived barriers to including children in mediation', *British journal of special education,* 32 (1), 35–41.

Soar, K., Gersch, I. and Lawrence, J. (2006), 'Pupil involvement in special educational needs disagreement resolution: a parental perspective', *Support for learning,* 21 (3), 149–155.

Tribunals Service (2008), *First-tier Tribunal – Health, Education and Social Care Chamber, Special Educational Needs and Disability, Statistical Information 2007–2008* http://www.sendist.gov.uk/Documents/Publications/AnnualReports/SENDISTAnnualReport2008.pdf [accessed 15 October 2010].

Tribunals Service (2010), *Annual Report and Accounts 2009–10,* HC239, London, TSO.

Vermeulen, B.P. (2004), 'Regulating school choice to promote civic values: Constitutional and political issues in the Netherlands', in P.J. Wolf and S. Macedo (eds), *Educating Citizens. International Perspectives on Civic Values and School Choice* (Washington DC: Brookings Institution Press), pp. 31–66.

Wallace, H. and Mulcahy, L. (1999), *Cause for Complaint. An evaluation of the effectiveness of the NHS complaints procedure* (London: Public Law Project).

Welsh Assembly Government (2008), *Voices and Choices. A proposed right for children to appeal to the Special Educational Needs Tribunal for Wales* Consultation Document 051/2008 (Cardiff: Welsh Assembly Government).

Welsh Assembly Government (2009a), *Education (Wales) Measure). Explanantory Memorandum* (Welsh Assembly Government) http://www.assemblywales.org/ms-ld7759-em-e.pdf [accessed 29 October 2010].

Welsh Assembly Government (2009b), *Voices and Choices Consultation. Summary of Responses* (Welsh Assembly Government) http://voicesandchoicesresponses090122voicesresponsesen.pdf [accessed 29 October 2010].

Whitty, G. and Wisby, E. (2007), DCSF Research Report DCSF-RR001 *Real Decision Making? School Councils in Action* (London: DCSF).

Chapter 2
Dispute Resolution in Education: Roles and Models

Neville Harris

Introduction

This chapter looks at the forms and specific functions of the principal dispute resolution mechanisms particularly relevant to cases concerning special educational needs. It devotes particular attention to what has become one of the principal 'non-traditional' alternative formal processes, attracting considerable political and judicial attention, mediation. The arrangements for dispute resolution operating in various national jurisdictions are discussed in detail in chapters 3–6, including their historical background and the legal, administrative and policy frameworks. Their importance comes primarily from the considerable potential for conflict between parents and public authorities over education decisions and the propensity for transformation of dissatisfaction and disagreement in this context to disputes, as discussed in the previous chapter. The various dispute resolution mechanisms have discrete roles (albeit with some overlap) in terms of handling specific forms of grievance and providing different remedies to complainants. Yet they can also be seen as having a broader collective function in this field. As discussed below, the ends served by dispute resolution in this area of governance, and indeed other areas, go beyond the traditional constitutional function of redress mechanisms, most notably courts and tribunals, in providing a check on executive power through accountability for unlawful action.

It is important also to consider how far dispute resolution mechanisms might be capable of reflecting the purposes and values that might be expected of them. This brings into play the important concept of administrative justice, which hangs in particular on the quality and effectiveness of both internal administrative decision making processes and external accountability mechanisms, as measured by their capacity for procedural fairness and the delivery of substantive justice in their decisions (Adler 2010b) (see below).

The role and functions of dispute resolution

A system for dispute resolution may be regarded as having both private and wider public purposes. Referring to civil justice, for example, Genn (2010, pp. 16–17) explains that there is a private function of 'providing peaceful, authoritative and coercive termination of disputes between citizens, companies and public bodies' and a public purpose of serving the interests of 'social justice, economic stability and social order', for example by reinforcing particular social values to do with fairness or maintenance of the rule of law. Within the field of education, dispute resolution may be seen as having a key role in finding the limits to individual substantive rights and power in specific circumstances where there is a clash of interests, seeking to balance the relevant interests in a way that is consistent with the law. However, the interests that are bound up in individual decisions go beyond those of the individual parties, who, in relation to education matters, for the most part will be the state – in the form of a publicly funded school or local or central authority – and a child and his or her parents or a group of individuals. Public authorities are also responsible for their decisions and actions to citizens in general. Education decisions will frequently be about, or will have an effect on, the allocation of public resources. This is particularly true of decisions about the education of children with learning difficulties and disabilities. Decisions may affect specific individuals but may also impact indirectly on the interests of others in the potential allocation of resources to them. Moreover, the public in general will have an interest in the implementation of the general policy surrounding the operation of public services and in ensuring that decisions by public authorities are taken fairly, rationally and in accordance with the law. Dispute resolution bodies may therefore be variously expected to provide a means for safeguarding such interests. Courts, through the process of judicial review in the UK and the constitutional or administrative courts found in many other jurisdictions, might represent the paradigm for this purpose, but within the general administrative and legal frameworks governing state provision 'different mechanisms are employed to hold public authorities accountable in different ways' (Woolf et al. 1999, p. 4). Ombudsmen, for example, are seen as having a constitutional role as part of a network of governance and accountability mechanisms for public authorities, provided they are valued by democratic institutions such as Parliament, have sufficient independence and are accountable themselves (Buck et al. 2011, pp. 230–231). As discussed below, one of the concerns about mediation is that it is a process designed to find a settlement between the individual parties and does not properly embrace this wider public accountability function. There is scope for debate over whether the availability of some of the non-traditional or alternative dispute resolution (ADR) mechanisms, such as mediation and conciliation, has served to protect or weaken the constitutional safeguards that redress is traditionally regarded as providing.

There is also a sense in which the ability to secure redress of grievance and hold the state to account provides a degree of empowerment to the individual. It has arguably been reinforced through the extension of opportunities to challenge decisions of public authorities via new and more accessible routes to redress. Rights to redress of grievance, in fact, fit within both of the principal conceptual frameworks used in defining the relationship between the user and provider of education and other public services: consumerism and citizenship. Potter (1988) saw redress as one of five elements of consumerism, the others being access; information; choice; and representation. All these elements are identifiable in the legal and policy frameworks governing state education that were developed in the UK, especially in England and Wales, post 1980 (see Harris 1993). Education consumers, for example, acquired equal access rights under anti-discrimination law; were presented with information on a range of matters including school examination results as a result of duties places on schools and local authorities; gained opportunities for increased choice in the context of school admission and special educational needs; and as a group had guaranteed representation on school governing bodies and local authority education committees. Consumerism also emerged, to a lesser extent, in the education system of the Netherlands, although against a dominant background of freedom of choice as a constitutional right (Dijkstra et al. 2004) and with a less fully developed framework of redress (Harris and Van Bijsterveld 1993). The reforms to public services in the UK during the 1980s were intended to generate more efficient provision through the operation of a competitive market and to reduce the imbalance of power between providers and users of services by rendering the former more accountable for service quality. While public services have continued to be organised around a broadly consumerist model (Vidler and Clarke 2005), there was also, in the 1990s, a fairly deliberate attempt by government to shift the policy discourse partly away from notions of consumerism towards the idea of citizenship, albeit with an emphasis on responsibilities. Citizenship is broadly considered to represent a status arising from a relationship between individuals and the state based around rights and responsibilities, albeit that there is no fixed definition to this somewhat multi-dimensional concept (Lister 2007). It is said to give rise to social belonging on the part of the citizen and a right of social, economic and political participation. It recognises that users have a stake in, and 'ownership' of, services and provision. The idea that all citizens have an opportunity to participate in the shaping of services and thereby make those services more responsive to needs is said to be conducive to social solidarity, but there is also a contractarian form of citizenship in which the individual has more freedom to exercise choice and is intended, in so doing, to contribute to greater efficiency and responsiveness in public services (Dean 2002, pp. 187–188).

The broad distinction between the consumer and citizenship models is based on the perception that the consumer acts self-interestedly, while the citizen must accept responsibilities to the community as a whole. However, both models have similar elements to them, especially choice and, as discussed below, redress. The concept of the 'consumer-citizen' recognises this common ground and the fact that people can engage directly with services as a consumer whilst also having rights and duties relating to them by virtue of their membership of the community, as per the citizenship model (Woods 1988, p. 327). Wilkins (2010) has shown how in exercising opportunities for choice, parents may not merely act as self-interested consumers but in some cases be driven by a sense of community interest associated with citizenship, while in these and other cases they may also act in furtherance of a moral commitment to exercise responsibility for their child's welfare. Wilkins concludes that this 'complicates' the perceived dichotomy between individuals who act as consumers in the marketplace and citizens in the public sphere and finds that the parents (in the case of his research, mothers) 'inhabit and negotiate a number of intersecting and crosscutting positions, which resist easy categorisation' (at pp. 185–186). Similarly, another study found that, in relation to claims for welfare provision, people tended 'to exhibit an ostensibly contradictory mixture of guarded altruism and pragmatic instrumentalism' and, while largely predisposed to the basic ideology of self-interest and contractarian citizenship, would value 'key elements of the solidaristic or collectivist principles on which the welfare state was originally founded' (Dean 2002, p. 188; see also Clarke et al. 2007). Moreover, in a very interesting study of the consumer and citizenship paradigms in the context of the student–university relationship, Ahier et al (2003) found that despite the commodification and marketisation of higher education, students tended to have a sense of belonging and collectivity, of 'sociality and mutuality', more consonant with notions of citizenship than consumerism. As we also saw in Chapter 1, those who pursue redress are not always motivated by personal benefit but in some cases, especially when bringing a complaint against a public authority, may also have an altruistic purpose in seeking community benefit by exposing faults and thereby deterring recurrences which might adversely affect others.

Redress of grievance is embedded within these consumer and citizenship models. Under both models a person can utilise redress to enforce his or her substantive rights, which can be instrumental in ensuring the accountability of a public authority. In relation to consumerism, redress reinforces the aims of a marketised system for public services by ensuring that key opportunities for choice and participation are not wrongly denied the user and that his or her increased power is not undermined. At the same time, redress is also central to the civil rights of the citizen and is closely linked to the status of social rights, since although the latter are difficult to enforce (indeed that is something which has invited a degree of scepticism about their status as rights: Plant 1992, p. 26), their realisation in fields such as education and social welfare will often be dependent on the successful utilisation of a dispute resolution process, a facet of the interdependence of the different classes of citizenship rights (see Fabre 2000, pp. 125–126). The emphasis on individual action through the initiation of a redress process also reinforces the element of responsibility central to the participatory dimension of citizenship that has received ever increasing policy promotion. One of the problems with this aspect of citizenship is that some people face barriers to participation, due to educational or social disadvantage, that place them in an unequal position to others vis-à-vis the enjoyment of citizenship rights. Various forms of support may be necessary to ameliorate this problem. For example, there are local authority-funded parent support services available to parents of children with SEN in England, as discussed in chapter 3, and assistance from voluntary sector bodies. Another possibility recently suggested in the UK is a kind of integrated 'triage-plus' process involving expert advice to citizens on enforcing entitlement and selecting an appropriate route to redress (see Law Commission 2007). Since there are a number of dispute resolution routes that can be pursued, public confusion about redress mechanisms is commonplace (National Audit Office 2005, para. 1.35) and advice and assistance may be needed to ensure effective access; indeed, this could be of 'fundamental importance' according to Buck et al. (2011, p. 239).

The rights, as configured, relating to parental views or choices concerning their child's education, form part of the framework for the allocation of resources. A market orientated system in particular rests on the idea that consumer demand will be linked to quality, so that if schools are funded on a per capita basis (that is, on the basis of pupil recruitment levels) parental choice brings resources to the school. In the same way, if the parents of a child with SEN express a preference for a school placement that involves additional expenditure for the local authority, they are potentially contributing to the process of resource allocation, although the local authority may be able to show legal grounds for denying their choice. Where disputes over such matters arise, the dispute resolution body must of necessity play its part in the determination of how the resources are allocated. Clarke et al. (2010, p. 39) have explained, that in relation to the demand for places at schools which are oversubscribed, so that parental choice for all cannot be guaranteed, the 'appeals system can be seen as an example of the failure of choice policy and practice to cope with the allocation of scarce resources'. The fair and equitable allocation of resources is something that is expected to be a normative aim of public services, but cannot be guaranteed where school choice is concerned. Thus, as Clarke et al. explain (2010, p. 42), 'the logic of administrative justice is summoned to restore the promise of equity and fairness'. By virtue of the independence and detachment of the appeals process, the tribunal is perceived to bring a measure of fairness and objectivity into the decision making process.

Even so, and notwithstanding adherence to various principles of procedural fairness such as the right to be heard and to receive a reasoned decision, tribunals may not be expected in themselves to rectify unfairness in the policy itself. The dispute resolution body can in fact be seen to be playing a role in the implementation of the policy, even if that might not be regarded as its primary purpose, by interpreting and applying rules which embody it. Thomas (2011, pp. 285–286), for example, in a study of asylum adjudication, argues that tribunals 'operate as adjudicatory mechanisms in the implementation of public policy' and that they serve an instrumental purpose, through adjudication, in furthering the realisation of policy goals. There is also an argument that the presence of a tribunal or other dispute resolution body brings increased legitimacy not only to decision-making by government agencies (Cane 2009, p. 215), by enabling unfair decisions to be corrected, but also to the policy in question; and it may be perceived to temper the policy's harsh effects, making it more 'palatable' (Prosser 1977, p. 44). On that basis, the use of a specialist panel for particular types of case, operating an objectively fair process that conforms to normative procedural expectations, becomes not so much a means of giving citizens confidence that their case will be dealt with expertly but rather as a means of generating greater acceptance of disadvantageous outcomes under policies which are incapable of satisfying every complainant's expectations. Especially where the law is tightly drafted and entitlements are predominantly rule based, tribunals have little scope for adapting policy but are placed in the position of having 'to decide whether the regulations have been applied correctly by officials, not whether justice has been done in the individual case' (Baldwin et al. 1992, p. 212). However, as the discussion in chapters 3 and 4 shows, the law of special educational needs is generally not tautly worded and leaves quite a wide scope for the exercise of discretion, albeit that in England and Scotland the policy is spelled out in official guidance and codes of practice to which the appeal tribunal must have regard.

The idea that dispute resolution has broader or secondary aims and a wide public purpose can also be seen in the way that it can impact on public administration. Adjudication via judicial review or other forms of litigation or in second-tier appeal bodies can provide declarations of law that ought to influence first-tier tribunals and decision makers, even though this cannot be guaranteed in practice and, where it does, the impact may be quite subtle and difficult to measure (e.g. Hertogh and Halliday 2004; Buck et al. 2005). Even first-tier tribunal decisions may be able to influence the way that some local decision makers approach their task (Baldwin et al. 1992, p. 88), although Adler (2010a, p. 415) finds their decisions to have a 'rather limited impact' in that respect and, as a consequence, views such tribunals as a 'not particularly effective' means of enhancing the quality of administrators' decision-making. There has, nevertheless, been quite a strong push in the UK in recent years for the guidance contained in decisions by tribunals to be fed back to first-tier decision makers so that lessons can be learnt and adjustments and improvements can be made in order to improve the quality of initial decision making (e.g. DCA 2004; HCWPC 2010; AJTC 2010). This function of assisting public bodies to 'learn the lessons' handed down by the dispute resolution process is particularly relevant to complaints processes (Harris 2007; Gulland 2010), both internal but more especially external, for example those operated by the Local Government Ombudsman or the Office of the Independent Adjudicator for Higher Education in England. Buck et al. (2011, pp. 226, 229) describe this function of ombudsmen as contributing to the capacity of public authorities in respect of 'getting it right' first time when making decisions affecting citizens and as distinct from their main function of 'putting it right' for citizens with a legitimate grievance. This function of feeding back such collective lessons is one which mediation, at least as it presently operates, would appear to be far less capable of performing.

Forms of dispute resolution

The range of different dispute resolution mechanisms and processes for special educational needs cases reflects the diversity of grievances that people experience and the kinds of remedies they need. However, there has been increasing general recognition of the value of a flexible approach to dispute resolution so that, for example, where there is scope for the settlement of a dispute as it progresses, the case may need to be diverted into a process conducive to it, such as mediation. There may also be a way of identifying cases which have entered a formal process of appeal but whose outcome is entirely predictable, rendering adjudication unnecessary. A method that has been trialled in the UK in some kinds of tribunal case is 'early neutral evaluation', which is discussed below. The principal processes used for redress of grievance, and their typical characteristics, are also described below, followed by a review of the forms of so-called 'alternative' dispute resolution (ADR), focussing in particular on mediation. Issues concerning the participation of children in dispute resolution processes were discussed in chapter 1.

Complaints

Complaints procedures, internal or external, play a key role in investigating grievances about how people are treated by the administration, such as being misinformed, subjected to unduly delayed decisions or being subjected to discourteous behaviour by an official or professional. The kinds of consequences that might flow from such problems could range from inconvenience or severe aggravation or upset through to financial expense or denial of a service. The factors that influence decisions to bring a complaint were discussed in chapter 1. The approach followed in complaints investigation tends to be inquisitorial and often does not involve a hearing. Depending upon the process, remedies can range from an apology through to payment of compensation, but for the most part the expectation is that these remedies would only be recommended.[1] Complaints procedures are generally easy to access and are probably the easiest for citizens to utilise without assistance, since the complaints body (particularly an external complaints body such as an ombudsman in England or Scotland) is able to play an active role in requesting further information from the complainant and the process may not involve the complainant's participation in person, although this may also constitute a drawback. Essentially there is a trade off between the demands of procedural fairness on the one hand, and economy, efficiency and speed on the other (although not all processes operate quickly in practice, and they may not have embedded time limits). Thus there is not likely to be any kind of oral hearing nor, especially at the internal stage, is it certain that the complaint will be investigated by an independent person or body. Unfortunately, as discussed in chapter 1, there are various barriers to the use of complaints processes in education, including ignorance and the inhibiting effect of fear of prejudicing the child's interests.

1 See in particular the discussion of complaints in chapter 3.

Appeals

Appeals against decisions by first-tier decision makers will typically involve fresh consideration of the merits of a decision by an independent adjudicator or tribunal (often with specialist members, such as the First-tier Tribunal in England and the Additional Support Needs Tribunal in Scotland) or by a court, such as an administrative court, as in the Netherlands, where such a court holds jurisdiction over disputes concerning education in state schools.[2] There is some variation with regard to the incorporation of processes designed to foster a resolution of the case at an early stage. For example, as discussed in chapter 6, a resolution session or sessions will be convened in a school placement dispute case in the US to provide an opportunity for resolution prior to the scheduling of a due process hearing, which is the equivalent of an appeal hearing. In England and Scotland, as discussed in chapters 3 and 4, there is no equivalent stage prior to an appeal, although the First-tier Tribunal in England is now under a duty to facilitate recourse to alternative dispute resolution (such as mediation) in an appropriate case.[3] As noted above, one technique that has been piloted in the UK (using disability allowance cases and employment cases) is that of 'early neutral evaluation'. It involves a prior review of appeal cases by a tribunal judge with a view to sifting out those which are very likely to fail or succeed and which may therefore be capable of being resolved without the need for a full tribunal ruling. The idea is that the judge would contact the party who was very likely to lose the appeal and, if that person was the appellant, he or she could decide whether it was worthwhile to continue with the appeal or could try to obtain further evidence prior to the appeal hearing to support it. If the loser was likely to be the executive body it could reconsider the case in the light of the judge's recommendations. It was found, in practice, that while early neutral evaluation did contribute to a more proportionate resolution of cases it did not bring overall costs savings nor did it reduce the overall time it takes for disputes to be resolved (Hay et al. 2010). There is, however, a plan to adopt it soon in England in relation to appeals concerning a local authority's refusal to agree to a formal assessment of a child, as discussed in chapter 3.

An appeal challenges the basis on which the decision maker reached his or her decision as well as the substance of the decision itself – its appropriateness in terms of its consistency with the evidence and the law. The appeal body is likely to have additional evidence that was not available to the initial decision maker. For example, in an SEN appeal case the parents of a child may have commissioned an expert report on their child's disabilities or learning difficulties to counter any assessment report prepared by the local authority. The appeal process involves adjudication and tends to operate on an adversarial basis although there is evidence that even where that is the case, inquisitorial techniques may be used (Adler

2 If it is a private school then the dispute would have to be taken to the civil court. See chapter 5.

3 See chapter 3.

2010a). There is generally an oral hearing which the parties are entitled to attend and at which they may make representations. The parties will enjoy a right to use a representative and in all the jurisdictions covered in this book legal representation is permitted. In some appeal processes, such as those in England, an informal approach at the tribunal hearing is encouraged. The appeal body's decision will be binding on the parties but there may be a second-tier appeal body or the possibility of a review of the decision by a court, on legal grounds.

Reviews

An appeal on the merits of the case is distinguishable from a review of a decision, where an internal or external person or body considers the appropriateness of a decision, usually on the basis of the information that was available to the original decision maker. In a special educational needs case it could include a review undertaken by the original decision maker or by a reviewer within the same authority. As discussed in chapter 5, in the Netherlands an application for an internal review, which will involve a reconsideration of the case by the decision maker (the school board), will be a pre-condition of making an appeal. That is not the case in the other jurisdictions covered in this book. Nevertheless, negotiations and representations in the early stages of a dispute may prompt an internal review. Although internal and external reviews are used in other areas of welfare decision making in the UK (such as entitlement to a social fund payment or access to housing provision as a homeless person) neither internal nor external review are formal mechanisms of redress in relation to education disputes. Judicial review is different from these other forms of review in that it is not concerned with the merits of decisions but with their legality. In the UK courts, judicial review provides a basis for the quashing of decisions by the administration which represent an abuse or misuse of power due to the decision maker exceeding his or her authority or misapplying his or her powers. It could consider unfairness in the way the power was exercised, for example questioning whether the decision maker paid regard to relevant evidence or applied the relevant legislation, such as the statutory criteria governing substantive entitlement, correctly in coming to its decision or instead made an error of law.

Lay adjudication

Judicialised appeal processes have tended to replace forms of adjudication involving non-lawyers as decision makers. For example, as discussed in chapter 3, local appeal panels deciding some kinds of special educational needs appeals in England prior to the mid-1990s comprised lay people, whereas since 1995 all appeals have been heard by a tribunal headed by a legally qualified chairperson and, latterly, a tribunal judge, although it is not required that the other two members of the panel are legally qualified people. Nevertheless, lay adjudication is used in some kinds of case where, although the original decision will have been made under an administrative framework governed by law, legal expertise is not thought to be needed and/or where the process itself is not judicial in character. A good example is the 'independent adjudication' process for additional support needs cases in Scotland, described in chapter 4. The adjudicators are appointed to a panel of adjudicators by the Scottish Ministers and must be 'individuals having such knowledge and experience of children or young persons with additional support needs and the functions of education authorities ... as the Scottish Ministers think fit' and 'may include a member of the staff of the Scottish Administration'.[4] They are independent of local authorities but are government appointees. Another example, in England, is the schools adjudicators who, among other things, adjudicate on objections to local school admission policies.[5] In the US, due process hearings, which are one of the mechanisms for resolving special education cases, are of a more quasi-judicial nature and perhaps because of this there is some diversity as between different states as to whether they are required to be conducted by people who are licensed attorneys or merely suitably qualified and experienced lay people.

Private law civil litigation

Civil litigation is also used to resolve particular kinds of SEN dispute, as the discussion in later chapters will show. In the United States it is used to bring claims over the financial consequences of various decisions or failures to act. In the Netherlands it is used in connection with grievances over education provided for children with SEN in private schools, while in the UK this process deals with claims concerning liability for professionals' negligence in handling children's needs.[6] It is not a major route to redress for parents in this field, since relatively few of the disputes involve contract or tort issues and are thus amenable to civil litigation of this kind. Legal expense may be a deterrent notwithstanding the availability in some cases of legal aid, legal expenses insurance or the possibility of contingency fee arrangements.

Negotiation

Negotiation often forms an important element in the relationship between parents and education officials in connection with the education of children with SEN, whether the negotiation is direct or conducted through a third party such as a parent partnership support officer in England or education counsellors in the Netherlands. Although negotiation between the parties over education matters concerning individual children plays a role in preventing disagreements from being transformed into disputes it may also continue during the course of a dispute. As

4 Additional Support for Learning Dispute Resolution (Scotland) Regulations 2005 (SI 2005/501), reg. 5(1).

5 School Standards and Framework Act 1998, ss. 25 and 88H.

6 See Chapters 1 and 3.

discussed in later chapters, a significant proportion of special educational needs appeal cases will be resolved without a formal determination due to the settlement of the dispute, which sometimes occurs very late in the day, usually after a period of negotiation. This is because there is usually a range of options for meeting a child's educational needs and even yes/no decisions can be arrived at on the basis of an agreement, such as whether a child should have their needs formally assessed or whether he or she should attend a mainstream or special school. Negotiation in this context is a private process over access to public resources. As such it gives rise to questions concerning the recognition and safeguarding of the public interest in such decisions by the state. This issue is equally applicable to mediated settlements of disputes and is discussed in that connection below. Negotiation will, of course, also play a role in the settlement of legal claims before the courts, which is how the majority of such cases are resolved.

Mediation

Mediation is a process whereby the parties identify and discuss the areas of disagreement between them and explore possible ways of resolving the dispute with the aid of an independent third party, the mediator. As described by an EC Directive promoting its use in civil and commercial disputes, it operates as a 'structured process'.[7] It tends to involve one or more bilateral meetings, preceded in some cases by a 'shuttle' process in which the mediator engages alternately with the parties. It is a voluntary and consensual process that aims to produce an agreement between the parties to resolve the dispute. Mediation is used for SEN disputes in all four jurisdictions covered by this book, but it has yet to become the mechanism of choice for most complainants even though it has many proponents and receives active policy promotion. As discussed in chapter 3, for example, mediation seems to be regarded as a pre-eminent ADR mechanism in England and is at the forefront of ideas about how to modernise dispute resolution through the use of more cost effective, accessible and 'proportionate' processes. Its use in family disputes in England is reasonably well established and while by no means does it attract unequivocal support (Herring 2009, pp. 135–145) and there remains user resistance to it (Roberts 2008; Westcott 2004) it has now become necessary, under provisions within the new Family Procedure Rules (2010) which came into force in April 2011, for the parties in such cases to consider mediation, via a mediation information and assessment session, prior to the start of any proceedings. Generally, rather than legally prescribed qualifications for mediators

7 *Directive 2008/52/EC of the European Parliament and of the Council of 21 May 2008 on certain aspects of mediation in civil and commercial matters,* OJ L 136/3, article 3(a): '"Mediation" means a structured process, however named or referred to, whereby two or more parties to a dispute attempt by themselves, on a voluntary basis, to reach an agreement on the settlement of their dispute with the assistance of a mediator'.

there are various accreditation schemes operating within the relevant fields;[8] and training for mediators is specifically encouraged by the EC Directive.[9]

Although mediation is generally seen as distinct from court or tribunal processes, judicial mediation is also used. Court-based mediation is used in some family cases in the UK and a mediating judge is used in Germany in social and administrative courts, including cases involving social benefits (Becker and Friedrich 2010). Judicial mediation has also been piloted in England in employment tribunals in three regions. The pilot, conducted in 2006–2007, involved the tribunal judge acting as a mediator in cases that were not part of their own caseload; they would not impose their views on the nature of an agreed settlement and could only outline various alternatives to the parties, leaving it to them to decide. The problem was that the process was found to be very expensive and seemed to have no statistical effect in terms of improving the rates of cases settled over a set time period or in the rates of resolution that avoided a hearing (Unwin et al. 2010).

The evidence on mediation suggests that it helps the parties in dispute to identify and focus on the important issues; can enable disputes to be resolved more quickly; offers very good prospects of settlement; is viewed positively by many of those who participate in it; attracts high levels of compliance; tends to be less stressful for the parties than an appeal; and, over the long term, helps the parties to maintain good relations and effective communication, which is important in the field of SEN given the strong emphasis often placed on a 'partnership' approach (Hall 1999; Gersch and Gersch 2003; Harris, Riddell and Smith 2008; Harris and Smith 2008; Tennant et al. 2008). Mediation is regarded as facilitating better understanding by the parties of each other's perspective and as helping to clarify the issues that lie at the heart of the dispute. Unlike appeals adjudication it is also said to facilitate interests-based solutions, not merely those based on rights, involving more creative and flexible outcomes (Stilitz and Sheldon 2007). Enabling the parents to become more directly involved in a decision about their child's education through mediation is also consistent with ideas of citizenship, referred to above, reinforcing the rights and responsibilities attached to it.

Mediation nevertheless raises a number of questions. In relation to SEN cases there are doubts about its cost effectiveness and as to whether it really extends the scope for settlement or speeds up the resolution of disputes (see Tennant et al. 2008, p. 46). There is also a more profound question as to whether mediation, as a

8 They generally seem to operate on a voluntary, industry-wide basis, such as the National Mediator Accreditation System in Australia, which is dependent upon voluntary compliance by mediation providers who will accredit mediators who meet the various agreed standards. Another example is the Law Society of England and Wales's Family Mediation Accreditation Scheme. While the latter scheme aims to provide an assurance of service quality for the public, it is a non-exclusive scheme and non-accredited solicitors etc. are not prohibited from acting as mediators: Law Society (2009).

9 Note 7 above, article 4.2. There is also a European Code of Conduct for Mediators: http://ec.europa.eu/civiljustice/adr/adr_ec_code_conduct_en.pdf [accessed 12 April 2011].

negotiated outcome to a dispute about fundamental rights, really serves the interests of 'justice' (Bondy and Mulcahy 2009; Stilitz and Sheldon 2007; Supperstone et al. 2006). In addition to concerns about procedural justice (below), there is a risk that a mediated outcome may neither deliver to the claimant his or her true substantive entitlement, nor ensure that he or she achieves an outcome which is consistent with that achieved by others. There is also a risk that the outcome might not be 'fair' to others, notably those parents and children who were not a party to the dispute but who may be less likely to have their needs fully met as a result of the allocation of scarce resources agreed via the mediation. On the basis of such objections there might, on the face of it, only rarely be a case for mediation. Yet mediation is widely favoured, so if it is to be used, when will it be suitable?

Richardson and Genn (2007) seek to identify the citizen-versus-state cases which would be suited to mediation as opposed to adjudication by a court or tribunal. They view adjudication as necessary for disputes which concern issues of liberty and personal status, given that they centre on basic rights of fundamental importance. They also consider that disputes about entitlement to a material benefit, such as social security, may also require adjudication since they concern legal questions related to satisfaction of statutory conditions – the claimant will generally either meet the condition(s) of entitlement or he or she will not. That seems a reasonable argument, especially since the interpretations of the law and the weighing up of evidence that are needed in such cases are judicial tasks. Obviously, however, even if mediation as a process could produce an appropriate outcome, it lacks the declaratory, binding effect that is needed where these kinds of issues fall to be determined. Richardson and Genn consider that the kinds of case for which mediation is particularly suitable lie in a third category concerned with 'entitlement to consideration', where the rights are less clear cut and are meant to be determined in individual cases with reference to a wide range of considerations, such as local resource constraints on service providers.[10] They regard SEN as such an area, such as a typical case where parental wishes for a particular form of provision have to be weighed up against issues of 'efficiency' and where individual interests have to be balanced against wider policy goals. In Richardson and Genn's view, the utility of mediation for such a case arises out of the lack of a single identifiable outcome that alone could be the 'right' one, although formal adjudication by a tribunal would be needed for intractable cases.

Nevertheless, there is an argument that an expert, independent tribunal would be a better forum to identify, through an objective assessment, the arrangements which would meet the child's needs and to determine how far the relevant authority is required by law to go in meeting them. Moreover, the right to education, especially for a child with SEN, is surely a fundamental right connected to human dignity and thus of considerable importance (O'Mahoney 2008) regardless of the basis

10 See also Adler (2006a, p. 81), who argues that 'mediation and conciliation may be may be appropriate in disputes that call for the exercise of discretion' but may be 'inappropriate where rights are involved'.

on which, and the means by which, its translation into actual provision is to take place. In England, for example, once special educational provision is determined in a statement of SEN[11] the child acquires a right to receive it by virtue of the statutory duty on the local authority to ensure that the specified provision is made.[12] Moreover, there is a basic requirement that the educational provision to be made for a child must be appropriate; the question is whether arrangements settled upon via mediation will guarantee that this is the case. Mediation may in any event be intrinsically unsuitable in some kinds of SEN case where there is little scope for a compromise, such as where the issue is whether there should be a formal assessment of a child's SEN.

It is also the case that, regardless of the nature or subject matter of the dispute, there is in citizen-versus-state cases an inherent imbalance of power between the parties. Adler argues that it 'would take a very skilled mediator' to deal effectively with power imbalances and inequalities in the process (Adler 2006b, p. 978). He is somewhat skeptical that this can be achieved. He argues that tribunals offer better prospects of correcting power imbalances between the parties, due to their pro-active and enabling approach. Stilitiz and Sheldon (2007, p. 165), on the other hand, have more faith in the capacity for 'a skilled and robust mediator' to place the parties on level ground. Moreover, according to Roberts (2008, p. 12), mediators have a 'fundamental ethical responsibility' to terminate a mediation session 'where it appears that unfairness would result because of the exercise of duress by one party on another or where cultural or other considerations deny a party the capacity to negotiate in their own right or at all'. This issue is considered further in chapter 3, where the results of a survey in England are discussed. They in fact lend some support to Adler's position on this matter. As discussed there and elsewhere, the availability of assistance to a parent, such as legal or lay representation, can help to reduce the inequality between the parties. Mediation, however, tends to operate on the premise that legal professional assistance is unnecessary, and it is discouraged in SEN mediations in some jurisdictions (but not in the US – see chapter 6). There is a concern that the inherent 'inequality of arms' will prejudice parties already at a disadvantage in the process of mediation, notably parents from more deprived socio-economic backgrounds as opposed to the middle class parents who are better able (and more likely) to access redress mechanisms (see e.g. Coldron et al. 2002).[13]

There is also concern that ADR approaches may weaken citizens' substantive rights by undermining their proper declaration and enforcement, the so-called 'vindication of individual rights' (Supperstone et al. 2006). The risk is that, in mediation, citizens might end up settling for less than their true entitlement, thus prejudicising the 'justice' in the outcome to the dispute. Genn (2010, p. 116) finds that the parties to mediation are required to 'relinquish ideas of legal rights

11 This is a formal document, prepared by the local authority, recording the child's needs and the special educational arrangements to be made for him or her – see chapter 3.

12 Education Act 1996, s. 324(5) – see chapter 3.

13 With regard to ethnicity, see the evidence relating to England in chapter 3.

during mediation and focus, instead, on problem solving'. While settling below their expectation may not necessarily result in an injustice if the parents have an unrealistic view of what it is their right to expect for their child, there will undoubtedly be cases where parental wishes are reasonably related to probable entitlement. A representative of a voluntary body interviewed for the ESRC research in England, which is discussed in chapter 3, commented that settling for too little was less of a risk where the issue was:

> 'black and white ... if it was for example a particular school that a parent was wanting and that's the only thing they'd be happy with, then there would be no harm in going to mediation because they'd either get it or they won't'.

On the other hand, if the parents were contesting the contents of the child's statement of SEN, which, among other things, sets out the arrangements for the child's special educational provision, 'they could be pushed into accepting something they don't want'. There is an inherent risk of this, particularly for citizens who may not be entirely knowledgeable about the law and in particular the criteria on which the decision might need to be decided by a tribunal or court. A solicitor interviewed for the ESRC research commented that she would advise parents entering mediation to 'know first what their fundamental rights are' and not 'go into mediation blindfolded'. While settling for too little may be a concern that is equally applicable to civil or judicial review litigation, given that the overwhelming majority of those cases settle (see e.g. Bondy and Sunkin 2009), one difference with regard to mediation is that, as intimated above, lawyers are much less likely to play a role.

The risk that the substantive justice in the dispute may not be realized through mediation stems from the nature and purpose of mediation itself. Genn (2010, pp. 117–118) argues that mediation is concerned with compromise, communication and relationships, 'but it is not about substantive justice'. She refers to the argument, used in the context of civil and commercial disputes, that mediation has a residual utility in that the kind of individual solution to a dispute it offers does 'no worse harm' than not resolving the dispute at all. Genn (2010, p. 118) is critical of this viewpoint, arguing that what is being suggested is that '[w]e should simply be measuring the outcome of mediation against doing nothing', which means that 'the access to justice contribution of mediation offers little more than closure of a dispute, however it is achieved'. In any event, the extent of the risk of settling too low is difficult to determine, since the outcome to a dispute may in part be based on evidence provided and perceptions arising during the proceedings themselves and the justice in the dispute may depend on how far the individual child's needs are capable of being met in the light of the local authority's resources. However, the ESRC survey discussed in chapter 3 provides some evidence that in a minority of cases parents do settle for too little, for less than they might have secured via a successful appeal to the tribunal. If this occurs, of course, it is the child's interests that are prejudiced. Indeed, one of the broader concerns about mediation of education disputes is, as discussed in chapter 1, whether there is sufficient attention to those interests as against the claims of the parents and the interests of the local authority.

Questions have also been raised at various points as to whether participation in processes such as mediation or indeed less structured forms of dispute resolution (perhaps negotiation), as processes of 'informal justice', has an 'empowering' effect on complainants individually or collectively and increases equality, thus being socially transformative (e.g. Abel 1992). Increasing the opportunities for redress may been seen as reinforcing the enjoyment of rights of citizenship, but at the same time substantive social rights and their enforcement may be placed at risk if and when mechanisms more capable of safeguarding them are avoided.

Administrative justice and the choice of dispute resolution process

As Adler (2010b) explains, 'administrative justice' has a procedural and a substantive dimension, being concerned with processes that operate in a fair manner and which deliver substantive justice in the sense of just outcomes expressing the inherent rights and entitlement of the citizen. Administrative justice is seen as being concerned as much with the actions of 'front line' decision makers as with the processes for correcting their decisions in order to prevent injustice (see e.g. Hertogh 2010; Van Aerschot 2011). Yet there is a link between the two, since the kind of mechanism or process that is best able to deliver administrative justice in the form of redress of grievance will depend, in part, on the kind of decision making occurring at the front line, as already noted in the discussion of mediation above. When it comes to the issue of which mechanism should be used for resolving disputes, it is important to take account of the kind of legal and administrative framework within which the decision maker is operating.

In education, decision making occurs against a very diverse range of statutory duties and powers. Some concern fundamental rights in respect of access to education, although most disputes, including those about SEN, centre on priorities and choices that parents make on behalf of their child where rights are conditioned by the wider responsibilities of education authorities to allocate resources and manage their administrative functions effectively. Mullen (2010, pp. 409–410) regards sensitivity to the context of decision making as important in identifying the appropriate form of redress mechanism that should be used for a particular kind of case. In particular, regard should be had to the policy area's goals, the roles of the various administrative agencies responsible for giving effect to them, and the kind of environment in which they operate. Mullen (p. 410) argues that 'an administrative system which relies heavily on professional judgment and experience may require a different approach to redress from one in which decisions are made according to detailed rules'. Yet in a field such as special educational needs many decisions involve both elements. As Kagan (2010, pp. 164–165) notes, while it is possible to distinguish between decision making constrained by legalism[14] from where it is subject to less legal control and the decision is based on expert judgment or is even (where hierarchical controls are weakest) dependent on negotiation, decisions may also involve some combination or sequence of the different elements and such differences may also exist between front-line and appellate decision making. There may, for example, be a need for diverse methods where, as in education, there are different kinds of grievance and various desired outcomes. A further factor, particularly in the field of SEN, is the importance of resolving disputes quickly. As Scott Baker LJ has commented: 'Cases that involve issues about the education of a child are par excellence cases that need to be heard and determined expeditiously … Otherwise there is a real danger that the child's best interests may be overtaken by the passage of time'.[15]

Mullen's distinction between professional judgment and rule-based decision making bears a relationship to the three models of administrative justice proposed by Mashaw (1983) (and later extended by Adler: see Adler 2010b). Mashaw's 'professional treatment' model (pp. 26–29) is one in which the decision maker reaches a decision on the basis of contextual interpretation and in doing so draws on professional expertise related to the needs of the client. Mashaw identifies the legitimating value of each of the models; and, in the case of professional judgment, it is 'service'. Mashaw's 'bureacratic rationality' model would be applicable to rule-based decision making, which aims to apply rules correctly in order to realise a policy's (Mashaw (p. 26) refers to 'society's') pre-established goals. The legitimating values of this model are accuracy and efficiency. The third of Mashaw's models, 'moral judgment' (pp. 29–31), which Adler (2010b) prefers to term a 'legal' model, has as its primary goal conflict resolution in respect of issues of entitlement under a neutral decision maker, a model that is associated with adjudication.

These different models can be identified not only across different fields of education decision making, but also within them. For example, within the field of SEN, bureaucratic rationality predominates in areas such a local authority's classification and assessment of SEN as applied to the children in its area and may have increased importance where, as in the UK, attempts are made by codes of practice to control the exercise of discretion in order to maintain consistency. Elements of professional treatment are most obvious when it comes to the determination of the contents of a statement of SEN, which is a process which draws on a multi-professional assessment. When there is an appeal which proceeds to a

14 Kagan (2010) distinguishes between 'bureaucratic legalism', in which centrally driven rule-making seeks to control decision making to ensure uniformity of approach, from 'adversarial legalism', where there is less hierarchical control and those who are the subject of decisions often have rights capable of being asserted and adjudicated upon. He argues that adversarial legalism may be used where, for example, there is a political distrust of decision makers on the basis that their legalistic, mechanistic approach might fail to have sufficient regard to the equity of a case.

15 H v Essex County Council and Others [2009] ELR 161, at para. 51.

decision, the tribunal makes an independent determination based on the contextual interpretation of law and facts, which epitomises the role of the moral judgment or legal model. It enables the exercise of professional discretion to thus be judged against legal norms (Blair 2000, p. 190). Mashaw sees his three models as in competition with each other. Thus, for example, bureaucratic rationality may be undermined by professional treatment's ethical concerns or by 'the highly textured search for moral deservedness inherent in traditional adjudication' (Mashaw 1983, p. 40). Riddell argues that such a tension between the models is evident in the field of SEN where the 'growing importance of the legal framework clearly represents a challenge to the dominant models of professionalism and bureaucracy', with local authorities concerned that decisions by the tribunal may skew resource allocations (Riddell 2003, p. 203).

The further development of Mashaw's typology by Riddell (2003) and Adler (2003) has introduced three additional models of administrative justice reflecting the influence of managerialism, consumerism and markets, which themselves largely reflect dominant trends in the governance of public services. Consumerism has the goal of active user participation. Its legitimating value is that of consumer satisfaction. Managerialism involves accountability based on judgments of performance. It has the legitimating goal of improved efficiency. Managerialism has had a growing influence in some education systems through target setting and regulation; the accountability mechanisms under this model would be various complaints procedures. The 'markets' model is identified by a degree of parental choice and, as with consumerism, has the legitimating goal of improved efficiency.

It is in fact quite difficult to decide where, if at all, a process such as mediation might fit within these administrative justice models. In one sense, because of the element of direct participation that it involves and the fact that the process aims towards an outcome that the parties will be satisfied with, it is consistent with the consumer model. On the other hand, this model appears to be more relevant to how people are treated by administrative processes, focusing, as Halliday (2004, p. 123, who in fact raises questions about some of the other models) sees it, on 'customer care' rather than 'substantive needs or desires'. However, mediation may have some features of other models, such as professional treatment, for example, where there is a facilitated process of negotiation (in particular, through the involvement of parent support services or education counsellors, as noted above and in later chapters, although professional dominance is in fact much more likely to emanate from the authorities' side). It also has features of the legal model, in the sense that the mediator is independent, the parties may assert rights, and, although not a decision maker, the mediator facilitates an outcome which will often, although not always, be decisive. There is, however, no certainty that the agreed outcome will conform to the norm of legality, which would be expected of this model.

While different models can be matched to the different kinds of SEN dispute and the particular context(s) in which they arise, there may be overriding principles or national priorities, based for example on issues of economy or efficiency, that call for the prioritisation of a particular approach to dispute resolution. As Adler (2010b, p. 151) explains, there may be trade-offs fought out between different institutional actors, such as civil servants in support of the bureaucratic model and lawyers and judiciary in support of the legal model. The drive for 'proportionate dispute resolution' in the UK may involve similar compromises. Thomas (2011), for example, has shown how the administration and adjudication of asylum appeals in the UK involves a somewhat uneasy trade-off between policy demands of speed and efficiency and the justice requirements for proper investigation and accurate assessment of facts and evidence. That does not mean, however, that fundamental principles of administrative justice should be ignored. For example, the independence of the dispute resolution body or the extent of its power to provide a suitable remedy (such as a binding ruling) will often be of crucial importance. However, there may similarly be tensions between them, as for example the Administrative Justice and Tribunals Council (AJTC) in England has identified in relation to efficiency and accessibility, which it identifies among its proposed principles for administrative justice (AJTC 2010).[16] The AJTC's principles include making users and their needs central to processes; operating independent, open and appropriate redress procedures; keeping people informed and empowering them to challenge decisions; providing well-reasoned, lawful and timely outcomes; and enabling disputes to be resolved proportionately and efficiently.

There may be a case for the different processes to be adapted to ensure that any of the factors necessary for disputes to be dealt with justly, both in terms of process and outcome, are preserved while enabling other policy goals to be served. Thus, for example, building mediation into an appeals process may result in greater overall efficiencies, by enabling some disputes to be resolved more quickly. It may also promote the participative resolution of a dispute, while ensuring that the dispute remains located in an adjudicatory framework. Similarly, an inquisitorial methodology employed by a tribunal which adopts an enabling approach to claimants could reduce the need for support such as legal representation to which the adversarial model is seen as giving rise. The use of early neutral evaluation in appeal cases, discussed above, may serve similar ends without necessarily compromising principles of fairness or access to justice.

Conclusion

This chapter has explained the role and forms of the different methods for resolving disputes and dealing with grievances that arise in the field of special educational needs, which are variously discussed in the specific national contexts in later chapters. Leaving aside complaints processes and private law civil actions seeking

16 For example, locating decision making in one place may be efficient but could deny access to people living far away from it. See also the discussion of complaints above.

compensation via the courts, which have their own discrete purpose in, primarily, redressing past wrongs, the principal models of dispute resolution that operate in the field of special educational needs, and which are concerned with prospective arrangements affecting children's education and well being, are adjudication by a court or tribunal, mediation and, often in combination with these two, negotiation. Mediation offers an alternative to such adjudication that accords with the increasing preference, at a policy level at least, for methods of redress that are less formal, confrontational and expensive and more accessible than court or tribunal processes. Negotiation and settlement, whether or not involving mediation, are dominant characteristics of civil dispute resolution in general. The idea that court or tribunal adjudication should be a last resort for dispute resolution is a largely accepted one, both in principle and at a practical level. Moreover, in relation to special educational needs, if the law provides sufficient flexibility with regard to some key areas of decision making such as on arrangements for the identification, assessment and addressing of needs, there is scope for a tailored outcome based on compromise. An adjudicated outcome may not be necessary. Unless the relevant substantive rights are placed in a rather more rigid legal framework than currently tends to be the case, settlement will retain its place. Where a negotiated settlement proves impossible, the underlying legal basis to the original first-tier decision means that a formal appellate process will often be needed to resolve the dispute.

Yet it is clear that the practical benefits of mediation, such as facilitating an early resolution of a dispute and interest-based outcomes, play against a broad range of deep concerns. The latter arise out of the perceived need for public vindication of rights and the issue of whether the interests of justice and fairness are sufficiently recognised and the rights of the child are likely to be adequately protected. The fact that mediated outcomes cannot be forced on anyone and that the citizen will often still be able to invoke the appeal process provides the relevant party with a safeguard but does not protect these wider interests. The administrative justice principle identified by the AJTC (2010, para. 33) that decisions should be 'publicly explained and justified' does not seem to be served by what is essentially a private negotiated outcome to a dispute which, in terms of any procedural requirement, does not need to be justified to anyone. On the other hand, this is equally true of the many appeal cases which, as discussed in later chapters (especially chapter 3), are settled leading to a withdrawal of the appeal and thus the absence of judicial scrutiny.

Another point to be borne in mind in respect of ADR mechanisms concerns their potential to improve equality of access to dispute resolution, given the known inequalities in connection with access to judicial mechanisms such as courts and tribunals. One of the interesting points made by Felstiner et al. is that social inequalities may affect the process of 'transformation' by which injurious experiences or grievances become disputes, which was discussed in chapter 1, so that efforts to improve access to justice 'will only give additional advantages to those who have already transformed their grievances into disputes' and will 'accentuate the effects of inequality at the earlier, less visible stages' (Felstiner et al. 1981, p. 637). Therefore if mediation is to be given a role to play at an early stage it is necessary to ensure that there is equal access to it and therefore social barriers will need to be minimised. Later chapters assess the role of mediation and other mechanisms for resolving SEN disputes in the individual jurisdictions.

References

Abel, R.L. (1992), 'The Contradictions of Informal Justice', in Abel, R.L., *The Politics of Informal Justice, Volume 1: The American Experience* (New York: Academic Press), pp. 267–320.

Adler, M. (2003), 'A socio-legal approach to administrative justice', *Law and Policy*, 25, 4, 323–352.

Adler, M. (2006a), 'The Leggatt Report, the White Paper and the Reform of Tribunals', *Journal of Social Security Law*, 13(2), 73–85.

Adler, M. (2006b), 'Tribunal reform: Proportionate Dispute Resolution and the pursuit of administrative justice', *M.L.R.*, 69, 6, 958–985.

Adler, M. (2010a), 'Social Security and Social Welfare', in P. Cane and H.M. Kritzer (eds), *The Oxford Handbook of Empirical Legal Research* (Oxford: OUP), pp. 399–423.

Adler, M. (2010b), 'Understanding and Analysing Administrative Justice', in M. Adler (ed.), *Administrative Justice in* Context (Oxford: Hart), pp. 129–59.

Ahier, J., Beck, J. and Moore, R. (2003), *Graduate citizens? Issues of citizenship and higher education* (London: RoutledgeFalmer).

AJTC (Administrative Justice and Tribunals Council) (2010), *Principles for Administrative Justice* (London: AJTC).

Baldwin, J., Wikeley, N. and Young, R. (1992), *Judging Social Security. The Adjudication of Claims for Benefit in Britain* (Oxford: Clarendon Press).

Becker, U. and Freidrich, N. (2010), 'Mediation in Bavarian Social Jurisdiction – Findings of a Model Project', in Max Planck Institute for Foreign and International Law (MPI), Report 2008–2009 (Munich: MPI), pp. 49–52.

Blair, A. (2000), 'Rights, duties and resources: the case of special educational needs', *Education and the Law*, vol. 12, no. 3, pp. 177–193.

Bondy, V. and Mulcahy, L. with Doyle M. and Reid V. (2009), *Mediation and Judicial Review: An empirical research study* (London: The Public Law Project).

Bondy, V. and Sunkin, M. (2009), *The Dynamics of Judicial Review. The resolution of public law challenges before final hearing* (Colchester: University of Essex).

Buck, T., Bonner, D. and Sainsbury, R. (2005), *Making Social Security Law* (Aldershot: Ashgate).

Buck, T., Kirkham, R. and Thompson, B. (2011), *The Ombudsman Enterprise and Administrative Justice* (Farnham: Ashgate).

Cane, P. (2009), *Administrative Tribunals and Adjudication* (Oxford: Hart).

Clarke, J., McDermont, M. and Newman, J. (2010), 'Delivering Choice and Administering Justice: Contested Logics of Public Services', in M. Adler (ed.), *Administrative Justice in Context* (Oxford: Hart), pp. 25–45.

Clarke, J., Newman, J. Smith, N., Vidler, E. and Westmarland, L. (2007), *Creating Consumer-Citizens: Changing Identities in the Making of Public Services* (London: Sage).

Coldron, J., Stephenson, K., Williams, J., Shipton, L. and Demack, S. (2002), *Admission Appeal Panels: Research Study in the Operation of Appeal Panels, Use of the Code of Practice and Training for Panel Members*, Research Report RR344 (London: DfES).

Dean, H. (2002), *Welfare Rights and Social Policy* (Harlow: Prentice Hall).

DCA (Department for Constitutional Affairs) (2004), *Transforming public services: Complaints, redress and tribunals*, Cm 6243 (London, TSO).

Dijkstra, A.B., Dronkers, J. and Karsten, S. (2004), 'Private schools as public provision for education: school choice and market forces in the Netherlands', in P.J. Wolf and S. Macedo, with D.J. Ferrero and C. Venegoni (eds), *Educating Citizens: International perspectives on civic values and school choice* (Washington DC: Brookings Institution Press, 2004), pp. 67–90.

Fabre, C. (2000), *Social rights under the constitution. Government and the decent life* (Oxford: Clarendon Press).

Felstiner, W.L.F., Abel, R.L. and Sarat, A. (1981), 'The Emergence and Transformation of Disputes: Naming, Blaming and Claiming…', *Law and Society Review*, 15(3–4), 631–654.

Genn, H. (2010), *Judging Civil Justice* (Cambridge: Cambridge University Press).

Gersch I.S. and Gersch A. (2003), *Resolving Disagreement in Special Educational Needs* (London: Routledge Falmer).

Gulland, J. (2010), 'Current developments in the UK – Complaints Procedures and Ombudsmen', in M. Adler (ed.), *Administrative Justice in* Context (Oxford: Hart), pp. 457–481.

Hall, J. (1999), *Resolving Disputes Between Parents, Schools and LEAs: Some Examples of Best Practice* (London: DfEE).

Halliday, S. (2004), *Judicial Review and Compliance with Administrative Law* (Oxford: Hart).

Harris, N. (1993), *Law and Education. Regulation, Consumerism and the Education System* (London: Sweet and Maxwell).

Harris, N. (2007), 'Resolution of student complaints in higher education institutions', *Legal Studies*, 27, 4, 566–603.

Harris, N. and Van Bijsterveld, S.C. (1993), 'Parents as "Consumers" of Education in England and Wales and the Netherlands: A Comparative Analysis', *International Journal of Law and the Family*, 7, 178–204.

Harris, N., Riddell, S. and Smith, E. (2008), *Special Educational Needs (England) and Additional Support Needs (Scotland) Dispute Resolution Project: Resolving and Avoiding Disputes Concerning Special Educational Needs, working paper 1: Literature Review* (CREID: Edinburgh).

Harris, N. and Smith, E. (2008), *ESRC Research: Resolving and Avoiding Disputes Concerning Special Educational Needs, working paper 6: A survey of local authorities and parent partnership services in England*, CREID, Edinburgh http://www.creid.ed.ac.uk/adr/pubs/adr_workingpaper6.pdf [accessed 17 September 2010].

Hay, C., McKenna, K. and Buck, T. (2010), *Evaluation of Early Neutral Evaluation Alternative Dispute Resolution in the Social Security and Child Support Tribunal*, Ministry of Justice Research Series 2/10 (London: Ministry of Justice).

HCWPC (House of Commons Work and Pensions Committee) (2010), *Second Report of Session 2009–10, Decision making and appeals in the benefits system,* HC 313 (London: TSO).

Herring, J. (2009), *Family Law* (3rd edn) (Harlow: Pearson).

Hertogh, M. (2010), 'Through the Eyes of Bureaucrats: How Front-Line Officials Understand Administrative Justice', in M. Adler (ed.), *Administrative Justice in Context* (Oxford: Hart), pp. 203–225.

Hertogh, S. and Halliday, S. (eds) (2004), *Judicial Review and Bureaucratic Impact* (Cambridge: CUP).

Kagan, R.A. (2010), 'The Organisation of Administrative Justice Systems: The Role of the Political Mistrust', in M. Adler (ed.), *Administrative Justice in* Context (Oxford: Hart), pp. 161–182.

Law Commission (2007), Housing: Proportionate Dispute Resolution – The Role of Tribunals, A Consultation Paper, Consultation Paper No. 180 (London: Law Commission).

Law Society, The (2009), *Family Mediation Accreditation Scheme. Criteria and guidance notes* (London: Law Society). http://www.lawsociety.org.uk/new/documents/accreditation/family-mediation-accreditation-scheme-guidance.pdf [accessed 12 April 2011].

Lister, R. (2007), 'Inclusive citizenship: realizing the potential', *Citizenship Studies*, 11, 1, 49–61.

Mashaw, J.L. (1983), *Bureaucratic Justice: Managing Social Security Disability Claims* (New Haven and London: Yale University Press).

Mullen, T. (2010), 'A Holistic Approach to Administrative Justice?', in M. Adler (ed.), *Administrative Justice in Context* (Oxford: Hart), pp. 383–420.

National Audit Office (Comptroller and Auditor-General) (2005), *Citizen's redress: what citizens can do if things go wrong with public services*, HC 21 Session 2004–2005 (London: TSO).

O'Mahoney, C. (2008), 'Special educational needs: balancing the interests of children and parents in the statementing process', 20, 2, *C.F.L.Q.*, 199–218.

Plant, R. (1992), 'Citizenship, rights and welfare', in A. Coote (ed.) *The Welfare of Citizens: Developing new social rights* (London: IPPR/Rivers Oram Press, 1992), 15–29.

Potter, J. (1988), 'Consumerism and the Public Sector: How Well Does the Coat Fit?', *Public Admininstration*, 66, 149–164.

Prosser, T. (1977), 'Poverty, Ideology and Legality: Supplementary Benefit Appeal Tribunals and their Predecessors', *British Journal of Law and Society*, 4, 39–60.

Richardson, G. and Genn, H. (2007), 'Tribunals in Transition: Resolution or Adjudication?', *Public Law,* 116–141.

Riddell, S. (2003), 'Procedural Justice and Special Educational Needs Assessments in England and Scotland', *International Journal of Inclusive Education,* vol. 7, no. 3, 201–23.

Roberts, M. (2008), *Mediation in Family Disputes. Principles of Practice* (3rd edn) (Aldershot: Ashgate).

Stilitz, D. and Sheldon, C. (2007), 'Meeting education disputes', *Education Law Journal*, 8, 3, 165–173.

Supperstone, M., Stilitz, D. and Sheldon, C. (2006), 'ADR and Public Law', *Public Law*, 299–319.

Tennant, R., Callanan, M., Snape, D., Palmer, I. and Read, J. (2008), *Special Educational Needs Disagreement Resolution Services*, Research Report DCSF-RR054 (London: DCSF).

Thomas, R. (2011), *Administrative Justice & Asylum Appeals: A study of Tribunal Adjudication* (Oxford: Hart).

Unwin, P., Karuk, V., Latreille, P., Michielsens, E., Page, L., Siara, B., Speckesser, S., Boon, A., and Chevalier, P-A. (2010), *Evaluating the use of judicial mediation in Employment Tribunals*, Ministry of Justice Research Series 7/10 (London: Ministry of Justice).

Van Aerschot, P. (2011), *Activation Policies and the Protection of Individual Rights* (Farnham: Ashgate).

Vidler, E. and Clarke, J. (2005), 'Creating Consumer-Citizens: New Labour and the Remaking of Public Services', *Public Policy and Administration*, vol. 20, no. 2, 19–37.

Westcott J. (ed.) (2004), *Family Mediation. Past, Present and Future*, Bristol, Family Law.

Wilkins, A. (2010), 'Citizens and/or consumers: mutations in the construction of concepts and practices of school choice', *Journal of Education Policy*, vol. 25, no. 2, 171–89.

Woods, P. (1988), 'A strategic view of parent participation', *Journal of Education Policy*, vol. 3, no. 4, 323–334.

Woolf, The Rt Hon The Lord, Jowell, J. and Le Sueur, A.P. (1999), *De Smith, Woolf and Jowell's Principles of Judicial Review* (London: Sweet and Maxwell).

Chapter 3

On the Right Track? The Resolution of Special Educational Needs Disputes in England

Neville Harris with Emily Smith

Introduction

This chapter examines conflict between parents and schools or local authorities in England in connection with a child's special educational needs (SEN) and the provision to meet them. It discusses the role of the dispute resolution mechanisms and one of the key issues on which it focuses is the impact of mediation in this field. Mediation is a process that English local authorities[1] are in effect required by statute to make available to parents who are in disagreement with a local authority or a school over any such matter.[2] Parents' right to opt for mediation gives them an alternative route of redress to the long established appeal route, discussed below.[3] Policy makers hoped that the availability of mediation would reduce the proportion of disputes in which there is an appeal to the tribunal.[4] The field of SEN dispute resolution in England represents a useful case study for considering the role of mediation and assessing its value as a dispute resolution mechanism for citizen-v-state disputes more generally.

---

1 In April 2010 all of the statutory functions of local education authorities (LEAs) became those of local authorities. The term 'local education authority' was replaced by 'local authority' under an array of education statutes. At the same time, 'children's services authority' was replaced with 'local authority' under various children statutes: Local Education Authorities and Children's Services Authorities (Integration of Functions) Order 2010 (SI 2010/1158); and the Local Education Authorities and Children's Services Authorities (Integration of Functions) (Local and Subordinate Legislation) Order 2010 (SI 2010/1172).These changes are intended to reflect the integration of local children's services post the Children Act 2004 and the previous Government's *Every Child Matters* policy and its *Children's Plan.*

2 Education Act 1996 (1996 Act), s. 332B – see below.

3 1996 Act, s. 332B(6): 'The arrangements [for dispute resolution involving mediation] cannot affect the entitlement of a parent to appeal to the Tribunal'.

4 See DfES (2001), para. 2:26, referring to the potential for mediation to limit long-term disagreements, thereby 'reducing, in time, the number of appeals going to the SEN Tribunal'.

Among the evidence on which this chapter draws are the findings from empirical research by the authors in 2008–2009 which aimed to discover how SEN mediation operated in practice and how it and the appeal process were viewed by professionals and parents. This research in England was part of an Anglo-Scottish project funded by the ESRC (RES-062-23-0803), the Scottish findings from which are discussed in chapter 4. There are significant differences between these two parts of the UK with regard to the legal and institutional frameworks and in the needs, as defined, that may be covered by the dispute resolution arrangements in question (Harris 2009; Riddell and Weedon 2009; Riddell et al. 2010). Nevertheless, the findings on the role and comparative value of appeals and mediation in each jurisdiction were very similar. This chapter concentrates on the research findings from England (referred to in this chapter as 'the ESRC research'), so that results can be analysed in the context of the government-commissioned Report of Inquiry by Sir Brian Lamb into *Special Educational Needs and Parental Confidence* in that jurisdiction (Lamb 2009) and the government's proposals for reform issued in March 2011 (DfE 2011).

The research in England involved interviews with 30 key professionals including mediation providers, representatives of voluntary organisations, tribunal chairs/judges, the President of the Special Educational Needs and Disability Tribunal (SENDIST), parent partnership officers, local authority officers and head teachers; a survey by postal questionnaire of all 150 local authorities (with a 40 per cent response rate) and all 148 parent partnerships services (PPS) (with a 57 per cent response rate), whose staff are often the gatekeepers for parental challenges to local authorities; and 25 in-depth case studies of disputes across three local authorities (referred to herein by the fictitious names 'Northborough', 'Middleshire' and 'Southside'). The parent case studies involved interviews with the parents and professionals who were involved in individual disputes. The parents in these cases were reluctant to grant permission to interview the child whose education was at issue; nevertheless some insights were gained into the children's views of their case from the parents and professionals. Generally, although there is encouragement for decision makers and adjudicators to facilitate children's participation in decisions and processes in this field,[5] it occurs infrequently, especially in the redress processes, for reasons explored in chapter 1 (and see below).

The ESRC research found some evidence that the number of disagreements or disputes concerning SEN in England has increased in recent years, even though this is not reflected in the appeal or mediation statistics, which have remained fairly static. An increase in disputes over the previous two to three years was reported by 39 per cent of the English local authorities, with 32 per cent reporting no change and 24 per cent referring to a decrease. However, more than half (53 per cent) of the parent partnership services, reported an increase in disputes and only 9 per

5 See eg. DfES (2001), part 3; Health, Education and Social Care Chamber, *Practice Direction, First-tier Tribunal, Health, Education and Social Care Chamber, Special Educational Needs or Disability Discrimination in Schools Cases* (Tribunals Service 2008), para. 15c.

cent a decrease, with 22 per cent reporting no change.[6] The lack of corresponding growth in the use of the formal dispute resolution processes for SEN disputes lends support to the conclusion that a high proportion of parent grievances are in fact resolved via local negotiation, as discussed below. It was noted in chapter 1 that many citizens are reluctant for various reasons to pursue a grievance, but that grievances concerning education are particularly likely to be acted upon because they centre on issues which have a more direct impact on families'/children's interests. It is also the case that in the field of education the involvement of parents in the taking of decisions about children is in fact encouraged and supported by various legal duties on local authorities, discussed below.

However, while these factors help to account for the propensity for SEN disputes to arise, they do not explain the apparent growth in disputes in recent years. Explanations which emerged during the ESRC research centre in part on increasing tensions over resource-related issues. Among PPS respondents to the ESRC survey in England, changes in local authorities' policy and practice, for example delegation of funding to schools and pursuit of central government policy to reduce the number of statements of SEN, were considered important factors in the increase in disputes. Local authorities, on the other hand, cited greater parental awareness of their rights and an increased willingness to challenge decisions, often encouraged by voluntary organisations and solicitors.

The SEN framework and 'battleground'

Children with learning difficulties comprised over 1.7 million children in England or almost 21 per cent of the school population in January 2010.[7] They face the greatest barriers to educational achievement and, to ameliorate their disadvantage, require varying levels of special educational provision. Such provision is defined under the Education Act 1996 (the 1996 Act) as provision which is additional to or different from that made 'generally' for pupils of the child's age in the local authority's mainstream schools in the area.[8] Children with SEN are also eight times more likely to be excluded from school, even though schools on the whole appear to tolerate a higher level of what they consider to be unacceptable behaviour from such pupils than others before excluding them

---

6 Approximately two-thirds of these responses were based on actual figures, the rest on estimates.

7 DCSF (2010c), *Special Educational Needs in England, January 2010, Statistical First Release SFR 19/2010* (London: DCSF) http://www.education.gov.uk/rsgateway/DB/SFR/s000939/sfr19-2010.pdf [Accessed 6 December 2010], Tables 1A and 1B.

8 That is, its schools other than special schools (Education Act 1996, s. 312(4)(a)). Special schools are schools designed to cater specifically for children with SEN. In the case of a child aged under two, any educational provision the child needs is special educational provision: s. 312(4)(b).

(Wilkin et al. 2005, p. 2). They are also around 30 per cent more likely than other children to be bullied by other pupils (Lamb 2009, para. 2.5).

The state's current education-related obligations towards children with SEN originated from the recommendations of the Warnock report (DES 1978), which led to the introduction of the rights-orientated framework initially under the Education Act 1981. Amendments were later made by the Education Act 1993. The law is now contained in the 1996 Act. Part 4 of that Act, as amended, prescribes what has become a somewhat elaborate statutory framework for provision and decision-making, explained in the SEN Code of Practice, to which local authorities and schools must have regard (DfES 2001). The government has recently described this thirty year old framework as 'no longer fit for purpose' (DfE 2011, p.15) on bases discussed below.

The aims of the current legislation are to ensure that each child with SEN is identified, their needs are ascertained and the level and form of educational provision that is required to meet them are determined. The key elements in the legislative framework, discussed more fully below, include a non-medical, defining, concept of 'learning difficulty' as the basis for SEN and a principle that children with SEN should be included within mainstream settings wherever possible, which was strengthened via amendments made by the Special Educational Needs and Disability Act (SENDA) 2001.[9] Also significant is the distinction between, on the one hand, the child who requires a statement of SEN (a formal document made by the local authority recording his or her needs and the provision required to meet them), and, on the other, the child with SEN but no statement, for whom an individual education plan (IEP) maintained by the school must suffice. Parental rights are also an important feature, such as to make representations in the assessment of the child's needs, to express a preference for school to be named as the child's placement in a statement, and to appeal against key decisions.[10] Such procedural rights reinforce the element of parent participation that is expected to be integral to these determinations. They underscore the normative parent and education provider partnership that is reflected in both policy rhetoric and practice principles and is premised on a view that effective parental involvement with their children's schooling brings positive benefits to their learning and helps professionals to meet needs effectively.[11] Parental involvement is also regarded as a 'powerful lever for raising achievement in schools' and something that needs to be properly embedded, which means that 'hard to reach' parents, who tend to be

---

9 See Education Act 1996, s. 316, as substituted by SENDA 2001, s.1, and the discussion in Harris 2007, pp.332–341. On the educational impact of inclusion, see Kalambouka et al. (2007).

10 See in particular 1996 Act ss. 325, 326, 328, 328A (added by the Children, Schools and Families Act 2010, s. 2), 329, 329A and Scheds 26 and 27. The grounds of appeal are set out in n. 65 below.

11 See for example DfES 2001, section 2 of which concerns 'Working in partnership with parents'.

concentrated within lower socio-economic groups, may need specific targeting for engagement strategies (Harris and Goodall 2007, pp. 5–6).[12] However, the realisation of partnership rests on agreement between the interested parties on aspects of education, yet where special needs and provision are concerned agreement can often prove elusive in practice.

It has long been acknowledged that within the SEN field there are in fact significant tensions that tend to render relations between the relevant partners rather brittle and engender 'mistrust' (HCESC 2007, p. 3). There is less scope for a one size fits all pattern of provision than in other fields and significant potential for genuine differences of view on what will work best for individual children. Parents of children with SEN have perhaps the greatest concerns about their children's educational and social progress and may have firm views on their child's requirements. Yet they can feel disempowered due to the dominance of professional viewpoints.[13] While some parents may submit to such viewpoints, others' resistance to them may lead them to draw on their framework of rights. A shifting discourse from one of professional judgment to legal rights in the field of SEN has been widely observed, reinforced by a range of policy and statutory developments, including the establishment of the tribunal, noted above, and various rights concerning the exercise of choice.[14]

It is therefore unsurprising that challenges to decisions are commonplace, as parents '"fight" to achieve a better outcome for their child' (HCESC 2006, para. 147). The fact that special educational provision for some pupils with SEN involves considerably more expense for local authorities than standard provision[15] raises the stakes in decision making and often leads to stern parental resistance. There is indeed a suspicion among some parents that the supposed 'honest' assessment of the individual child is 'tainted by the need to restrict costs'.[16] If challenged via an appeal the local authority will almost always defend its assessment of needs before the tribunal, even though a further strain on its budget may be incurred in doing so (HCESC 2007, para. 7).

The action demanded of local authorities and schools in response to a particular child's needs continues to be contingent on the application of judgement as much as on the determination and interpretation of facts. This is, for example, exemplified

12 Government has funded a programme entitled 'Engaging Parents in Raising Achievement'.

13 For a review of the literature, see Rogers et al. 2006, pp. 7–9.

14 Both developments occurred, initially, under the Education Act 1993.

15 While the average budgeted net expenditure per pupil with SEN is approx £3,500 per annum the average annual cost of a special education placement at a school outside a local authority's area among the 11,000 children who had such a placement in 2006 was £57,000: Audit Commission 2007, para. 17.

16 Sean O'Sullivan, a deputy head teacher, cited in HCESC (2007) at para. 7. The Committee regarded this as a 'serious problem' (para. 8). In its previous report it recommended that assessment and funding of SEN should not be functions carried out by the same body (the local authority): HCESC 2006.

by the statutory test for whether a child has or does not have SEN: whether he or she has a 'learning difficulty which calls for special educational provision to be made for him'.[17] A child is defined as having a learning difficulty if:

> '(a) he has a significantly greater difficulty in learning than the majority of children his age,
>
> (b) he has disability which either prevents or hinders him from making use of the educational facilities of a kind generally provided for children of his age in schools within the area of the local education authority, or
>
> (c) he is under the age of five years and is, or would be if special educational provision were not made for him, likely to fall within paragraphs (a) or (b) when over that age'.[18]

The largest categories of SEN, in terms of the numbers of children identified as having them, are 'moderate learning difficulty'; behavioural, emotional and social difficulties; speech, language and communication difficulties; autistic spectrum disorder; and 'specific learning difficulty' (primarily dyslexia) (Ofsted 2010, table 6). Warnock's overarching concept of SEN was intended to replace a medical impairment-based categorisation of children with one based on the level of need. Nevertheless, despite this intention, 'parents find that obtaining a specific diagnosis for their child, such as autism, establishes his or her educational need, rather than the other way round' (Fortin 2009, p. 44).

The notion of a special need, and the idea of categorising children in accordance with it, remains contested at a philosophical level (e.g. Vehmas 2010).[19] The central issue remains the appropriateness of labelling a child as a member of a group whose needs differ in a significant way to those of others who are considered to represent an idealised norm (Monk 2000; Adams 2003). In a pragmatic sense, however, its application as a legal construct has the essentially altruistic and instrumental goal of ensuring that individuals requiring special assistance are identified, through a broad definition, noted above.[20]

It should perhaps be stressed at this point that as a legal construct the concept of SEN is distinct from that of disability per se. As a recent report on SEN and disability by Ofsted (the Office for Standards in Education, Children's Services

17 1996 Act, s. 312(1).

18 1996 Act s. 312(2), as amended.

19 The way that the law separates out special educational needs from other needs is also regarded as problematic due to its practical consequences: see King and King (2006).

20 Cf. the position in Sweden, which adopts a similar principle of inclusion to the UK, where 'there are no explicit criteria expressed in the … school law or in other mandatory regulations that must be fulfilled in order to establish that a pupil has special educational needs': Isaksson et al. (2010).

and Skills) notes, '[n]ot all disabled children have special educational needs' (Ofsted 2010, p. 77). Disability is defined under discrimination law as a 'physical or mental impairment' which 'has a substantial and long-term adverse effect on [a person's] ability to carry out normal day-to-day activities'.[21] Discrimination in schools on the grounds of disability, including a failure to make reasonable adjustments to prevent disadvantage to a disabled child, is proscribed under this legislation[22] and complaints can be taken to the First-tier Tribunal.[23] Cases can even be brought alongside appeals concerning SEN, which shows the close inter-relationship between the two sets of rights. Nevertheless, the primary aim of the law of SEN differs from that of disability discrimination law. As noted above, the former seeks to ensure that every child with learning difficulties receives an appropriate form of educational provision, with a strong presumption that it should occur in a mainstream setting. Disability discrimination law has a somewhat broader aim of facilitating greater equality of opportunity and widened social participation through reductions in the barriers to full participation in educational institutions (see further Harris 2007, p. 166).

There are in fact wide and currently insufficiently unexplained variations in the proportion of children in different localities classed as having SEN.[24] Authorities with the highest levels of social deprivation, however, seem to have the highest proportion of pupils with SEN.[25] Ofsted caused some controversy by concluding that a significant number of pupils are wrongly classed as having SEN when 'their needs were no different to those of most other pupils' (Ofsted 2010, p. 9).[26] The government has said that such over-identification as having SEN 'harms children who do not have SEN' because it is seen as explaining a lack of progress in the child and generating a 'culture of low expectations for these children' (DfE 2011, para. 3.40, p. 67). The current definition is pivotal to the specific range of duties local authorities owe to such children: for example, having to ensure that all who teach the child are made aware of the child's needs, use their 'best endeavours' to ensure that the child receives the special educational provision their needs call for and, normally (and in all cases where there is no statement) provide for the child to

21 Equality Act 2010, s.6 and schedule 1. This Act is replacing the Disability Discrimination Act 1995.

22 Ibid. (2010 Act), ss.84–89.

23 Ibid., s.116 and schedule 17.

24 See Ofsted 2010 para. 22. This variation prompted the DCSF to commission research into this issue: http://www.dcsf.gov.uk/research/programmeofresearch/projectinformation.cfm?projectid=15311&resultspage=1 (accessed 8 March 2010).

25 Unpublished report by J. Lewis, A. Mooney, L-M. Brady, C. Gill, A. Henshall, N. Willmott, C. Owen, K. Evans and J. Statham (in draft) *Why the Difference? SEN and disability: understanding local variation in service provision and support* (DCSF commissioned research), cited in Lamb (2009), paras 4.1–4.2.

26 Challenging Ofsted's conclusion, Lord Low of Dalston has referred to the 'florid misinterpretations of Ofsted – to the effect that as many as half of children with SEN might be wrongly diagnosed as such': House of Lords Debates 21 October 2010, at col. 960.

be educated in a mainstream school[27] (which is where 55 per cent of children with statements were being educated in January 2010).[28]

If the child has, or is believed probably to have, SEN a further pivotal distinction may need to be made as to whether it is 'necessary' for the local authority to determine the special provision that is required to meet the child's needs. If the conclusion drawn is that such necessity does *not* exist, which is normally the case, it will be for the school to decide how the child's needs are to be met (a process known as 'School Action'), and whether outside advice and support are needed ('School Action Plus'). In January 2010, 11.4% of the school population in England were identified as being at School Action level and 6.2% at School Action Plus, but the government plans to replace these separate categories with a new single one which they suggest would less confusing and also reduce the overall numbers identified as having SEN by ending the relevance of 'how support is provided' for the child in his or her categorization (DfE 2011, pp.18 and 68). The arrangements would be set out in an IEP. If, on the other hand, a local authority determination *is* considered necessary, the authority would be expected to carry out a formal multi-professional assessment of the child's needs, a process in which an element of parental participation is facilitated by the law.[29] The local authority must decide, following the assessment, whether it is necessary to 'determine' the special educational provision that the child requires. Such provision and other prescribed matters including details of the needs themselves are to be included in a statement, to be maintained by the local authority.[30] Among children with SEN but without a statement, who comprise just over 18 per cent of pupils enrolled at school in January 2010, approximately two-thirds receive help via School Action and one-third via School Action Plus. The pupils with statements represent 2.7 per cent of the total school population.[31]

Parents have various rights under the statementing process. They must initially be sent a draft statement. They have a right to make representations, request a meeting with an officer of the authority and express a preference for a school to be named as the child's placement.[32] Since the 1993 Act there has been a duty to adhere to the parents' preference, if expressed and if relating to a *state maintained* school, but not if the school is unsuitable for the child or the child's attendance would be incompatible with the efficient use of resources or efficient education

27 1996 Act, ss. 316, 316A and 317. If the child has a statement the duty to educate in a mainstream school will not apply if such a placement would be incompatible with the parents' wishes or the provision of efficient education for other children: s. 316(3).

28 DCSF (2010c), Tables 1A and 1B. The rest were placed at a mainstream special school (38 per cent), independent schools (4 per cent) or at non-maintained special schools or pupil referral units (3 per cent).

29 1996 Act, s. 323 and schedule 26. The parent has a right to make representations, and submit written evidence, to the local authority and may attend the examination of the child.

30 Ibid., s. 324.

31 DCSF (2010c), Tables 1A and 1B.

32 1996 Act, schedule 27, paras 2–4.

for the other pupils.[33] The only legal imperative to adhere to parental requests for an *independent* (private) school placement, which is almost certainly going to be more costly, arises from the long-standing general principle under statute that children should be educated in accordance with their parents' wishes. However, local authorities can avoid it on efficiency and expenditure grounds (that is, that it would not be compatible with efficient education or would give rise to 'unreasonable public expenditure').[34]

So local authorities in effect have considerable discretion over the kind of provision they consider will meet the child's needs, including the school or type of school that the child should attend. Many parents nevertheless want their child to have a statement, finding that it gives them 'confidence to ask questions and challenge when things are not happening for their child or when something is going wrong' (Lamb 2009, para. 6.30). This confidence stems from the authority's duty to ensure that any educational provision specified in a statement is made for the child.[35] As Baroness Grey-Thompson said in a recent House of Lords debate on SEN: 'Rightly or wrongly, a statement is the only way that parents can feel that their child's rights are protected and cannot be ignored. What parent would not want to be in a position to do this?'[36] However, this protection can be viewed as undermined if, as often occurs, an authority attempts to avoid a high level of specificity in the educational provision set out in the statement. Many disputes about this issue have received judicial consideration, with the courts confirming that although specified provision must match the needs that have been identified, local authorities enjoy a degree of latitude in deciding on provision and can often make out a case for there to be flexibility in the stated arrangements.[37]

Although the decision to make a statement is meant to hinge on whether a school would or would not be able to make the necessary provision for the child from its own resources,[38] it will in practice be greatly influenced by resource considerations at the authority level, as noted above. This has led the architect of the current system, Baroness Warnock, to add her voice to those who see a need to separate the assessment and funding functions that currently rest with local authorities. Recently she admitted that her committee in 1978 had been:

---

33 1996 Act, schedule 27 para. 3(3).

34 1996 Act s. 9, originating in the Education Act 1944, s. 76.

35 1996 Act, s. 324(5)(a)(i). See *R(N) v North Tyneside Borough Council* [2010] EWCA Civ 135. The authority also has a discretion to arrange for non-educational provision: 1996 Act s. 324(5)(a)(ii).

36 House of Lords Debates, 21 October 2010, at col. 956.

37 See e.g. *R (Wiltshire County Council) v YM and SENDIST* [2006] ELR 56; *T v Devon County Council and SENDIST* [2007] ELR 79; and *R (N) v North Tyneside Borough Council* [2010] ELR 312 (CA); for a review of the earlier case law, see Harris (2002).

38 If it would not, a statement would be needed. This is the test for when a statement is 'necessary' as stated in the code of practice: DfES (2001), para. 8:2.

> 'extraordinarily short-sighted ... not to realise, that if a local authority had to assess a child and its needs for a statement, and the same body had to fund those needs, it would in the end look not to what the child needed but to what it thought it could get away with: what it thought it could possibly afford'.[39]

The level of support for a particular child could well be difficult for an authority to justify to itself if it exceeds that made for other children with similar needs or if it means that the obligations owed towards other children cannot be properly met. The authority's more polycentric view of a case therefore plays against the parent's not unreasonably narrower focus on the needs of his or her child and, in some cases, his or her strong ideological wish or predilection for a particular kind of treatment – for example, the inclusion of the child with other children in a mainstream setting. Such a preference has not, however, attracted much protection under the European Convention on Human Rights, in particular Article 2 of Protocol 1 (no-one is to be denied the right to education and respect is to be given to parents' right to ensure their child's teaching conforms to their religious or philosophical convictions) and Article 8 (the right to respect for privacy and family life). As discussed in chapter 1, the dominant judicial view has been that these Convention rights do not guarantee individual parents an education of their choice for their child, in view of the state's authority to determine how to deploy necessarily limited resources in the wider interest (see Harris 2007, pp. 347–348). Authorities will, of course, be influenced by their established policies or practices. They are a significant and long standing cause of the continuing wide variations across authorities in the identification of children as having SEN, in the arrangements made for those with similar needs (Ofsted 2010), and in the proportions of children who are assessed as requiring a statement (HCESAC 1987, para. 33; Audit Commission 2002, para. 32; Pinney 2004, p. 15). The legality of local policies that are irrational may, however, lead them to be struck down by the courts via judicial review.[40]

Reform

There is currently a significant momentum towards the reform of the special educational needs framework in England. The Lamb Inquiry recommendations are already proving to be influential, the government having expressed the intention to take into account recent independent and other reviews of SEN policy.[41] The Lamb report does not propose any dismantling of the current

39 House of Lords Debates, 21 October 2010, col. 947.

40 See, e.g. *R v London Borough of Hillingdon ex p. Governing Body of Queensmead School* [1997] ELR 331.

41 Sarah Teather, speaking at the Every Disabled Child Matters event 5 July 2010. http://www.education.gov.uk/childrenandyoungpeople/specialeducationalneeds/a0061713/next-steps-on-special-educational-needs-and-disabilities [accessed 15 November 2010]. See also DfE 2011, p.16.

legislative framework, but rather improvements: a 'radical overhaul', but not a complete re-design (Lamb 2009, p. 1). One of Lamb's central messages (2009, para.5.62), also reflected in separate research findings (Penfold et al. 2009, para. 5.1), is that the kind of relationships that parents have with local authorities and schools affects their confidence in the system and this in turn has a critical bearing on the likelihood of a dispute. Lamb makes a number of key recommendations designed to increase parental satisfaction and improve the responsiveness of the system to children's needs. In particular, ways of fostering better engagement and communication with parents are identified (such as consulting them on schools' SEN policies and considering their information needs annually). Lamb also advocates greater support for parents, such as establishing an independent advice line and re-launching PPS as providers of high quality advice, more conversant with the statutory framework; and better standards of monitoring and inspection. Change should involve 'enhanced rights and a cultural shift in the way in which schools, local authorities and other professionals work with parents and children' (Lamb 2009, p. 1). One of the principal concerns is the widely divergent experience of parents and children in different locations. The system is supporting some children well; but for the families of others it 'represents a battle to get the needs of the child identified and for these to be met' (Lamb 2009, p. 2).

The previous government's response to Lamb included a range of commitments for reform under an 'implementation plan' (DCSF 2010a). Part of this would have involved the introduction of an independent right of appeal for children (mirroring developments in Wales: see Harris 2009). The previous government also included proposals for a 'pupil guarantee' in the Children, Schools and Families Bill, with an 'ambition' for all children to be able to go to a school 'where they are taught in ways that meet their needs, where progress is regularly checked and where particular needs are identified early and quickly addressed'.[42] However, the pupil guarantee provisions did not survive in the 'washing up' process for Bills in the run-up to the general election in 2010. However, the residual Act places a new duty on school inspectors, in reporting on how far a mainstream school meets the needs of the range of its pupils, to consider in particular the needs of disabled children and children with SEN.[43] This addresses a shortcoming identified by Lamb, which found that inspection reports left parents with 'little information on which to base decisions about choice of school' (Lamb 2009, paras 5.21 and 5.33).

The present government has now promised that parents will be given 'better support and more control' (DfE 2011, p.42). Parents would not only have a right to express a preference for any 'state-funded' school, therefore bringing Academies

42 The pupil guarantee was defined as document setting out what the pupil 'is entitled to expect with regard to the school', to be 'framed with a view to realising the pupil ambitions', which included the one cited above and also, inter alia, that their school will be one where 'they are able to express their views ...': clause 1.

43 Children, Schools and Families Act 2010, s. 1, amending the Education Act 2005, s. 5.

within the scope of this right, but would also be provided with more information about the options available to them (DfE 2011, pp.17 and 52). They would receive a local offer describing the additional or different provision made in schools in their area (pp.45-46). The government has also promised a 'new approach to statutory assessment' (DfE 2011, p.34), including greater transparency and tighter time limits for the various stages (pp.39-40). A radical proposal would involve replacing the current SEN statutory assessment and statement of SEN with a 'single statutory assessment process and "Education, Health and Care Plan", from birth to age 25' (p.36). The plan would be 'transparent about funding for the package of support'. The idea of a wholly integrated approach to assessment and planning of provision is a logical one but one that may be difficult to put into practice. It also raises difficult questions regarding the design of the dispute resolution process, particularly if the assessment for entitlement to social security disability benefits, currently governed by a separate appeal process, is also included as has been suggested (DfE 2011, p.37). Parents may also be given a 'personal budget', which might take the form of a notional sum which can be allocated by the parent to the cost of services they wish for their child (pp.46-47). The proposal is that all parents whose child has an Education, Health and Care plan would have a right to a personal budget by 2014 covering education, health and social care (p.49).

Such reforms, along with the government's aim of reducing bureaucracy within the system, would require changes to the law. The government has tacitly acknowledged the importance of the legislative framework in setting in place the various important duties in this field. Therefore the plan is to provide straightforward and practical advice for professionals and give parents a 'clear and accessible explanation' of the framework and the duties within it. The SEN Code of Practice will therefore be retained but it will be streamlined (DfE 2011, p.98, paras 5.19 and 5.20).

Arguably, if parents better understand their rights and receive additional support to navigate the system they may in the future be even more willing to pursue redress if dissatisfied. As discussed below, the government has made it clear that there is no plan to remove the right of appeal in SEN cases – indeed the conferment of a right of appeal on children themselves (an issue, including the problematic position of 'looked after' children, that was discussed in chapter 1) will be introduced on a pilot basis in England – although at the same time it wants to encourage the use of mediation (DfE 2011, pp54-56, para 2.59 et seq.).

Redress and SEN

Introduction

The considerable scope for disagreement between parents and local authorities in the field of SEN, particularly in relation to assessment and statements, is reflected in the establishment of rights of redress, which are the most highly developed across all areas of education in England. Of particular significance is parents' (including foster parents'[44]) right of appeal to the First-tier Tribunal and from there, on a point of law, to the Upper Tribunal. Neither tribunal tier has a jurisdiction in relation to other areas of education decision making, other than cases involving complaints of disability discrimination against schools. Additionally, parents have a unique right to request mediation in connection with any matter related to SEN functions on which they disagree with the child's school or local authority (see below). These opportunities for redress in this field complement those, such as negotiation or the investigation of complaints, which are available for education disputes more generally.

The more robust framework for redress of grievance concerning SEN relative to other areas of education is a legacy of the importance attached by the Warnock Committee to parental rights, central to the idea of an education system responsive to individual needs. Redress was also accorded a key role under the post-1979 Conservative Government's broad consumerist vision of an education system operating on a quasi market basis and guided by parental choice (Harris 1993). However, SEN has a distinct status as a field in which individualised educational arrangements are often legally necessary and a likely source of conflict. The Lamb Inquiry in fact perceived the role of redress to be not confined to righting wrongs in individual cases but as also to have a 'policing' function. There is, however, criticism of both aspects: 'parents need better forms of redress than the system currently offers' and the processes are, in themselves, inadequate to ensure proper accountability within the SEN system (Lamb 2009, p. 5). Parents were considered to need more information and assistance to be able to make effective use of the redress mechanisms. It was always likely that the government would support increased use of alternative dispute resolution (ADR), and this has proved to be the case. In particular, the government is proposing that parents and local authorities should 'always try mediation' before the parent would be being permitted to register an appeal, but at the same time it does not want to impede the exercise right of appeal, including the meeting of any time limits for an appeal to be lodged (DfE 2011, p. 55 para. 2.62).

Parent partnership and voluntary services

The Lamb report acknowledged the importance of parent partnership services (PPS) as advisors and providers of information to parents. It wanted to see them strengthened and their role reinforced (Lamb 2009, R. 18). PPS can both facilitate the exercise and enforcement of rights by parents and be instrumental in the resolution of disagreements, although principally through informal means rather than in appeal or formal mediation processes. In the ESRC research, PPS reported that the number of clients per service in any year ranged from 80 to over 3,000.

44 Foster parents are classed as parents for this purpose: *Fairpo v Humberside County Council* [1997] ELR 12, [1997] 1 All ER 183.

While these figures may not have been totally accurate in every case (and some were only estimates) they are consistent with other evidence indicating that many parents receive PPS help (Rogers et al. 2006), although Lamb reported that PPS 'reach only a fraction of the parents who may want or need support' (Lamb 2009, para. 3.54).

PPS were in effect put on a statutory footing as a result of the Special Educational Needs and Disability Act (SENDA) 2001: local authorities must make arrangements for 'the parent of any child in their area with special educational needs to be provided with advice and information relating to those needs' and to make the services known to parents and others.[45] However, some of the ESRC research PPS respondents complained that parents did not know about their service, often because schools lacked information about it. PPS have in fact been active in helping parents resolve their disagreement with a school or local authority since at least the late 1990s (Hall 1999). However, at that time they were not viewed as independent of local authorities. Since then the Code of Practice has indicated that local authorities do not have to provide PPS themselves and can wholly or partially buy them in instead; but if they do provide a service in-house it must be 'at arm's length to ensure parental confidence' (DfES 2001, paras 2.16–2.17). In the ESRC research, 73 per cent of the respondent PPS were provided by the local authority, 21 per cent by a voluntary organisation and 6 per cent by private or other providers.

PPS are seen by many parents as 'empowering' them (Rogers et al. 2006, p. 48), but professionals' views of the quality of service they provide are rather mixed (Rogers et al. 2006). Minimum standards for PPS are specified by the SEN Code of Practice, including the provision of 'accurate, neutral information' to parents on 'their rights, roles and responsibilities within the SEN process' (DfES 2001, para. 2.21), but they are not interpreted uniformly across different PSS. The main cause seems to be the diversity of staffing and budget levels (Rogers et al. 2006; Harris and Smith 2009). In the ESRC research 75 per cent of the PPS respondents considered themselves to be understaffed.

A core role of PPS is 'to prevent difficulties from developing into disagreements' (DfES 2001, para. 2.22). PPS are also expected to help parents to make 'informed decisions' (DfES 2001, para. 2.19). However, only a minority of the PPS respondents in the ESRC research would advise parents which route of redress to take or on the likely outcome of a tribunal hearing. Also, they do not always help parents prepare appeal documentation and generally will not be able to offer legal expertise (Penfold et al. 2009, p. 50). Furthermore, a sizeable minority of the ESRC research PPS did not see their role as extending to attendance at mediation meetings or tribunals. Even where they do attend, they tend to act as adviser or supporter rather than representative. Local authority based PPS members seem to be inhibited by reason of their employer being one of the parties to the dispute. Some PPS will refer the parent to a voluntary organisation such as

45 Education Act 1996, s. 332A, inserted by SENDA 2001, s. 2.

IPSEA (Independent Panel for Special Education Advice) for additional help in connection with an appeal. Contrastingly, in the field of school admissions, school choice advisers[46] would be expected to assist parents in seeking redress, including the preparation of an appeal, attendance at an appeal hearing and, subject to local agreement, presentation of the appeal (DCSF 2010a, Appx 5 para. 18).

Two PPS members' descriptions of how they perceive their role are typical:

> We see our role as being a mediatory one rather than [that of] a formal mediator. We empower parents to take an active and informed role in their child's education. A large part of our work is in preparing parents for meetings with schools and other professionals. We may accompany a parent to a meeting but our role is not to take an active part in the meeting but to support a parent in doing this. We may ask for clarification, remind a parent about issues that they have not raised, take informal notes for the parent and provide emotional support (PPS 16)

> Where relationships have broken down between parents and schools or [local authority] we would talk to both parties and arrange meetings as appropriate to try to build relationships up, all the work we do is around getting all parties to work together for the best for the child (PPS 120).

This informal, go-between, role was constantly reiterated by respondents. PPS are involved in bringing the parties together and, as one PPS member put it, helping by 'negotiating between parties' (PPS 122) and (according to most respondents) informally mediating. Yet there is evidence that parents regard voluntary bodies such as IPSEA, one of a number that play a key role in supporting parents, as more independent and expert sources of help than PPS (Penfold et al. 2009, p. 51). However, local authorities can be wary of succumbing to the pressure that some voluntary organisations seek to exert.

Mediation

Mediation arrangements The impetus to establish a framework for the independent mediation of SEN disputes arose from a finding in the DfEE-commissioned research by Hall (1999) that although PPS (above) were playing a useful mediation role they were often insufficiently separate and independent from the local authority. Hall (1999, p. 53) outlined three models for independent mediation services: a panel of trained mediators from whom services could be bought in; an expanded form of existing local mediation services, with the acquisition of SEN expertise; and the establishment of regional panels funded by a number of neighbouring local authorities, to provide mediation services to those authorities.

46 Required, with a role of assisting parents, under School Standards and Framework Act 1998, s. 86(1A), inserted by the Education and Inspections Act 2006, s. 42.

Prior to the publication of Hall's report the Government issued its Programme of Action on SEN in which it accepted the need for independent dispute resolution (DfEE 1998, chap. 1 paras 8 and 11). Subsequently it expressed its commitment to dispute resolution services independent of the local authority (DfEE 2000, Annex B para. 5). The proposed legislation also met the need highlighted by Hall (1999, p. 41) for mediation to be underpinned by a statutory duty on local authorities if it was to become properly established. Also incorporated was the idea that mediation should be permitted to run alongside the appeal process,[47] that the two processes should not be mutually exclusive.

SENDA 2001 placed local authorities under a duty to:

> 'make arrangements with a view to avoiding or resolving disagreements between authorities (on the one hand) and parents of children in their area (on the other) about the exercise by authorities of their functions under [part IV of the 1996 Act]'.[48]

There is also a similar duty in respect of disagreements in schools between a parent and the school's governors or, in the case of independent schools, the proprietor.[49] Disagreement avoidance measures reported by ESRC research local authorities typically focused on communication, including providing parents with verbal or written explanations, inviting parental contact to discuss concerns and offering parents a meeting. The arrangements made by local authorities 'cannot affect the entitlement of a parent to appeal to the Tribunal' and so parents have a choice of redress mechanism but can initiate both processes.[50] Local authorities must make the arrangements, and the fact that the right of appeal is not affected, known to parents when they inform them about a decision and their right of appeal.[51] Entry into mediation is voluntary.

'Independent persons' must be appointed for the purposes of the arrangements.[52] The three approved models of 'independent mediation' are essentially those identified by Hall (above). It was admitted by the government that it was likely that a mediator could well have had previous dealings with the relevant school or local authority. It was felt that to bar the appointment of people with no local connection, requiring other people to be found, would represent a 'nightmare scenario for the new services'.[53]

47 Hansard, House of Lords Debates, vol. 622, Special Educational Needs and Disability Bill, CWH 112, 29 January 2001, per Lord Davies of Oldham

48 Education Act 1996, s. 332B(1), inserted by SENDA 2001, s. 3.

49 Education Act 1996, s. 332B(2) and (8).

50 Ibid., subs. (6).

51 Education (Special Educational Needs) (Consolidation) Regulations 2001 (SI 2001/3455), regs 12 and 17.

52 Education Act 1996, s. 332B(3).

53 Hansard, HL Debs, col 690, 20 February 2001, per Baroness Blackstone, Under-Secretary of State.

The official guidance is somewhat ambiguous in this regard, indicating at one instance the need for 'an independent element' whilst at another stressing that to maximise confidence in the arrangements they should be 'genuinely independent' (DfES 2001, paras 2:25–2:26). Separate guidance explains that the facilitators should not be officers of the local authority in question nor have an involvement in decisions concerning the child or a vested interest in the outcome of the dispute, since '[p]erceived bias is likely to cause resentment and hinder progress towards resolving disagreements' (DfES 2002, section 3 para. 27). Impartiality has been found to be 'crucial to a positive experience of independent mediation' (Tennant et al. 2008, p. 45).

The basic expectation is that local authorities will use outside organisations and work in partnership with them in developing the mediation services (DfES 2001: 2:29–2:30). Post the 2001 Act, mediation was initially provided through the nine Regional Partnerships which had been established in the late 1990s to improve regional co-ordination of SEN services (Fletcher-Campbell et al. 2006). Their costs were funded for two years by central government. In the subsequent period many local authorities opted for alternative arrangements, although according to the ESRC research, some 65 per cent of the local authorities had continued with the same mediation providers throughout. A minority of local authorities had separate contracts to buy in services from individual organisations. Around half of local authorities pay for services under a case inclusive service level agreement with the provider: the authority meets administrative costs and is entitled to a set number of mediations. Around one quarter, however, pay an amount per mediation. Some local authorities use their PPS as a dispute resolution service and, more commonly, may enter into reciprocal arrangements with other authorities, which at least offers a more independent element, although runs the risk of a 'cosy' relationship. A further course adopted by some authorities is to use mediation services which have been bought in previously for work in other dispute areas, such as child or family welfare. The above arrangements seem to work well, according to the ESRC research local authorities. However, authorities' need to pay for mediation services can undermine public perceptions regarding those services independence (Tennant et al. 2008, p. 2).

The reference in the 2001 Act (above) to 'disagreements' as opposed to 'disputes' is interesting. There is a clear intention that the arrangements should foster early resolution: 'disagreement resolution can be entered whenever relations between parents and the school or LEA are becoming strained, or misunderstandings are developing' (DfES 2002, section 3 para. 36).[54] Speedy resolution would prevent the damaging effects of delay which might be especially detrimental to a child with SEN due to their educational disadvantage and inherent vulnerabilities. Practical solutions, agreed upon as soon as possible by the parties, should be sought in order to minimise disruption to children's education (DfES 2001, para. 2.26). It

54 See also the comments reported in Hansard, House of Lords, Committee Reports, Special Educational Needs and Disability Bill, CWH 112, 29 January 2001, per Lord Davies of Oldham, at CWH 111–112.

is clear that although practice varies across different local authorities, mediators can often be involved in attempting to broker an agreement before the formal process of mediation is underway, through 'early stage mediation' or 'informal pre-mediation', usually involving telephone contact without the need for a face to face meeting (Tennant et al. 2008, pp. 41–43).

Whichever system is used, the role of the mediator is the same: to bring about a settlement through a 'structured process' of disagreement resolution (DfES 2002, sect. 3 para. 18). The mediator's role is not to impose a settlement but to bring the parties together in a way that facilitates discussion and, it is hoped, achieves an agreed outcome. 'Shuttle' mediation is recommended, whereby the mediator meets with each of the two parties individually before perhaps bringing them together for face to face meetings. This can help to prevent confrontation and promote frank discussion. However, it can also generate suspicions of partiality, adds to the overall time taken, and gives scope for the mediator to manipulate the process (Roberts 2008, p. 133). A typical start to the process in London is a plenary session involving the range of interested parties (Ruff 2004). It will help the mediator to understand the key points of disagreement, although could be intimidating to the parent (Roberts 2008, p. 132). Legal representation per se is considered by the guidance to be 'contrary to the spirit of informal disagreement resolution' (DfES 2002, sect. 3 para. 41), but this view arguably underplays the perceived formality of the process from the parent's perspective. More tolerated are 'less formal advocates' such as an independent parental supporter, introduced to the parents by PPS, although even here there is an emphasis on ensuring that parents 'are enabled to speak for themselves' (DfES 2002, sect. 3 para. 41). Having some form of support available has been found to be valuable to parents entering into the mediation process, particularly among those such as lone parents who could feel more anxious about coping on their own (Tennant et al. 2008, p. 46).

Take-up of mediation Parents are not taking up mediation in the numbers that might have been anticipated when the arrangements were introduced and especially when their provision in effect became mandatory. (Local authorities and schools may also refer a case to mediation, but this hardly ever occurs.) The returns from the local authorities participating in the ESRC research indicated a very low take-up of mediation. In each of the years 2005/06, 2006/07 and 2007/08 approximately one half of the local authorities had *no* special educational needs mediations. In 2007/08 only one in seven of the authorities had three or more mediations and only two authorities had four or more mediations. Altogether, there were in 2006–2007 only 72 mediations across 54 respondent authorities and in 2007–2008 there were 58 mediations across 55 authorities. This take-up rate, at just over one mediation per authority, is even lower than the average of 1.7 per authority shown in mediation provider figures over a similar period cited by Tennant et al. (2008, tables 3.1 and 3.2), which also show that an average of two cases per authority were resolved prior to formal mediation, with the intervention of the mediation provider. The number of appeals lodged with the tribunal in each of those three years (a full set of appeal figures is cited below – see figure 3.1) was 3,110 in 2006/07 and 3,392 in 2007/08. The number of cases in which a decision was reached by the tribunal (i.e. where there was no withdrawal of the appeal due to prior settlement or other reason and the appeal was not struck out for want of jurisdiction or other reason such as lateness) in 2007–2008 was just under 1,000. This translates as an average for each local authority of just over 20 appeals per annum that were lodged and just under 7 appeals that were heard. There are unexplained variations in the level of use of mediation and in the rate of appealing in different local authorities, with no direct correlation between the two: some authorities had an above average level of both appeals and mediations, some had low levels of both, and some had high rate of one and a low rate of the other.

A number of factors lie behind the low take-up of mediation. One of them is clearly the relatively high proportion of the disagreements or disputes that are resolved through local negotiation, often involving PPS, or in some cases with the intervention of the school. Aside from that, one of the main factors identified in the ESRC research is that local authorities have not sufficiently publicised or promoted mediation. They are advised that they should inform parents of mediation when, for example, a statement or amended statement is issued or when a decision refusing formal assessment of a child is communicated (DfES 2001, paras 2.25 and 7.29). Eighty per cent of the local authorities in the ESRC survey considered that parents would know about mediation, primarily from such decision letters. However, these letters are only sent in specific circumstances and tend not to tell parents that mediation is also available for disagreements with their child's school. Some local authorities are reluctant to promote mediation because they perceive it to lack value. In their view, discussions can take place and agreement can be reached without it (Tennant et al. 2008, p. 25), while in some other cases a definitive ruling by the tribunal is considered necessary. Some of the local authorities in the ESRC research also identified their reorganisation into integrated children's services authorities as a distraction. Additionally, the cost of mediations, especially where the authority pays on a per case basis, can be a disincentive. The promotion of mediation in a particular case may also be dependent on the availability to the authority of a specialist tribunal or appeal officer who can predict a potential defeat for the authority at a tribunal, but not all authorities have them. Schools also fail to promote mediation, either due to a lack of awareness, a wariness of any form of external intervention in their affairs, and an unwillingness to commit staff time to it.

Parental misunderstanding of the nature and role of mediation is another factor affecting take-up, compounded by poor knowledge of it among some local authority SEN and school staff (Tennant et al. 2008, pp. 25 and 30). In two of the ESRC case studies the parents were ignorant of mediation and in another case the parent misconstrued informal meetings as part of formal mediation. Another parent participated in mediation over the contents of her child's SEN statement but mistakenly thought she had been to the tribunal. Take-up will also be affected by parents' doubts over the independence of the mediator and by their past experience of dealing with the local authority. If there are tense and difficult relations with the authority, which is a common experience (Penfold et al. 2009), the parents may view the authority as unsympathetic and unlikely to be swayed other than by a tribunal ruling. Parents will also be influenced by the negative experience of others, especially if they are in self-help groups. One of the ESRC case study parents had been told by another parent that mediation was a waste of time. In any event, parents often want their 'day in court', regardless of alternatives.

Mediation is also going to be hindered by the possibility that the local authority refuses to participate in it, although this not all that common (see below). Also, advisers and especially interest groups often promote the appeal route in preference to mediation because the tribunal's decision is binding and may provide an outcome more favourable to the parent. Furthermore, many of the professionals in the ESRC research considered that mediation is less suitable in some cases than others. For example, it will be ineffective if the matter at issue gives little or no scope for compromise, such as a dispute over school placement or whether to make a statement of SEN. In three of the ESRC case studies there was a dispute over a refusal to conduct a formal assessment of the child, each of which went to mediation but only one of which was successfully resolved through it. However, two other mediation cases, concerning the contents of statements, led to an agreement.

Views of mediation As noted in chapter 2, mediation is regarded as having a number of advantages over court or tribunal adjudication in terms of being cheaper, aiding the identification of the key areas of conflict, facilitating mutual understanding and earlier resolution, assisting in the maintenance of good long-term relations and enabling interest-based solutions to disputes, which are often more 'subtle and complicated' than would otherwise be attainable (Graham 2008, p. 128). Many of these advantages, particularly those relating to communication and mutual understanding, are said to make mediation particularly suitable for disputes involving children's interests (Roberts 2008, p. 132). Mediation is also considered to be less stressful for parents and tends to be valued by users. It is also seen as conducive to ideas of citizenship by facilitating parental involvement.

The mediation model received much support from local authorities and professionals in the ESRC research: two-thirds of the authorities were satisfied or very satisfied with it. Most local authorities (87 per cent) considered that mediation facilitates better mutual understanding of the parties' perspectives, which can aid compromise and improve relations. Through mediation, parents may be able to understand why the local authority feels unable to accede to their wishes, while the authority may appreciate the precise circumstances of the child and family. For example, in one case in Northborough, the diagnosis of the boy's condition was clarified at mediation, leading to the increased allocation of support for the child. This links into another advantage which was also confirmed, that by focussing widely mediation often gets to the heart of the dispute. The importance of this stems from the fact that some grievances are not directly tied to the statutory grounds of appeal. For example, in one of the cases in Middleshire the mediation meeting revolved around a teenage boy's non-attendance at a school where he was bullied.

There was less support for the view that mediation leads to an earlier resolution of the dispute. Mediation can be organised quite quickly and so can obviate the need for an appeal hearing, which in 2008–2009 did not occur until, on average, 6.4 months after the appeal was registered (Tribunals Service 2009, para. 1.1). Moreover, as discussed below, many appeals are withdrawn (over 40 per cent in 2008–2009: Tribunals Service 2009, para. 1.4), usually due to settlement which often occurs at a very late stage. Early mediation, if successful, might reduce expenditure of the tribunal's time and resources. But while mediation forces parties to confront the issues together earlier than would occur in an appeal, local authorities in the ESRC research had mixed views on whether it tended to resolve disputes quickly: 28 per cent thought it did, 40 per cent thought it did not and 31 per cent were unsure. Of course, the parents may know that they can proceed to the tribunal if mediation fails to offer them what they want, with the result that the dispute could become protracted. Although, as noted above, an aim of introducing mediation was to reduce the proportion of disputes going to the tribunal, only one third of the local authorities considered that mediation reduced the likelihood of an appeal, whereas 50 per cent did not believe that this was the case. One factor is that some parents enter mediation in the belief, reinforced by their advisers, that this will give them a moral premium at the tribunal hearing. There is, however, no evidence that such a benefit accrues; and in any event tribunals do not specifically enquire about the parties' prior or concurrent participation in mediation.

Mediators clearly aim to defuse tension and minimise outward expressions of conflict between the parties, but the idea that mediation is significantly less confrontational than an appeal was not wholly borne out by the experience of the case study parents who used it, as discussed below. Nevertheless, mediators and voluntary organisations were of the view that mediation is less adversarial than the appeal process. This may partially account for the reportedly lower levels of stress that parents participating in mediation experience compared to when appealing, also referred to by the vast majority (83 per cent) of local authorities in the ESRC survey.

As to whether mediation is cheaper than an appeal, while that could be the case for a parent who, for an appeal, might hire a legal representative or commission an independent assessment of their child, it may not be the case for the local authority. Although authorities themselves used legal representation in one in six appeal hearings in 2008–2009 (Tribunals Service 2009, para. 1.13), they obviously do not maintain the tribunal, which is the responsibility of central government. They do have to pay for mediations, but a majority (54 per cent) of ESRC local authority respondents thought that, on a case by case basis, mediation took up less staff time and cost them less than appeals. We are not aware of any comparative costings for the two processes in this field, but as mediation involves a single facilitator as against both a three person panel and a potentially protracted series of procedural steps involving the preparation and processing of written information, it is very likely to involve less overall cost. On the other hand, if mediation fails to reach a settlement and the case proceeds to an appeal the overall cost will obviously be higher than if only one process has been used (see Advice Services Alliance 2007). Certainly research into court-referred or -linked mediation suggests that this will be the case; parties and representatives were particularly likely to regard both costs and time taken up as increasing when there was no settlement at mediation and being saved where settlement was reached (Genn et al. 2007, pp. 178–182).

Despite the important, although not always clear-cut, advantages of mediation in SEN cases, there are also a number of significant drawbacks to it. In chapter 2 it was noted that there are concerns about whether mediation sufficiently safeguards individuals' substantive rights and protects the public interest in disputes by enabling state agencies to be held to account for incorrect or unfair decisions. The issue of whether mediation is able to correct or compensate for imbalances of power between state and citizen parties to disputes was also discussed. With regard to the issue of accountability, one of the obvious drawbacks to mediation is that it is an essentially voluntary process, a characteristic that is reinforced in relation to tribunal-recommended mediation by the incorporation of the principle of consent into tribunal rules.[55] A local authority may decline to enter mediation. In the ESRC research 13 per cent of local authorities had refused to participate in mediation in at least one case. The main reason for refusal was that they considered that mediation would be unlikely to succeed, for example because the law or the authority's policy left no scope for settlement.

There is also the risk that the local authority will not adhere to the agreed settlement or that the parents will have a subsequent change of heart. In the ESRC research approximately half of the local authorities regarded the non-binding nature of mediation settlements as a disadvantage for both of the parties. There were several cases where the mediated settlement was not honoured by the local authority, although we were also informed of cases where the parents changed their mind after the mediation. Another problem was that the officer participating in the mediation on behalf of the local authority may not have the power to agree formally to a concluded settlement. The matter would have to be taken back to the authority for someone else to do this, which could cause a delay or even the unravelling of the agreement. The effectiveness of the mediation process itself is also sometimes affected by the non-attendance of key people.

Also raised in chapter 2 was the 'vindication of rights' argument, namely that the absence of a definitive ruling, such as a tribunal or court can provide, means that there is no authoritative declaration of parents' rights. However, it is difficult to judge objectively whether legal rights are denied as a result of mediated settlements, since SEN law does not prescribe a particular level of provision for the child. Moreover, a comparison with a decision by a tribunal is unlikely to be possible since most cases that are settled by mediation will not proceed to a tribunal hearing and decision. Nevertheless, in the ESRC research one third of local authorities considered that the parent's rights may be less well safeguarded by mediation.

55 Tribunals, Courts and Enforcement Act 2007, s. 24, discussed below.

Only a very small minority of authorities felt that parents had settled for less in mediation than an appeal would have given them, although one fifth of PPS officers reporting having had at least one such case. This therefore does lend some credence to the suggestion, discussed in chapter 2, that parents may in some cases place their rights at risk when entering mediation. Parents may also be disadvantaged by an 'inequality of arms' during the mediation process (see chapter 2), especially with the absence of legal representation and the unwillingness of PPS to represent them, noted above. More than one in four of the PPS respondents in the ESRC research considered that the parents would be at a disadvantage during mediation, mainly due to their inexperience or lack of skill, although nearly 70 per cent considered that mediation is not inherently more advantageous to one party than another.

A final problem with mediation is that it does not facilitate the participation of the child. The arguments and broader evidence concerning this were discussed in chapter 1. Neither mediation nor the appeal process has a good record in this regard, although improvements have occurred in relation to the tribunal (see below). Hall found that children were 'not usually involved in discussions between their parents and their school or LEA' and did not participate in mediation meetings, although they were consulted 'as and when required' (Hall 1999, para. 7.14). Yet in this field there is almost universal agreement that the child's views are important and should be taken into account and that, wherever possible (bearing in mind the child's age, understanding and vulnerabilities) the child should be heard and listened to. Hearing children's own perspectives is considered important to understanding the nature of their needs and assessing the suitability of proposed educational arrangements. However, there is no requirement for the child's view to be fed into the mediation. Yet while it is officially acknowledged that children 'may not be involved directly' in mediation meetings they 'should be consulted to determine their wishes, needs and views' and their view should be established early in the process (DfES 2002, part 3 para. 45). In the ESRC research, mediators said they made an effort to elicit the child's perspective on the case prior to the meeting, but few local authorities considered that mediation facilitated the taking into account of the child's views.

The appeal process

Background Parents first acquired a right of appeal in SEN cases under the Education Act 1981. Prior to this they could merely make a request to the Secretary of State to cancel a local certification that a child required special education.[56] The grounds of appeal under the 1981 Act were, however, limited and there was not always a guarantee of a binding ruling. There were two separate appeal routes.[57] One, for cases where a statement was refused, involved appeal to the Secretary

56 The power to cancel was in the Education Act 1944, s. 34(6). The local authority's medical officer could also cancel it.

57 Education Act 1981, ss. 5 and 8.

of State. If the appeal was upheld the Secretary of State could only direct the local authority to reconsider its decision. The other route, for appeals concerning statement contents, including an amendment, involved a hearing by a local appeal committee appointed by the local authority. The committee could either confirm the decision or remit the case to the authority for reconsideration. The rationale for not empowering the issuing of binding rulings was that consideration of the many different factors relevant to the drawing up of statements and determination of school placements required specialist expertise which the appeal panel might not possess (see Harris 1997, pp. 17–18). There was a further right of appeal in such cases, again to the Secretary of State, who could for example amend or terminate a statement, but the whole process was protracted. Relatively few appeals reached the Secretary of State under either of these routes in the period 1984–1991, although there was a steady increase in the combined annual total from 39 to 146 over this period; and an estimated 300–400 SEN appeals were dealt with by local appeal committees (Harris 1997, p. 19).

The growing recourse to redress was to some extent indicative of the incomplete realisation of partnership ideal envisaged by Warnock (1978) (Wolfendale 1994; Harris 1997). However, it became clear that the appeal system was seriously flawed, with procedural shortcomings (see Harris 1997, p. 20). There were significant delays, compounding the time parents had to wait for completion of the various stages of assessment and statementing (see Audit Commisssion/HMI 1992). Cases had also become more complex and contentious (DfE 1992, para. 20; Council on Tribunals 1993, para. 2.11). Increasingly, significant numbers of parents were resorting to judicial review to challenge SEN decisions, with 120 applications in 1992 (Harris 1997, p. 21, citing the *T.E.S.*, 15 January 1993). The Government accepted the need for a more judicial approach which could offer parents 'a clear, timely and effective means of redress for their grievances' (DfE 1992, para. 21). Accordingly, under the Education Act 1993 a new tribunal was established on a national basis, under a President: the Special Educational Needs Tribunal (SENT). SENT was the first tribunal dealing with education matters that was required to have a legally-qualified chair. The other two members of the tribunal were drawn from a 'lay panel' of persons appointed by the Secretary of State from among persons with knowledge or experience of children with SEN *or* local government.[58] The members initially appointed to the lay panel for the tribunal's first year were predominantly people with local authority experience, as senior officers and advisers. Despite concern that they might be overly sympathetic to the local authority's case, research suggested a 'broad picture of neutrality' and there was a legitimate reason for ensuring that people with relevant experience were appointed, in view of the premium necessarily placed on specialist knowledge to inform decision making (Harris 1997, pp. 43–44 and 52). In any event, when new

58 Special Educational Needs Tribunal Regulations 1995 (SI 1995/3113), reg. 3.

regulations were introduced in 2001 the reference to local government knowledge or experience was omitted.[59]

After the jurisdiction of the tribunal was subsequently widened under SENDA 2001 to include complaints of disability discrimination, lay members' qualifying knowledge and experience was in respect of children with SEN *or* children with disabilities, or both.[60] The tribunal's name was altered to the Special Educational Needs and Disability Tribunal (SENDIST), to reflect its newly extended role, and it adopted the case management framework for appeals which was established during the final year of SENT. This involved a 'case statement period' during which, after an appeal was lodged, both parties had to prepare statements of their case. The idea behind this replacement of the traditional approach whereby one party lodges their case and then the parties may respond to each other's pleadings in turn, is to encourage 'constructive forward thinking about the child's education ... in preference to confrontation' (Aldridge 2001, p. 131). It was also at this time that greater recognition was given to the importance of listening to the views of the child, first through the conferment on children of a right to attend the tribunal hearing and be heard[61] and secondly through a requirement that the local authority's statement of its case should set out the child's views or, if it was not possible to ascertain them, why that was the case.[62]

The rules governing appeals obviously gave the process a degree of formality, but the original intention had been that 'the tribunal's procedures should be as informal as possible' (DfE 1994, para. 35). Articulating an approach which has now also become strongly associated with mediation in these cases, the President explained that the tribunal would aim to ensure that there was a 'non-confrontational atmosphere' and that 'tribunal proceedings do not add rancour to the relations between the parents and the LEA', since a reasonable ongoing relationship would be 'in the interests of the child' (Aldridge 1995, p. 12). Initially, informality was not written into the rules governing the hearing, which the tribunal was nevertheless required to conduct in a manner that was conducive to 'clarification of the issues' and consistent with 'just handling of the proceedings'.[63] Research suggested that while parents found the tribunal helpful and the proceedings not legalistic, the goals of informality and reduced confrontation were in competition with the demands of time and efficiency, particularly with regard to ensuring that all relevant evidence and the arguments were properly advanced and considered (Harris 1997, pp. 153–158). There was, in

59 Special Educational Needs Tribunal Regulations2001 (SI 2001/600), reg. 3.

60 Special Educational Needs and Disability Tribunal (General Provisions and Disability Claims Procedure) Regulations 2002 (SI 2002/1985), reg. 3. Wales has had its own tribunal, the Special Educational Needs Tribunal for Wales, since 1 September 2003 (Education Act 1996, s.336ZA, inserted by the Education Act 2002, Sch. 18 para. 5), from which there is a right of appeal, with permission, to the Upper Tribunal.

61 Special Educational Needs Tribunal Regulations 2001 (SI 2001/600), reg. 30. See Chapter 1.

62 Special Educational Needs Tribunal Regulations 2001 (SI 2001/600), reg. 13(2)(e)

63 Special Educational Needs Tribunal Regulations 1995 (SI 1995/3113), reg. 28(2).

any event, variation between tribunal chairs as to the level of formality in hearings. When the new rules were introduced in 2001 they retained these requirements but the tribunal was also subjected to a duty 'as far as appears to it appropriate, to seek to avoid formality in its proceedings'.[64] The issue of how far the tribunal has operated in a user friendly way since then is discussed in the next section.

The grounds of appeal to the SENT under the 1993 Act were wider than those under the 1981 Act. For example, they included a right of appeal against a decision not to carry out a formal assessment or a decision to cease to maintain a statement. They were extended still further under SENDA 2001 and, more recently, under the Children, Schools and Families Act 2010.[65] The 1993 Act introduced a right of appeal against a tribunal decision to the High Court, on a point of law (by 1997 there had been 101 such appeals), with the result that the judicial review process became much less important.[66] On 3 November 2008 the SENDIST jurisdiction was incorporated into the new First-tier Tribunal (Health, Education and Social Care Chamber) and new procedures came into operation, as discussed below.[67]

---

64 Special Educational Needs Tribunal Regulations 2001 (SI 2001/600), reg. 32(2).

65 The full list of decisions in respect of which there is a right of appeal is now: (i) not to make a statement (1996 Act, s. 325); (ii) to make, amend or not to amend a statement (s. 326) (the appeal may be against the description of the assessment of SEN, the specified provision (including the school) or the fact that no school is specified); (iii) not to comply with a request by a parent of a statemented child that the child be further assessed (s. 328); (iv) not to comply with a request by a parent of a child for whom there is no statement, that the child's needs be formally assessed (s. 329); (v) not to comply with a request by the head teacher that the needs of the child (whether statemented or not) be formally assessed (s. 329A, introduced under SENDA 2001, s. 8); (vi) not to comply with a request for the naming of a different school in a statement of special educational needs (Schedule 27 para. 8); (vii) to cease to maintain a statement (Schedule 27, para. 11) (the LEA may not cease to maintain a statement until the determination of the appeal: para. 11(5), added by s 6 of 2001 Act); and (viii) where the authority determines, following a review of the child's needs, not to amend a statement (s. 328A, inserted by s. 2 of the 2010 Act from 1 September 2010; see the Act's Commencement No.1 Order 2010 (SI 2010/1817)).

66 As Popplewell J states, 'the present law is that if there is a statutory right of appeal it is to be exercised and, save in exceptional circumstances, judicial review will not be granted where the statutory right of appeal exists and has not been exercised': *R v Special Educational Needs Tribunal ex parte F* [1996] ELR 213, QBD, at 217. Judicial review in this field is now pretty much only relevant to broader challenges to policy, e.g. with regard to funding of SEN provision (as in *R v London Borough of Hillingdon ex parte Governing Body of Queensmead School* [1997] ELR 331, QBD), issues concerning failure to meet non-educational needs per se (as they lie outside the appeal jurisdiction), or enforcement action to compel implementation of a tribunal's decision (through an application for a mandatory order).

67 See the First-tier Tribunal (Health, Education and Social Care Chamber Rules) 2008 (SI 2008/2699) and the Health and Social Care Chamber, *Practice Direction, Health and Social Care Chamber, Special Educational Needs or Disability Discrimination in Schools Cases* (2008).

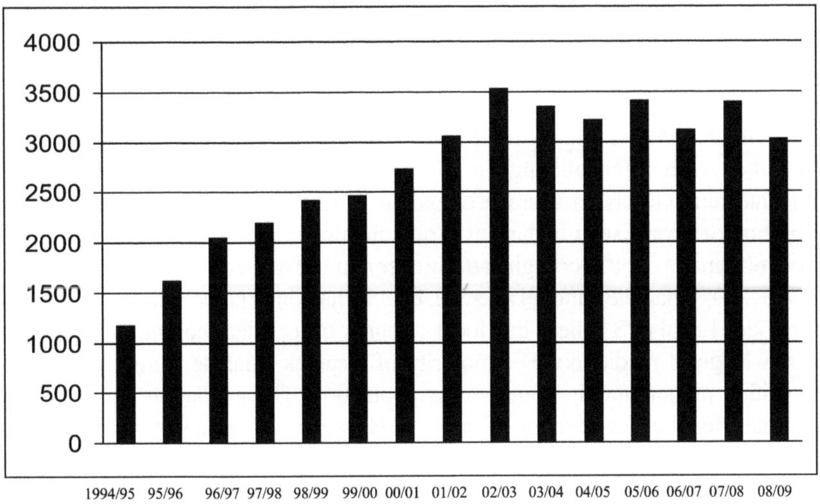

Source: Totals drawn from annual reports by the SENT and SENDIST Presidents and the Tribunals Service.

Figure 3.1 Number of appeals registered with SENT and successors in England 1994–1995 to 2008–2009

The tribunal was always likely to inspire higher levels of confidence among parents than the processes it replaced, because of its independence and expertise, its power to make binding decisions, and the prospects of a more consistent approach under prescribed procedural rules. With additional grounds of appeal, raised parental expectations resulting from the new right to nominate a school for the child, and new responsibilities on local authorities to inform parents of their right of appeal, it was not surprising that recourse to the tribunal proved popular. Post the introduction of SENT the number of appeals increased by a significant amount each year. The increase levelled out by 2002 but has remained fairly constant since then: see Figure 3.1. The Government sees mediation as having the potential to prevent long-term disagreements over SEN, thereby 'reducing, in time, the number of appeals going to the SEN Tribunal' (DfES 2001, para. 2.26). It does not seem to have had that effect on appeal numbers (SENDIST 2007, p. 2), although see the view of Middleshire local authority below.

The figures for 2008–2009 are the first that relate to the First-tier Tribunal (although the first two months of that period relate to SENDIST). Although the numbers were at their lowest for eight years they were still within the 3,000-plus range that has prevailed since 2001. There is in fact considerable variation across different local authorities in the number of appeals relative to the pupil population. In the three ESRC case study authorities, for example, the number of appeals per 10,000 school population in 2006–2007 was 2.26 in Northborough, 1.36 in Middleshire and 12.15 in Southside. The socio-economic, demographic and local authority policy and practice profiles shed some light on these variations.

Northborough is a largely rural county with a lower than average proportion of children with SEN, although a slightly above average proportion of pupils with statements. It has an average employment rate and a slightly below average proportion of people with higher level qualifications. The main area of disputes is school placement. Northborough had a higher number of mediations (eight meetings in 2006–2007) than the national average, but this has since fallen following a change of provider. Local PPS believe that local authority officers lack commitment towards or knowledge of mediation. The majority of disputes emanate from a part of the area with a predominantly middle class population. The mediation rate may help to account for the low number of appeals. However, the authority also claims to have been very active in meetings and negotiations with parents, although some parents reported that it had not been all that helpful or communicative. The authority admitted that engagement with parents can sometimes come rather late in the day. There is also some variation across the area in the quality of PPS support and their degree of involvement in disagreement resolution.

Middleshire combines rural and urban areas. Only around 2.5 per cent of the population comprises people from minority ethnic backgrounds. Its very low appeal rate (above) in part reflects the below average proportion of children who have SEN (at 15.4 per cent). It has an average statementing rate, although there have been falls in recent years. Like Northborough (above), which also has a low appeal rate, there has been a conscious effort by the local authority in recent years to meet with and engage parents, a process strengthened by improved staffing levels. One benefit has been a reduction in disputes concerning assessments, to which the local authority's increased tendency to concede to parental requests has contributed. In addition, the authority has sought to bring parents and PPS into contact with each other and considers that it has a very good relationship with the PPS. The high number of mediations (ten in 2006–2007, lower than in the previous two years) is considered by the local authority and PPS to have contributed to the low appeal rate, which has fallen by two-thirds over the previous two years. Both the local authority and PPS have a positive view of mediation but consider the appeal system to be unfair, both in the way it tends to favour parents but also in how it calculates the cost differentials between different placements.

Southside is urban and has quite a high proportion of residents of minority ethnic origin and recent immigrants. The area is mixed in terms of affluence. It has many well educated residents in professional occupations and a high overall rate of employment. The school population has a higher proportion of children with SEN than the national average but a lower than average proportion of children with statements. There was only one mediation in 2006–2007. Among local authority staff there is a degree of uncertainty regarding the value of mediation. Local PPS are considered by the LA to be relatively weak and under-utilised by parents. One of the most active voluntary organisations supporting parents is distrustful of PPS and antipathetic towards mediation. These factors are likely to have contributed to the high appeal rate, but a further element could be the numbers of middle class parents; such parents are more likely than less advantaged persons to bring challenges to local authority decisions concerning education (Coldron et al. 2002; Lange and Riddell 2000, p. 141; Evans and Vincent 1997, pp. 109–110; Harris 1997, p. 76).

The key message from these three case study authorities seems to be that local authority and PPS practice vis-à-vis communicating with and supporting parents can have a strong impact on the appeal rate, confirming other research findings (Penfold et al. 2009). A secondary factor could be the social class profile of the area, in that the link between social advantage and propensity to use formal dispute resolution processes especially appeal routes is reaffirmed. Local authorities' and PPS' view of mediation and promotion of it also seem to have influenced its take-up.

In terms of the kinds of SEN to which appeals to the tribunal nationally relate, the largest categories in 2008–2009 were: autistic spectrum disorder; behavioural, emotional and social difficulty; specific learning difficulty; moderate learning difficulty; and speech, language and communication needs (Tribunals Service 2009, para. 1.6). A relatively high proportion of appeals are upheld across all categories of case, as shown in Table 3.1 below (many are withdrawn: see below). The final column shows the proportion of decided appeals which were upheld.

Table 3.1 Appeals upheld by SENDIST/First-tier Tribunal in England in relation to different subject matters, 2008–2009

Subject	Resolved	%	Appeals decided	Appeals upheld	%
Refusal to assess	1072	36	134	88	66
Refusal to statement	182	6	41	24	59
Refusal to re-assess	40	1	5	3	60
Ceasing statement	34	1	14	9	64
Contents of statement	1639	55	597	526	88

Source: Tribunals Service 2009, paras 1.7 and 1.8.

The success rates for appeals concerning statement contents need to be viewed cautiously, since they do not necessarily indicate that the appellant gained everything they had hoped for. Nevertheless, they show that a reasonably high proportion of appeals are upheld. This not only indicates that appealing is often very fruitful for parents but may also imply that local authorities ought to be more pliant in their negotiations. On the other hand, the cases that are decided represent only a minority of the registered appeals (see below) and thus they will mostly be ones where local authorities feel unable to give more ground. Apart from in the very smallest categories, such as refusal to re-assess, the success rates were more or less the same in 2007–2008 (Tribunals Service 2009, para.

1.8), indicating that, thus far, the introduction of the First-tier Tribunal (below) has not materially affected the chances of an appeal being upheld.

The reform of tribunals The impetus towards the establishment of the largely unified tribunal service that exists today came in large part from the recommendations of the report into tribunals by Sir Andrew Leggatt (2001). The report advanced a vision of a coherent, independent and efficient tribunal system in place of the 70 plus separate tribunals operating in various fields. It proposed a single judicial structure and a focus in tribunal procedures on the user. It focused on the need for tribunals to be accessible to users and assist them, although it acknowledged that for full participation many users would need additional help from others (Leggatt 2001, para. 4.15). ADR methods, such as mediation, were considered to have a potential role, but the report was cautious about advancing them too wholeheartedly. The report referred to the fact that where opportunities arise for settlement of a case through informal discussion it can avoid the number of contested cases coming before tribunals. The report cited SEN cases resolved at the door of the tribunal as an example. ADR techniques might be particularly helpful in cases where the parties needed to maintain good long term relations, but they should be utilised on the basis of careful consideration of the kind and circumstances of individual cases (Leggatt 2001, paras 8.19–8.20 and 8.23).

Greater backing for ADR (whose use government has long committed itself to for disputes (contractual or other claims) involving itself and its agencies which might otherwise end up in court[68]) was given in the Department for Constitutional Affairs' subsequent White Paper (DCA 2004). More significantly, the idea that for citizen redress there should be 'proportionate dispute resolution' was strongly promoted. The White Paper contended that approaches such as mediation, conciliation or arbitration can often offer quicker and more cost effective resolution of grievances than judicial bodies, which tend to be less accessible to ordinary citizens. Disputes, it argued, can be avoided or resolved by more proportionate means:

> The aim is to develop a range of policies and services that, so far as possible, will help people to avoid problems and legal disputes in the first place; and where they cannot, provides tailored solutions to resolve the dispute as quickly and cost effectively as possible (DCA 2004, para. 2.2).

The White Paper also backed Leggatt's ideas about a unified tribunal system and for better information and support for tribunal users. Legislation was needed for many of the structural reforms, but not for the establishment of the Tribunals Service as an executive agency within the Ministry of Justice, under whose umbrella a range of

68 The government issued a Dispute Resolution Pledge to this end in 2001 and subsequently published annual monitoring reports. In May 2011 the pledge was replaced by the Dispute Resolution Commitment, the minister stressing that the government was 'leading by example by resolving issues away from the courts', using alternatives: Ministry of Justice Press Release, 23 June 2011.

tribunals (including SENDIST) were placed in April 2006; the Service was integrated into the new Her Majesty's Courts and Tribunals Service established in April 2011.

The First-tier Tribunal (Health, Education and Social Care Chamber) The jurisdiction of SENDIST was transferred to the Health, Education and Social Care (HESC) Chamber of the First-tier Tribunal (FTT) on its establishment on 3 November 2008. The grounds of appeal were not changed although, as noted above, an additional ground was added in 2010.[69] The composition of the tribunal for SEN and disability cases is unaltered, but chairs are now members of the tribunal judiciary. The HESC Chamber was one of three created on that day (three other chambers have since been added).[70] Each is headed up by a President. The government did not support the idea of a dedicated Children Chamber, which might have incorporated the SEN and disability jurisdiction, because children's issues such as child benefit and child support appeals were considered to be best placed in the Social Entitlement Chamber (Ministry of Justice/Tribunals Service 2008, p. 11). At the head of the new tribunals structure is a Senior President of Tribunals, who oversees both the FTT and the new second-tier appellate body, the Upper Tribunal (UT). The UT has four chambers. Its Administrative Appeals Chamber hears SEN and disability appeals on a point of law in place of the former appellate jurisdiction of the High Court.[71] In its first two years the UT's caseload in SEN and disability cases in England appears to have been broadly similar to that of the High Court before it.[72] The UT may also exercise a judicial review jurisdiction.[73] Unlike the High Court, it may itself be subject to judicial review,[74] albeit

69 See n. 65 above.

70 Tribunals, Courts and Enforcement Act 2007; Transfer of Tribunal Functions Order 2008 (SI 2008/2833) and the First-tier Tribunal and Upper Tribunal (Chambers) Order 2008 (SI 2008/2684). See further, Senior President of Tribunals (2008) and Adler (2006). The other five chambers are: Social Entitlement; Immigration and Asylum; General Regulatory; Tax; and War Pensions and Armed Forces Compensation.

71 First-tier Tribunal and Upper Tribunal (Chambers) Order 2008 (SI 2008/2684). The other three chambers are: Tax and Chancery; Lands; and Immigration and Asylum. Those wishing to appeal to the Upper Tribunal must apply first to the First-tier Tribunal for permission which, if refused, can be renewed before the Upper Tribunal itself. When it receives an application the FTT must first consider, subject to the 'overriding objective' (see note 85 below), whether to undertake a review of the decision: Tribunal Procedure (First-tier Tribunal) (Health, Education and Social Care Chamber) Rules 2008 (SI 2008/2699) (L. 16), rr. 46 and 47. See further note 77 below.

72 In the first 11 months of 2010 there appear to have been 13 published decisions of the UT relating to SEN or disability cases originating in England. This compares, for example, with 14 High Court decisions (including referrals back to the FTT) in 2006–2007 and 8 in 2007–2008: Tribunals Service 2008, paras 1.13 and 2.10.

73 See the Tribunals, Courts and Enforcement Act 2007, ss. 15–19; Supreme Court Act 1981, s. 31A. Some categories of judicial review have been transferred to the Upper Tribunal under powers in the 2007 Act: see Senior President of Tribunals (2010), paras 48–50.

74 The Government had left that matter to be decided by the courts: Ministry of Justice/Tribunals Service (2008), p. 13.

on a reduced basis to that which normally lies against public bodies and inferior courts or tribunals.[75]

One of the potential benefits of the new structure is a more consistent approach between different first-tier tribunal jurisdictions (Tribunals Service 2007). The establishment of a Tribunals Procedure Committee,[76] instrumental in the development of rules of procedure, has contributed to a more coherent procedural framework across the service (tribunals) as a whole. Even though there are separate sets of rules for each chamber, there is considerable common ground between them. Indeed, there has been a tendency to omit jurisdiction-specific rules in the interests of greater overall coherence, although some are needed, such as on the attendance of and giving of evidence by children at a hearing.[77] In addition, Chamber Presidents have a power to issue Practice Directions.[78] The Practice Direction on SEN and disability cases,[79] for example, includes the local authority's duty formerly in the SENDIST procedure regulations (above) to set out the child's view of issues raised by the proceedings. The child continues not to have a right of appeal in his or her own right,[80] although, as noted above, this is set to change, at least on a pilot basis. The basic rules governing the making of appeals (such as the normal 28 day time limit) and the duty of the local authority to issue a response containing prescribed information (normally within 21 days) are essentially preserved from the SENDIST procedures.

One of the HESC Chamber rules that is common to other chambers concerns ADR. It reflects the way that the use of ADR is included in the legislative framework as a whole. In particular, the Senior President of Tribunals must have regard to 'the need to develop innovative methods for resolving disputes that are of a type that can be brought before tribunals'.[81] Additionally, members of tribunals

75 The test should be whether the case involves an important point of principle or practice or there is some other compelling reason justifying the higher court's scrutiny of the decision: *R (Cart) v The Upper Tribunal* [2011] UKSC 28, e.g. paras 52–57. Cf the position of the election court: *R (Woolas) v The Parliamentary Election Court and Others* [2010] EWHC 3169 (Admin).

76 See Tribunals, Courts and Enforcement Act 2007, Sched 5.

77 Tribunal Procedure (First-tier Tribunal) (Health, Education and Social Care Chamber) Rules 2008 (SI 2008/2699) (L. 16), rules 24(b) and 48. The rules also contain a general power to review a decision when permission to appeal is sought and there has been an error of law: ibid., r. 49. Such a general review power is also found, for example, in the Social Entitlement Chamber's rules: Tribunal Procedure (First-tier Tribunal) (Social Entitlement Chamber) Rules 2008 (SI 2008/2685), r. 40.

78 Tribunals, Courts and Enforcement Act 2007, s. 23.

79 *Practice Direction, Health and Social Care Chamber, Special Educational Needs or Disability Discrimination in Schools Cases* (2008).

80 *S v Special Educational Needs Tribunal and the City of Westminster* [1996] ELR 228, CA.

81 Tribunals, Courts and Enforcement Act 2007, s. 2(3)(d).

are permitted to act as mediators in disputes.[82] Despite its various references to ADR in general, or to mediation specifically, the legislative framework is generally regarded as facilitating not promoting ADR. Vernon (2008, pp. 21–22) argues that it does not reflect a commitment to mediation, nor does it envisage 'compulsory or judicially directed mediation'. In general, it seems to be attuned to the growing support for ADR in appropriate cases while addressing the concern that appellants should not be denied a fair hearing for the resolution of their dispute (e.g. HLSCC 2006, para. 14). ADR was still considered to be 'in its infancy' in the tribunal world (Tribunals Service 2007, p. 54). Moreover, many tribunals regarded ADR as inherently unsuitable for their particular jurisdiction. A survey by the Administrative Justice and Tribunals Council (AJTC) on the use of ADR in tribunals found that SENDIST saw its role as 'decision-making rather than brokering a compromise between parties' (AJTC 2008). In the ESRC research, however, there was some support from within the SEN tribunal system towards at least encouraging agreement between the parties.

The HESC Chamber Rules give the parties a further 'nudge' towards ADR. Rule 3 places tribunals under a duty to:

> 'seek, where appropriate–
>
> (a) to bring to the attention of the parties the availability of any appropriate alternative procedure for the resolution of the dispute; and
>
> (b) if the parties wish and provided that it is compatible with the overriding objective, to facilitate the use of the procedure'.[83]

The rule is therefore consistent with the requirement in the Tribunals, Courts and Enforcement Act 2007 that those making tribunal procedural rules or practice directions covering mediation must take account of the principle that mediation is to be on the basis of a consensus.[84] The rule requires the tribunal to give consideration to the appropriateness of alerting the parties to the possibility of using mediation and to allow sufficient time for mediation to be concluded. However, the 'overriding objective' referred to in rule 3 is that the case should be dealt with 'fairly and justly'.[85] Two of the elements of that are the avoidance of delay and the

82 Ibid.

83 Tribunal Procedure (First-tier Tribunal) (Health, Education and Social Care Chamber) Rules 2008 (SI 2008/2699) (L. 16), r. 3. This rule is also in the Tribunal Procedure (First-tier Tribunal) (Social Entitlement Chamber) Rules 2008 (SI 2008/2685), r. 3.

84 Tribunals, Courts and Enforcement Act 2007, s. 24.

85 Tribunal Procedure (First-tier Tribunal) (Health, Education and Social Care Chamber) Rules 2008 (SI 2008/2699) (L.16), r. 2.

seeking of flexibility.[86] They could in fact be in conflict because if mediation does not resolve the case the parties may well have to return to the appeal process. The overall effect could be to prolong the process and the uncertainty for the parents and child. The government seems to have acknowledged this problem underlying its proposal in the 2011 Green Paper that 'parents and local authorities should always try mediation before a parent can register an appeal with the Tribunal', because it does 'not want this to affect the time that parents have to appeal' (DfE 2011, p.53, para.2.62).

Another factor in the overriding objective involves dealing with the case in ways which are proportionate to, inter alia, the complexity of the issues. This suggests that evidentially or legally complex cases may be unsuitable for ADR. The appropriateness of recommending mediation may also depend on whether mediation arranged by the local authority has already been tried but failed. However, it is reported that HESC now sends a letter to *each* parent who lodges an appeal with the FTT urging them to 'consider mediation today' (Ruff 2011). Such a blanket approach does not seem to be what the tribunal rules envisage, especially since in some cases mediation will already be underway or the local authority may in fact have refused to participate in it. HESC is, however, going to monitor the uptake of mediation and, if it continues to be low, may consider asking parents for their reasons for not opting for it (Senior President of Tribunals 2011, p.45).

In any event, the lodging of the appeal itself often facilitates a negotiated outcome, since parents frequently appeal with the aim of putting the local authority under pressure. As discussed earlier, a high proportion of appeal cases are settled. Some parents feel it is 'necessary to have made an appeal ... before the [local authority] would actively engage in discussions with them via mediation' (Tennant et al. 2008, pp. 52–53). According to the Deputy Chamber President for HESC, around one third of the appeals which do not proceed to a hearing are resolved shortly after the appeal is lodged and another third within a short time of the hearing date or even on the day of the hearing.[87] Some of the voluntary organisations interviewed for the ESRC research indicated that local authorities often back down only at the eleventh hour; this corresponded with the evidence from the individual cases. Building mediation into the tribunal process had some support. It could increase the number of early settlements and make a corresponding reduction in the number occurring at the last minute. One would not, however,

86 Ibid. The rest are: utilizing the tribunal's expertise effectively, 'ensuring, so far as practicable, that the parties are able to participate fully in the proceedings', 'dealing with the case in ways that are proportionate to the importance of the case, the complexity of the issues, the anticipated costs and the resources of the parties' (see below), and 'avoiding unnecessary formality in the proceedings'.

87 Presentation by John Aitken in the session 'SEN/ASN and dispute resolution: policy and judicial perspectives' at Dispute Resolution and Avoidance in Education: A Study of Special and Additional Support Needs in England and Scotland Dissemination Conference, University of Manchester, 28 October 2009.

anticipate that it would take the form of 'judicial mediation', discussed in chapter 2, nor does it seem likely that rule 3 of the HESC rules contemplates that. Judicial mediation has in fact been specifically rejected for a proposed process designed to forge settlements in cases where parents have appealed against a local authority's refusal to agree to a formal assessment of their child. Instead the process will be one of 'early neutral evaulation' (described in chapter 2) using the specialist lay members of the tribunal to advise parents on the prospects of success with their appeal. It has been revealed that at present some 84% of such cases tend to be conceded by the local authority prior to the appeal hearing and so the scheme's other stated objective is to identify the local authorities which are likely to settle (Senior President of Tribunals 2011, pp. 45–46).

Views of the appeal process The tribunal has enjoyed a good reputation among professionals and academics for its fairness, independence and expertise (Harris 1997, Evans 1998, Penfold et al. 2009). Genn et al. (2006) found in SENDIST no evidence of ethnic bias for or against appellants in relation to the outcome of cases. They also found that tribunal users were treated well, as confirmed by a majority of appellants within all ethnic groups. Other research also confirmed that in general parents were satisfied with the tribunal and that although preparation was difficult and stressful the hearing itself offered 'a good experience' (Penfold et al. 2009, p. 52). In addition the case management process is considered to work well in enabling the tribunal to ensure that it has the right evidence before it, the key issues are identified, and hearings are conducted within the required timescale (Lamb 2009, para. 5.70).

Local authorities, on the other hand, have tended to hold negative views of the tribunal. Almost half of the ESRC research local authority respondents did not think that the tribunal made a positive contribution to dispute resolution. They did not object to the right of appeal per se, indeed few were opposed to it, but they considered the appeal process costly to them in terms of time and resources. They also regarded it as a dispute catalyst, serving to encourage challenges. Some thought that the tribunal was overly generous in the degree of procedural flexibility it allowed parents, for example over time limits, and in its support for individual children, which had a tendency to skew resource allocation. The local authority responses also echoed the sector's prevalent view in the tribunal's early years that the process tended to favour parents (Harris 1997, p. 170). Overall, local authorities considered that they were more likely to achieve an outcome favourable to themselves via mediation than at the tribunal. The relatively high success rate for parents at the tribunal was commented upon earlier. In relation to the issue of fairness to the parties, only 30 per cent of local authorities considered that the tribunal was equally fair to both, whereas 90 per cent thought this to be true of mediation. These views make it even more difficult to understand why local authorities do not do more to make parents aware of mediation and seek to increase their understanding of it.

Even though parents seem to value the experience of attending the tribunal hearing, they often find the appeal process difficult, as noted earlier. Concerns have been expressed about its inherent formality and legalism. In the ESRC research almost all local authorities thought the appeal process was stressful for parents and more than half considered it was also stressful for them. The essential problem is that although the tribunal often acts inquisitorially,[88] the appeal process itself still has an inherently adversarial character, with the parties adopting individual positions and having to respond to each other's case. Lamb observed that 'many parents are finding appeals too difficult and complex and feel unable to pursue their claim without legal support' and recommended that legal aid exceptional funding be made available (Lamb 2009, para. 5.80). In 2008–2009 18 per cent of appellants had legal representation at their SEN and disability appeal hearing and an identical proportion had lay representation, while the same proportion received legal assistance throughout the appeal process and 6 per cent had support from a voluntary organisation throughout. However, legal aid is not available other than exceptionally for legal representation at this hearing, although at present parents on very low incomes may qualify for legal advice and support in connection with the appeal process and this is set to continue despite other cutbacks to legal aid announced by the government (see below). Research has indicated that in SEN appeals pre-hearing advice is even more important than representation at a hearing, as unrepresented appellants who had received such advice were found to have had more success than those who were represented, while representation gave appellants no added premium as against being unrepresented (Adler 2009).

In November 2010 the Government announced an intention to end all legal aid funding for education cases apart from judicial review cases and the few which may attract exceptional funding (Ministry of Justice 2010, paras 4.18–4.187). It argued that education issues, such as SEN provision, are not as critical as those involving an immediate threat to life, safety, liberty or having a roof over one's head and so should not be accorded the highest priority for funding. The Lord Chancellor also commented that some education cases 'can be turned into enormous legal battles, which seems to me very far removed from the object of ensuring that a child is best educated in school'.[89] It was assumed that parents could turn to alternative sources of advice and assistance, including PPS and voluntary sector bodies (Ministry of Justice 2010 para. 4.185). However, as discussed earlier, PPS often do not provide assistance specifically in connection with formal dispute

88 For example, in *DR v London Borough of Croydon* [2010] UKUT 387 (AAC) (26 October 2010), a disability discrimination case, Judge Wikeley (at para. 29) refers to the FTT (HESC)'s 'inquisitorial function' in disability discrimination cases. An inquisitorial approach is one where the court (or tribunal) is actively involved in establishing the facts as opposed to merely acting as a referee inter partes, as in an adversarial system: see Ministry of Justice 2010 p. 34, note 34. The FFT (Social Entitlement Chamber) hearing social security appeals is also considered by the Government to adopt an inquisitorial approach: Ministry of Justice 2010, para. 4.217.

89 House of Commons Debates, 15 November 2010, col. 668.

resolution, while voluntary sector bodies are not well funded and may not have the requisite legal expertise.

Sensibly, however, the government has since decided to retain legal aid funding for advice on SEN matters (specifically preparation for a tribunal appeal) and for representation at a second-tier appeal, to the Upper Tribunal, as confirmed in the Legal Aid, Sentencing and Punishment of Offenders Bill. There was a belief that: restricting legal aid for SEN cases could simply lead to more disability discrimination cases (attracting possible legal aid); consistency was needed with community care cases, which raise similar issues regarding support needs; difficult family circumstances of many families with a child with SEN should be recognized; and if mediation take-up increased, it would be only the more complex and intractable cases, where legal assistance would be most valuable, that would progress to the tribunal (Ministry of Justice 2011, paras 63–66).

A further problem with the appeal process is that it operates relatively slowly in many cases. While sufficient time is needed to help the parties compile the evidence and prepare the documentation that is needed to ensure a sufficiently thorough review of the issues, delay prolongs uncertainty, as noted earlier, which may be particularly detrimental for the child. In the ESRC research 78 per cent of local authorities considered the timescale to be a negative feature of the appeal process. As noted above, in 2008–2009 the average time from registration of an appeal to a decision was 6.4 months, an increase from the 2007–2008 average of 5.8 months (Tribunals Service 2009, para. 1.1). No corresponding figure has been published for 2009–2010, but it has been reported that 75 per cent of cases were resolved within 22 weeks, which naturally means that 25 per cent took longer (Tribunals Service 2010, p. 142). While there may be good reasons for this timescale, there clearly seems to be room for improvement. However, in the ESRC research several voluntary sector interviewees explained that local authorities do not always mind the relative slowness of the appeal process because it delays the commitment of any resources needed for compliance with a tribunal's decision.

Some mediation and appeal case studies

The three case studies summarised below are drawn from the ESRC research to illustrate the experience of parents in utilising various redress mechanisms. All the names are fictitious.

Mrs L White is the mother of Edward, aged 12, who has autism. After Edward's statutory assessment a dispute arose over the number of teaching assistant hours the local authority had allocated him. Mrs White received help from PPS and an independent parent supporter (IPS). Mrs White found the school and PPS particularly helpful, mainly because they were able to explain matters to her. She opted for mediation on the school's recommendation and contacted the mediation provider by telephone. She had various discussions with the mediator prior to the mediation meeting. The meeting was held at a library and lasted approximately 45 minutes. Although the local authority's senior assessment officer (SAO) initially did not accept that there had been a diagnosis of autism, he acknowledged it following clarification at the meeting. The school's SENCO (special educational needs co-ordinator)[90] reported that the SAO was unpleasant, aggressive and intimidating at the mediation. The IPS spoke at the meeting on behalf of Mrs White, who lacked confidence although contributed towards the end. Edward did not participate and his views were not included in the process although he had contributed to his annual reviews. Mrs White found the mediator 'very helpful' and would recommend mediation to others. She had known about the tribunal and would have pursued an appeal if the mediation had not worked. The local authority agreed to provide between 12–14 hours of 'emergency' teaching assistant support. When the statement was eventually made, after a period of 12 months in all had elapsed (a timespan which the SENCO described as 'ridiculous'), it provided for long term support of ten hours per week, exceeding the parents' expectation.

Mrs J Hall is the mother of Andrew, aged 13. The local authority was reluctant to diagnose Andrew's problems. Mrs Hall commissioned an independent report by an educational psychologist, at a cost of £350, which confirmed moderate to severe dyslexia. When Andrew was aged nine there was a dispute over the local authority's refusal to make a statement. Mrs Hall decided against mediation because the school advised her that the authority was opposed to making statements and the educational psychologist said that she would need to go to the tribunal for one. A voluntary organisation (VO) also advised her against mediation. An appeal to the SENDIST was unsuccessful, although some support was subsequently given by the local authority. In his final year at primary school Andrew was still not progressing sufficiently and a further appeal was made when a statement was refused and a note in lieu was issued.[91] Mrs Hall then applied for judicial review, with legal aid, to challenge the note in lieu as unlawful. Before the application was heard the local authority capitulated and made a statement. Andrew moved to secondary school but it was not a good transition and Mrs Hall was not happy with the circumstances at the school. She appealed against the contents of the statement, on the advice of the VO, which provided representation. The tribunal agreed with Mrs Hall, who wanted an independent school, where Andrew had had a trial placement, named in his statement. Mr and Mrs Hall believed that the speech and language report that had been prepared

90 Every school is required to designate a member of the school's staff as a SENCO: Education Act 1996, s. 317(3A), inserted by the Education and Inspections Act 2006, s. 173. See also the 1996 Act s. 317(3B) and the Education (Special Educational Needs Co-ordinators) (England) Regulations 2008 (SI 2008/2945), as amended.

91 A 'note in lieu' is made when the local authority concludes that a statement is not needed. The note explains why a statement is not being made, making reference to the findings of the statutory assessment. It will discuss the child's needs and any special help the child requires, but will not have the same status as a statement.

on Andrew by the NHS but ignored by the local authority swung the case in their favour. Andrew joined the independent school and progressed well. In Mrs Hall's view the tribunal had been a 'nightmare' and 'stressful' experience but both hearings had been fair and the tribunal had focused on the main issues. Andrew had attended the second tribunal hearing. The panel interviewed him in a separate room in a 'friendly' way and made several references to his views, in the main hearing.

Ms T Redgrave is the mother of Lucy, aged 10, who has a range of learning difficulties. Lucy attended a mainstream school, where she was supported via School Action Plus. Ms Regrave took up Lucy's lack of progress with the local authority and met with them, but no changes were made. Ms Redgrave opted for mediation on a friend's recommendation. At mediation it was agreed that the local authority's annual review of Lucy's progress should be brought forward by several months. However, what Ms Redgrave really wanted was a statement for Lucy. She said at the end of the meeting: 'this has been a waste of time really'. According to the mediator, the authority's officer who attends mediations is not able to offer a final agreement to anything, only to make a case to the authority's panel. Ms Redgrave found the meeting itself intimidating. There were quite a number of people present, including the form teacher, head teacher and a couple of local authority staff, neither of whom she knew, who 'just seemed to be sitting there'. She said: 'It was just really horrible and I just thought "why am I being put through this?"' Although the mediator had been good and had sought to keep everything relaxed, Ms Redgrave found the school and local authority very defensive. After the mediation meeting and before the panel review further information on Lucy's problems came to light and the local authority decided to make a statement. Ms Redgrave felt that she had had to battle unaided to resolve matters appropriately: 'You have to know what you want and just keep ploughing forward ... there should be someone guiding you along'. Ms Redgrave was helped by PPS, but they did not become involved in the mediation.

Discussion The three cases above are typical of those in the ESRC study. All three show that using mediation or appealing can be difficult for some parents, particularly those lacking confidence and support. Mrs White's case nevertheless illustrates how the mediation meeting may clarify the issues in a way that is conducive to a successful outcome. Both of the mediation cases reinforce the need for parents to have support during the process. Mrs White, for example, clearly benefited from the involvement of the IPS to speak on her behalf. The mediation cases also illustrate the failure of that process to involve the child. Indeed, Ms Redgrave considered that the local authority's defensiveness deflected attention away from the child's interests. This contrasts with Mrs Hall's case, where the tribunal had ensured that the child's views were elicited and taken into account. It demonstrates the tribunal's inherent ability to involve the child, although the child's participation does not occur all that often in practice, for reasons discussed in chapter 1. The lack of a binding outcome to mediation and the problem where a local authority representative is unable to settle on the authority's behalf is illustrated by Ms Redgrave's mediation case. All three cases illustrate how parents need to be very determined and that dispute resolution can often be a protracted and stressful process for them.

Complaints

Parents of children with SEN have for many years had the right to pursue a complaint via the Local Government Ombudsman (LGO), whose jurisdiction covers complaints of maladministration by local authorities.[92] Typical SEN-related complaints brought under this process concern delays in carrying out an assessment or reassessment, in meeting the 26-week time limit for issuing a statement,[93] or in setting in place appropriate educational arrangements.[94] Clearly, as discussed in chapter 2, the complaints route has a different purpose to an appeal or mediation process, since it is mainly concerned with the way in which the local authority has conducted its business and treated the complainant. It is generally not concerned with changing a substantive decision, although in some instances a recommendation or settlement may require the local authority to re-run its decision making process. In a case where an injustice has been found to have resulted from the maladministration the LGO might typically recommend an award of compensation and/or one of a range of possible other options such as an apology or the carrying out of some form of remedial action.[95] In some cases the local authority will be recommended to change its procedures in order to prevent recurrences of maladministration.[96] In 2009–2010 there were 2,136 complaints to the LGO concerning education, constituting 12 per cent of all complaints that year. Two-thirds of the education complaints were about school admissions, but another one in seven (298) concerned SEN. Statistics on redress for injustice in the education cases alone are not available, but the percentage for all LGO complaints was 27.7 per cent, inclusive of local settlements (LGO 2010,

92 Local Government Act 1974, s. 26 and Schedule 5.

93 See for example, Reports 98/C/4894 (Salford City Council) (2000); 03/A/09667 (Norfolk County Council) (2005); 05/A/13627 (Surrey County Council) (2007). In 2008–2009, 9 per cent of statements were not issued within 26 weeks, or 18 per cent where exceptional cases were discounted. The lowest proportion of statements finalised within 26 weeks by an individual authority that year was 54 per cent (excluding exceptional cases) or 30 per cent (all cases). See DCSF (2009), tables 1 and 2.

94 See e.g. Report 03/B/12830 (Bedfordshire County Council).

95 In *R (Gallagher and McCarthy) v Basildon District Council* [2010] EWHC 2824 (Admin) the court held that a local authority's refusal to act on a recommendation by the LGO to pay compensation can be challenged as unlawful (e.g. for lack of rationality) via an application for judicial review.

96 See e.g. Report 03/B/12830, note 94 above, where the authority was recommended to undertake a review of its arrangements concerning the education of children with emotional and behavioural difficulties.

tables 1 and 2 and table on LGO website[97]). One quarter of all complaints were locally settled in 2009–2010.

Lamb (2009, paras 5.50–5.57) envisaged the LGO playing a more effective policing role and supported the idea of extending its jurisdiction to include complaints concerning schools. This idea has since been acted upon: since January 2010 the LGO has been able to deal with complaints about SEN at school, because complaints related to the internal organisation, management or discipline of a local authority maintained school are no longer excluded.[98] Another change, introduced on a pilot basis in four areas from April 2010[99] and extended to 10 other areas on 1 September 2010,[100] but currently threatened with repeal under the Education Bill 2011 (see below), enables the LGO to investigate complaints of 'injustice' due to an act by the governing body or due to the head teacher's exercise or failure to exercise a prescribed function, other than related to admissions.[101] No specifically SEN-related head teacher functions have been prescribed, but almost all SEN functions at school level are the responsibility of the governing body and are therefore covered, including the duty to use their best endeavours to ensure that all children with SEN receive the special educational provision they need.[102] Complaints about matters covered by a prescribed right of appeal are, however, excluded,[103] ostensibly in the interests of minimising the number of discrete avenues of redress (DCSF 2008, para. 83). However, the AJTC found no case for the two processes to be mutually exclusive (AJTC 2009). Complaints of disability discrimination at school, although not strictly 'appeals' as such, are prescribed as covered by this process along with appeals concerning exclusion from school.[104] No date has been set for the piloted jurisdiction to be rolled out nationally. Where it operates it replaces the existing local complaints system which requires the governing body to investigate complaints about any matter related to

97 www.lgo.org.uk/publications/annual-report/ (accessed 14 September 2010).

98 Apprenticeships, Skills, Children and Learning Act 2009, s. 261, amending the Local Government Act 1974, Schedule 5 para. 5(2), with effect from 12 January: the Apprenticeships, Skills, Children and Learning Act 2009 (Commencement No. 1 and Saving Provision) Order 2009 (SI 2009/3317).

99 The four authorities are Barking and Dagenham, Cambridgeshire, Medway and Sefton. A further group of authorities is covered from September 2010.

100 See the Apprenticeships, Skills, Children and Learning Act 2009 (Commencement No. 3 and Transitional and Transitory Provisions) and (Commencement No. 2 (Amendment)) Order 2010 (SI 2010/1151 (C. 75)).

101 Apprenticeships, Skills, Children and Learning Act 2009, Part 10, Chapter 2.

102 Education Act 1996, s. 317(1).

103 Apprenticeships, Skills, Children and Learning Act 2009, s. 206(3)(b).

104 The Complaints against Schools (England) Regulations 2010 (SI 2010/853).

the school[105] and offers parents the possibility of taking them to the Secretary of State if they are not resolved.[106]

Under the new complaints process, the LGO may decide not to investigate if it considers that the governing body has responded satisfactorily to the complaint. The LGO sets its own procedure for an investigation, although it must be conducted in private[107] and a mediator may be appointed to assist. On upholding a complaint the LGO may make recommendations to the school on remedial action and the prevention of similar problems in the future and the governing body must issue a response indicating what it intends to do. The LGO can require the governing body to publish an 'adverse findings notice' and, in default, the LGO may publish it.[108] This ensures a degree of public accountability. Although the LGO has no enforcement powers for its recommendations the Secretary of State can direct the governing body to comply, and in the event of default can pursue enforcement via the courts. The Secretary of State also has long pre-standing general powers of intervention in response to complaints concerning education, exercisable where a school or local authority act in default of their duty or 'unreasonably',[109] but they were regarded as being of limited value for school complaints, since the threshold for legitimate intervention by the Secretary of State is high (DCSF 2008). These general powers cannot now be exercised in any case covered by the new LGO school complaints process until that process has been exhausted. The previous government estimated that 2,200 of the complaints it received each year would be dealt with under the new LGO jurisdiction, at an additional annual cost of £1.65m (Gillie and Hubble 2009, p. 127).

The LGO has a reputation for a thorough and independent investigation, but the process can take a long time to reach a conclusion, depending on factors such as the complexity of the case.[110] It has not been clear as yet how quickly the LGO is dealing with school complaints in the pilot areas.

---

105 Education Act 2002, s. 29. Note that under the Education (Special Educational Needs) (Information) Regulations 1999 (SI 1999/2056), reg. 3 and Schedule 1, school governing bodies are also under a specific duty to publish information about the school's arrangements for the treatment of complaints about SEN provision.

106 Under the 1996 Act ss. 496 or 497 (below).

107 Ibid., s. 209(2).

108 Ibid., s. 212.

109 Education Act 1996 ss. 496 and 497. In *Secretary of State for Education and Science v Tameside MBC* [1977] AC 1014 the test of unreasonableness was whether a local authority adopted conduct 'which no sensible authority acting with due appreciation of its responsibilities would have decided to adopt' (per Ld Diplock at p. 1064).

110 In 2009–2010, 56.8 per cent of complaints were determined within 13 weeks, but it unclear whether that percentage was inflated by cases dismissed for being outside the LGO's jurisdiction. Some 122 live cases were more than 52 weeks old: http://www.lgo.org.uk/publications/chapter-3-performance-against-business-goals/ [accessed 2 December 2010].

Take-up of the new complaints route in the pilot areas has, however, been low: in the year from April 2010 fewer than 100 complaints were received by the LGO.[111] The government regards this and the cost of the new jurisdiction as justifying a proposal, set out in the Education Bill 2011, to withdraw the arrangements, at a saving (as against a nationally rolled out system) of £2m–£6m per annum.[112] Such a step, however, would represent a lost opportunity to develop a coherent and independent framework, capable of operating consistently, for resolving complaints in this field.

Under a separate complaints procedure introduced in 2007, Ofsted may investigate written complaints, provided they have already been pursued under the school's complaints procedure.[113] However, this process is designed to facilitate complaints which relate to the school as a whole rather than the treatment of an individual child. This limitation, along with the absence of a specific remedy for a complainant, has caused some disappointment and surprise among parents (Ofsted 2007, Annex). The lack of a remedy in fact conflicts with one of the core principles of good complaints handling identified by the Parliamentary and Health Service Ombudsman (PHSO 2009). The process covers complaints about prescribed matters, including the quality of education, leadership and management; pupils' spiritual, moral, social and cultural development; and the school's contribution to pupils' well-being and to 'community cohesion'.[114] The process applies to all categories of state school, including special schools.[115] As part of the investigation Ofsted may convene a meeting with parents at the school. Ofsted's report of the investigation must be sent to the governing body which, in turn, must provide copies to parents. This reflects the previous government's attempt to make schools more accountable to parents, which has been carried through into their successor's plans to enable parents with concerns about pupil behaviour to request an Ofsted inspection (DfE 2010, para. 3.24). However, only 25 of the 1,394 complaints made were investigated under the Ofsted complaints process in 2008 (Henry 2009). Most were considered to fall outside the procedure's remit, suggesting that parents have little understanding of it. There was also, reportedly, concern among parents that if they made a complaint their child would suffer some form of backlash (Henry 2009).

The Ofsted process is specifically stated to be open to parents. The legislation does not give pupils an independent right of complaint. This exemplifies the general failure of education law in England to accord children equivalent complaint rights

111 House of Commons Public Bill Committee: Education Bill, 31 March 2011, col. 841, per Mr J. Hayes (Minister for Further Education, Skills and Lifelong Learning).

112 Education Bill, Explanatory Notes (May 2011), para. 344.

113 Education and Inspections Act 2006, s. 160, inserting ss. 11A–11C into the Education Act 2005.

114 Education (Investigation of Parents' Complaints) (England) Regulations (SI 2007/1089), as amended by SI 2008/1723.

115 As defined above: see n. 8.

to those which they enjoy in connection with local authority welfare services.[116] However, in relation to the school complaints process (above), children are not specifically excluded. Moreover, the new but now under threat LGO procedure may be used by parents *or* pupils;[117] the stated rationale is that the procedure should be consistent with the general jurisdictions of the LGO and the Secretary of State, neither of which have age restrictions (DCSF 2008, para. 40).[118] Envisaging the possibility that there could be a clash between the child and parent over a complaint, the LGO is expected to use its discretion, having regard to the child's age and understanding (DCSF 2008, para. 40). The practical reality is that almost all complaints will be made by parents and that, given the nature of their needs and difficulties, many children with SEN would lack the capacity to complain in their own right. A fear of repercussions may also inhibit children from complaining (Gorierly and Williams 1997, p. 32).

Negligence claims

Redress may also be pursued via a claim of negligence relating to the performance of professional duties concerning SEN. The case law, which is of fairly recent origin, has made an important contribution to the development of the law on the liability of public authorities in tort. What follows is a necessarily brief review of the key legal developments.

Building on the principles it established in 1995 in *X (Minors) v Bedfordshire County Council*[119] the House of Lords confirmed in *Phelps v London Borough of Hillingdon* in 2000[120] that a teacher or other educational professional may owe a duty of care at common law towards a child in relation to his or her education and welfare; it followed that where the required standard of care[121] was not met, the professional and their employer may incur liability in damages for harm suffered, provided the necessary elements of negligence, in particular a breach of duty and causation, could be established. The Court of Appeal added in *Carty* that an education officer employed by a local authority could also owe a common law duty of care to a child with SEN.[122] *Phelps* held that if an educational psychologist is called in to advise on assessment and future provision for a specific child, and

116 Children Act 1989, s. 26.

117 Education Act 1996, ss. 496 and 497.

118 However, the LGO's website as at 2 December 2010 continues to head the section on complaints about schools: 'What if I am concerned about my child's school?'. http://www.lgo.org.uk/publications/fact-sheets/complaints-about-schools/

119 *X (Minors) v Bedfordshire County Council* (and linked cases) [1995] ELR 404, HL.

120 *Phelps v London Borough of Hillingdon; Anderton v Clwyd County Council; G v London Borough of Bromley; Jarvis v Hampshire County Council* [2000] ELR 499.

121 Namely the standard of an ordinarily competent and skilled member of that profession acting in accordance with practice accepted by a responsible body of professionals in that field: *Bolam v Friern Hospital Management Committee* [1957] 1 WLR 582.

122 *Carty v London Borough of Croydon* [2005] EWCA Civ 19, [2005] ELR 104.

it is clear that the parents can be expected to rely on that advice, a *prima facie* duty of care will arise. In *Phelps* a psychologist employed by the local education authority had negligently failed to diagnose the claimant's dyslexia when the claimant had been a child. The authority was held vicariously liable. The House of Lords was not swayed by a range of policy arguments against liability.[123] The court, as in *X (Minors)*, held that local authorities and their employees may not be liable for action taken under statutory powers, since that could unduly hinder the performance of their statutory functions, but they could owe a duty of care in respect of the exercise of general professional duties. The question of direct liability was left fairly open. Lord Slynn said that while an authority would not be directly liable for the way it had established arrangements to meet its statutory duties towards, say, children with SEN, it might be directly liable if it employed professionals who were not qualified or competent to undertake their duties.[124]

This approach was followed in *Carty*,[125] where an education officer had failed to carry out a formal re-assessment of the child within a specific 12 month period prescribed by regulations and, in the light of it, to substitute a suitable school in his statement. It was held that the failure could not give rise to negligence liability since Parliament did not intend to confer a right to seek damages for breach of a statutory duty. The court nevertheless held that 'where an education officer, in the exercise of his or her statutory functions, enters into a relationships with or assumes responsibilities towards a child, then he or she may owe a duty of care to that child'.[126] Dyson LJ said that:

> 'The nature of the statutory function and the difficulty of decisions such as the assessment of the needs of a child with [SEN] and the determination of special provision that should be made are such that a court will usually only hold that it is fair, just and reasonable to impose a duty of care to avoid decisions that are plainly and obviously wrong'.[127]

The court further stated that in view of 'the complexity and the delicacy of the decisions that education officers and education psychologists have to make' the courts should 'not find negligence too readily'.[128]

---

123 Namely the risk of vexatious claims, the financial burden on local authorities of having to defend claims, the risk of a defensive approach to professional practice developing, the unfairness of singling out a particular professional among a number responsible for a child's education, and the general issue of policy as to whether the existence of a duty is fair, just and reasonable.

124 At p. 521D-H.

125 Note 122 above.

126 Ibid., at para. 43, per Dyson LJ.

127 Ibid.

128 Ibid., para. 78.

The House of Lords in *Phelps* also confirmed that these kinds of negligence claims could proceed as personal injury cases.[129] Awards of damages where there is a breach of the duty of care could be based on the consequences of a failure to diagnose a congenital condition, such as the child's reduced attainment levels and weakened future employment prospects and earnings. In *Skipper v Calderdale Metropolitan Borough Council and the Governors of Crossley Heath School*,[130] for example, there was an alleged failure by persons responsible for the claimant's primary and secondary education to identify her as suffering from dyslexia and to take steps to ameliorate her condition or mitigate its effects. The claimant said she had been humiliated at school by being unable to keep up with other children and considered lazy by teachers. She suffered from reduced confidence and lower self-esteem as a result. She claimed that but for the negligence she would have obtained higher A level grades and in due course secured better paid and more congenial employment. Her claim was struck out for having low prospects of success, but the Court of Appeal reinstated it. Latham LJ held that *Phelps* was:

> 'authority for the proposition that if it can be shown that a claimant's disability had a real effect on his or her ability to cope with school and work, or has otherwise interfered significantly with his enjoyment of life, that will be a loss of amenity which can properly sound in damages'.[131]

Although a number of similar cases followed *Phelps,* that judgment did not open the floodgates to negligence claims in this field or education more generally. There has, however, been a small group of cases in which the courts have held that the prevention of reasonably foreseeable harm as a result of bullying by other pupils could give rise to negligence liability (see Harris 2005).

The main problem for negligence actions in the context of education is that fault is difficult to prove. School records might not be adequate and recollections some time after the event might be unreliable. Showing a causal connection between the alleged negligence and the alleged loss and assessing the loss might be problematic. Several of the post *Phelps* cases concerned adults who were seeking damages for what happened to them at school. As Longmore LJ said in *Smith*, in such cases although the claim is for personal injury and the limitation period is therefore three years, 'the trial has to consider events that occurred about a decade or more earlier'.[132] In *Carty* (above), for example, the alleged negligence occurred between 1991–1993 but the case did not reach initial judgment in the High Court until 2004. The limitation period runs from the age of 18 and in any

129 *Phelps*, n. 120 above, at page 529.

130 [2006] EWCA Civ 238, [2006] E.L.R. 322. See also, as regards quantum of damages, *Clarke v Devon County Council* [2005] E.L.R. 375 CA.

131 [2006] EWCA Civ 238, [2006] E.L.R. 322, at para. 27.

132 *Smith v Hampshire County Council* [2007] EWCA Civ.246, [2007] E.L.R.321 CA, at para. 1.

event only from when the claimant had knowledge that he or she had a claim. Although the court has a discretion to extend time it is reluctant to do so where the acts or omissions in question occurred a long time ago.[133]

Establishing liability is therefore difficult and few claims are likely to succeed. The courts are keen to prevent undue interference with the carrying out of local authority functions towards children with SEN that might result from litigation of this kind if less restricted. Whether the pursuit of negligence claims over SEN matters will diminish further if proposed cutbacks to legal aid for personal injury cases occur remains to be seen. The original proposals indicated that negligence claims against public authorities would be potentially eligible for legal aid if they concerned 'very serious negligence', namely 'acts or omissions falling very far below the required standard of care' (Ministry of Justice 2010, paras 4.52–4.53). The government has since dropped this head of eligibility altogether, for being too wide. Legal aid for non judicial review claims against public authorities is being restricted to cases involving abuse of position or power or a 'significant breach of Convention rights' (i.e. rights under the ECHR) (Ministry of Justice 2011, para. 18; see also the Legal Aid, Sentencing and Punishment Bill 2011, schedule 1). Although the government considers that some personal injury claims may still be covered under these heads, relatively few seem likely to qualify.

Conclusion

The SEN system in England seeks to ascertain the kind and level of a child's needs and match them to particular level of provision. It leaves scope for interpretation and flexible application to take account of factors which it would be impracticable to attempt to prescribe legislatively. It also enables the provision made for individual children to be dependent on resource availability and allocation under local policy frameworks. Consequently, beyond important procedural guarantees of participation and the expression of preference, parents enjoy rights which are highly contingent. Nevertheless, parents receive messages of encouragement from the legal and procedural framework to press for provision that they consider their child needs or deserves. Local authorities, as providers and decision makers, tread carefully in responding to individual demands for fear of hampering their overall capacity to target resources effectively. Conflict is inevitable and it requires resolution. For parents, dispute resolution can be an important part of a 'struggle' to establish and enforce their rights (Lamb 2009, p. 6). Some parents (due to their

133 *Robinson v St Helens MBC* [2002] E.L.R. 681 CA. The limitation period was also considered in *Meherali v Hampshire CC* [2002] EWHC 2655 QBD, *Adams v Bracknell Forest BC* [2003] E.L.R. 409 CA; *Rowe v Kingston-upon-Hull CC and Essex CC* [2003] E.L.R. 771 CA and [2004] E.L.R. 459 HL; *Smith v London Borough of Havering* [2004] E.L.R. 629; and *Smith v Hampshire County Council* [2007] EWCA Civ.246, [2007] E.L.R.321 CA.

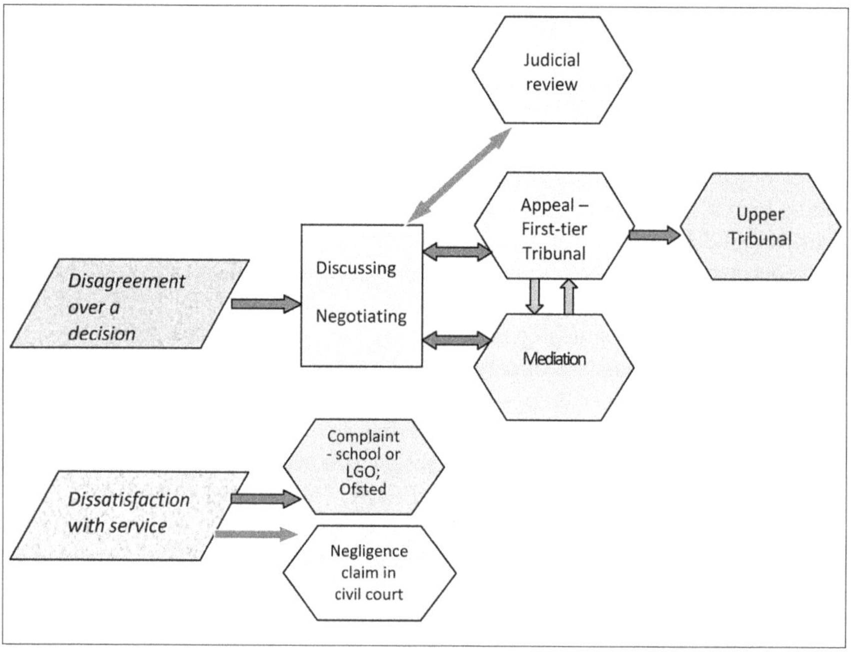

Figure 3.2 Main routes to redress of grievance: special educational needs and provision in England

social and educational background or financial position) are better equipped for it than others.

There are two basic tracks that redress of grievance will start along, as shown in Figure 3.2 (below). Redress in respect of dissatisfaction with the quality of service would be pursued via a complaint, for which several different processes exist. Negligence claims can be pursued via civil litigation. If there is disagreement with an SEN decision, which is not resolved via any discussion or informal negotiation which takes place, the matter may proceed as a dispute to formal mediation and/or, if the relevant grounds are invoked, the appeal process. Judicial review applications are pursued in a small number of cases not covered by the grounds of appeal or to enforce a tribunal decision; many are settled (Bondy and Sunkin 2009).

Despite its mandatory availability in SEN cases mediation has yet to establish a position as the primary dispute resolution mechanism in England. Clearly, if the policy intention is that it should be used in many more cases, thereby reducing recourse to the tribunal, much more could be done to improve knowledge and understanding of the process. This will be just as important, if not more so, if the government concludes that the answer to the question on which it has recently consulted – '[s]hould mediation always be attempted before parents register an appeal to the First-tier Tribunal (SEN and Disability)?' – is 'yes'. Meanwhile, whether more appeal cases divert into mediation via the operation of rule 3 of the HESC tribunal rules and, if this occurs, there are quicker and more long lasting settlements than those resulting from last minute settlements at the door of the tribunal, remains to be seen. However, the fact that currently many appeals are settled, and settled so late in the day, would suggest that perhaps the tribunal should go further than merely encouraging parents to try mediation, which in itself could be a factor in the recent increase in settlement rates (a 7.3% increase in the year to 31 March 2011, compared to a 2.8% increase in the number of hearings in this period),[134] and involve itself more directly in mediation, although, as noted above, a judicial mediation pilot in employment cases has suggested that the process may be costly and of limited effect in increasing settlement rates. In any event, ultimately those who are concerned to see a reduced incidence of tribunal cases should look at some of the reasons that parents bring an appeal. Certainly, it is used to gain some leverage, especially since advisers tend to stress to parents the good prospects of a favourable outcome. Professionals interviewed for the ESRC research indicated that exercising the right of appeal continues to be regarded by parents and advisers as the primary strategy to try to force the local authority to give ground. However, parents have also been found to be more motivated to appeal where the quality of communication from the local authority is poor and the authority lacks empathy and understanding, and less inclined to do so where the parties have developed more a constructive relationship (Penfold et al. 2009). These are clearly areas that need to be worked on.

While few professionals perceive there to have been any reduction in the number of disagreements or disputes, the fact that there has been no increase in either the number of mediations or appeals suggests that a higher proportion of parent grievances are being resolved via local negotiation and settlement. Such negotiation, often including informal mediation by parent partnership services, plays a very important role in dispute resolution or avoidance in this field. Yet there is no guarantee of procedural justice; a professional process of mediation will be far better able to provide one. Judicial oversight of such a process could enhance it further. The development of formal mediation in this field builds on a tradition of negotiated settlement to disputes about children's special educational needs in England. Yet it too carries a danger to the interests of social and distributive justice, as discussed in chapter 2, notwithstanding the strong policy arguments in its favour as a more proportionate process and potentially more accessible route of redress.

---

134 Based on unpublished statistics on numbers of hearings (765 in 2009–10 and 787 in 2010–11) and numbers of cases settled (2230 in 2009–10 and 2392 in 2010–11) kindly provided by HESC to the author.

References

Adams, J. (2003), 'Provision: who needs special needs?', in J. Swain, S. French and C. Cameron, *Controversial Issues in a Disabling Society* (Buckingham: Open University Press).

Adler, M. (2006), 'Tribunal reform: Proportionate Dispute Resolution and the pursuit of administrative justice' (2006) 69(6) *M.L.R.* 958–985.

Adler, M. (2009), 'Self representation, just outcomes and fair procedures in tribunal hearings', paper at Senior President's Conference for Tribunal Judges, 20 May.

Advice Services Alliance (2007), *Recent Developments in Alternative Dispute Resolution* (London: Advice Services Alliance).

AJTC (Administrative Justice and Tribunals Council) (2008), 'The Use of Proportionate Dispute Resolution in Tribunals', *Adjust* February http://www.ajtc.gov.uk/adjust/08_02.htm [accessed 1 December 2010].

AJTC (2009), *Department for Children, Schools and Families. A New Way of Handling Parents' Complaints about School Issues* (London: AJTC).

AJTC (2010), *Principles for Administrative Justice. The AJTC's approach. Consultation draft* (London: AJTC).

Aldridge, T. (1995), *Special Educational Needs Tribunal Annual Report 1994/95* (London: SENT).

Aldridge, T. (2001), 'Special Educational Needs Tribunal: New Procedure', *Education Law Journal*, 2(3), 131–133.

Audit Commission (2002), *Special Educational Needs: A Mainstream Issue* (London: Audit Commission).

Audit Commission (2007), *Out of Authority Placements for Special Educational Needs* (London: Audit Commission).

Audit Commission/HMI (1992), *Getting In On the Act – Provision for Pupils with Special Educational Needs – The National Picture* (London: HMSO).

Bondy, V. and Sunkin, M. (2009), *The dynamics of judicial review. The resolution of public law challenges before final hearing,* Colchester: University of Essex.

Coldron, J., Stephenson, K., Williams, J., Shipton, L. and Demack, S. (2002), *Admission Appeal Panels: Research Study into the Operation of Appeal Panels, Use of the Code of Practice and Training for Panel Members*, Research report RR344 (London: DfES).

Council on Tribunals, *Annual Report 1992/93* (London: HMSO, 1993).

DCA (Department for Constitutional Affairs) (2004), *Transforming Public Services: Complaints, Redress and Tribunals* (London: The Stationery Office).

DCSF (Department for Children, Schools and Families) (2008), *A New Way of Handling Parents' Complaints About School Issues* (London: DCSF).

DCSF (2009), *Special educational needs: Statements issued within 26 weeks* (London: DCSF) (http://www.dcsf.gov.uk/rsgateway/DB/STR/d000901/NI103Text.pdf [accessed 8 March 2010].

DCSF (2010a), *Improving parental confidence in the special educational needs system: an implementation plan* (London: DCSF).

DCSF (2010b), *School admissions code*, London: TSO.

DCSF (2010c), 'Special Educational Needs in England, January 2010, Statistical First Release SFR 19/2010' (London: DCSF) http://www.education.gov.uk/rsgateway/DB/SFR/s000939/sfr19-2010.pdf [Accessed 6 December 2010].

DCSF (2010d), *Support for All: the Families and Relationships Green Paper*, Cm 7787 (London: DCSF, 2010).

DES (Department of Education and Science) (1978), *Special Educational Needs* (London: HMSO, 1978).

DfE (Department for Education) (1992), *Special Educational Needs: Access to the System – A Consultation Paper* (London: Department for Education).

DfE (2010), *The Importance of Teaching*, Cm 7980 (London: TSO).

DfE (2011) *Support and Aspiration: A new approach to special educational needs and disability. A consultation* Cm 8207 (Norwich: TSO).

DfEE (Department for Education and Employment) (1998), *Meeting Special Educational Needs: A Programme of Action* (London: DfEE).

DfEE (2000), *SEN and Disability Rights in Education Bill. Consulation Document* (London: DfEE).

DfES (Department for Education and Skills) (2001), *Special Educational Needs Code of Practice* (London: DfES).

DfES (2002), *SEN Toolkit* (London: DfES), updated version at http://www.teachernet.gov.uk/_doc/4608/Toolkit%203%20Text.pdf [accessed 19 November 2010].

Evans J. (1998), *Getting it Right: LEAs and the Special Educational Needs Tribunal* (Slough: NFER).

Evans, J. and Vincent, C. (1997), 'Parental choice and special education', in R. Glatter, P.A. Woods and C. Bagley, *Choice and Diversity in Schooling* (London: Routledge), pp. 102–115.

Fletcher-Campbell, F. et al. (2006), *Evaluation of the Special Educational Needs Regional Partnerships*, DfES Research Report RR724 (Annesley: DfES).

Fortin, J. (2009), *Children's Rights and the Developing Law* (3rd edn) (Cambridge: CUP).

Genn, H. (2010), *Judging Civil Justice* (Cambridge: CUP).

Genn, H., Lever, B., Gray, L., Balmer, N. and National Centre for Social Research (2006), *Tribunals for Diverse Users*, DCA Research series 1/06 (London: DCA).

Genn, H., Fenn, P., Mason, M., Lane, A., Bechai, N., Gray, L. and Vencappa, D. (2007), *Twisting arms: court referred and court linked mediation under judicial pressure*, Research Series 1/07 (London: Ministry of Justice).

Gillie, C. and Hubble, S. (2009), *Apprenticeships, Skills, Children and Learning Bill: provisions for children, education and learners*, Research Paper 09/15 (London: House of Commons Library).

Goriely, T. and Williams, T. (1997), *Resolving Civil Disputes: Choosing Between Out-of-Court Schemes and Litigation. A Review of the Literature* (London: Lord Chancellor's Department).

Graham, J. with Graham, N. (2008), *Autism, Discrimination and the Law* (London: Jessica Kingsley).

Hall, J. (1999), *Resolving Disputes Between Parents, Schools and LEAs: Some Examples of Best Practice* (London: DfEE).

Harris, N. (1993), *Law and Education: Regulation, Consumerism and the Education System* (London: Sweet and Maxwell).

Harris, N. (1997), *Special Educational Needs and Access to Justice* (Bristol: Jordans).

Harris, N. (2002), 'Special educational needs – the role of the courts', *C.F.L.Q.*, 14(2), 137–156.

Harris, N. (2005), 'Pupil bullying, mental health and law in England', in N. Harris and P. Meredith (eds), *Children, Education and Health – International Perspectives on Law and Policy* (Aldershot: Ashgate), pp. 31–58.

Harris, N. (2007), *Education, Law and Diversity* (Oxford: Hart).

Harris, N. (2009), 'Playing Catch-up in the Schoolyard? Children and Young People's "Voice" and Education Rights in the United Kingdom', *International Journal of Law, Policy and the Family*, 23(3), 331–366.

Harris, A. and Goodall, J. (2007), *Engaging Parents in Raising Achievement – Do Parents Know they Matter?* DCSF RW-004 (London: DCSF).

Harris, N. and Smith, E. (2009), 'Resolving Disputes about Special Educational Needs and Provision in England', *Education Law Journal,* 10, 2, 113–132.

HCESAC (House of Commons, Education Science and the Arts Committee) (1987), Session 1986/87, *Third Report, Special Educational Needs: Implementation of the Education Act 1981*, Vol. 1 HC201-1 (London: HMSO).

HCESC (House of Commons Education and Skills Committee) (2006), *Special Educational Needs, Third Report of Session 2005–06, Vol.1,* HC 478-I (London: TSO), para. 147.

HCESC (2007), *Tenth Report of Session 2006–07, Special Educational Needs: Assessment and Funding*, HM 1077 (Norwich: TSO).

Henry, J. (2009), 'Hundreds of complaints from parents about schools – but less than 2% investigated' (21 February), http://www.telegraph.co.uk/education/educationnews/4741105/Hundreds-of-complaints-from-parents-about-schools-but-less-than-2-investigated.html [accessed 2 December 2010].

HLSCC (House of Lords Select Committee on the Constitution) (2006), *First Report Session 2006–07. Tribunals, Court and Enforcement Bill, Report with Evidence* (London: The Stationery Office).

Isaksson, J., Lindqvist, R. and Bergström, E. (2010), 'Pupils with special educational needs: a study of the assessments and categorising processes regarding pupils' school difficulties in Sweden', *International Journal of Inclusive Education,* 14(2), 133–151.

Kalamboka, A., Farrell, P., Dyson, A., and Kaplan, I. (2007), 'The impact of placing pupils with special educational needs in maninstream schools on the achievement of their peers', *Educational Research,* 49(4), 365–382.

King, M. and King, D. (2006), 'How the law defines the special educational needs of autistic children', *Child and Family Law Quarterly*, 18(1), 23–00.

Lamb, Sir B. (2009), *Lamb Inquiry, Special Educational Needs and Parental Confidence* (London: DCSF).

Lange C. and Riddell, S. (2000), 'Special educational needs policy and choice. Tensions between policy development in the US and UK contexts', in M.J. McLaughlin and M. Rouse (eds), *Special Education and School Reform in the United States and Britain* (London: Routledge), pp. 126–146.

Leggatt, Sir A. (2001), *Tribunals for Users. One System, One Service* (London: The Stationery Office).

LGO (2010), *Local Government Ombudsman. Annual Report 2009–10* (sic) (London: Commission for Local Administration in England). www.lgo.org.uk/publications/annual-report/ [accessed 14 September 2010].

Ministry of Justice/Tribunals Service (2008), *Transforming Tribunals. Implementing Part I of the Tribunals, Courts and Enforcement Act 2007. The Government's Response* (2008), http://www.justice.gov.uk/docs/cp3007-response.pdf [accessed 30 November 2010].

Ministry of Justice (2010), *Proposals for the Reform of Legal Aid in England and Wales*, Cm 7967 (London: The Stationery Office).

Ministry of Justice (2011), *Legal Aid in England and Wales: the Government Response*, Cm 8072 (London: The Stationary Office).

Monk, D (2000), 'Theorising Education Law and Childhood: Constructing the ideal pupil', *British Journal of Sociology of Education*, 21(3), 355–370.

Ofsted (2010), *Special educational needs and disability review – a statement is not enough*, ref 090221 (London: Ofsted).

Penfold, C., Cleghorn, N., Tennant, R., Palmer, I. and Read, J. (2009), *Parental Confidence in the Special Educational Needs Assessment, Statementing and Tribunal System* DCSF-RR117 (London: DCSF) http://www.dcsf.gov.uk/research/data/uploadfiles/DCSF-RR117.pdf [accessed 22 November 2010].

PHSO (Parliamentary and Health Service Ombudsman) (2009), *Principles of Good Complaint Handling* (London: PHSO).

Pinney, A. (2004), *Reducing Reliance on Statements: An Investigation into Local Authority Practice and Outcomes*, Research Report RR508 (London: DfES, 2004),

Riddell, S., Harris, N., Smith, E. and Weedon, E. (2010), 'Dispute resolution in additional and special educational needs: local authority perspectives', *Journal of Education Policy* (2010), 25, 1, 55–71.

Riddell, S. and Weedon, E. (2009), 'Approaches to dispute resolution in additional support needs in Scotland', *European Journal of Special Needs Education* (2009), 24, (4), 355–369.

Roberts, M. (2008), *Mediation in Family Disputes. Principles of Practice* (3rd edn) (Aldershot: Ashgate).

Rogers, R. et al. (2006), *Evaluation of the Special Educational Needs Parent Partnership Services in England*, DfES, Research Report, RR719 (London: DFES).

Ruff, A. (2004), 'SEN mediation – the way forward,' *ACE Bulletin*, No. 122, 8.

Ruff, A. (2011), 'Mediation: Its Role in Special Educational Needs and Disability Cases', *Education Law Journal,* 12(1), 00–00.

SENDIST (2007), *President's Annual Report 2006–2007* (London: SENDIST).

Senior President of Tribunals (2008), *Second Implementation Review October 2008* (London: Tribunals Service).

Senior President of Tribunals (2010), *The Senior President of Tribunals' Annual Report: Tribunals Transformed* (London: Ministry of Justice).

Senior President of Tribunals (2011), *The Senior President of Tribunals' Annual Report* (London: Ministry of Justice).

Tennant, R., Callanan, M., Snape, D., Palmer, I. and Read, J. (2008), *Special Educational Needs Disagreement Resolution Services*, Research Report DCSF-RR054 (London: Department for Children, Schools and Families). http://www.education.gov.uk/research/data/uploadfiles/dcsf-RR054.pdf [accessed 22 November 2010].

Tribunals Service (2007), *Transforming Tribunals: Implementing Part 1 of the Tribunal, Courts and Enforcement Act 2007* (London: The Stationery Office).

Tribunals Service (2008), *First-tier Tribunal: Health, Education and Social Care Chamber – Special Educational Needs and Disability, Statistical Information 2007–2008* (Tribunals Service), http://www.sendist.gov.uk/Documents/Publications/AnnualReports/SENDISTAnnualReport2008.pdf [accessed 30 November 2010].

Tribunals Service (2009), *Special Educational Needs and Disability Tribunal Annual Report 2008–2009* (Tribunals Service), http://www.sendist.gov.uk/Documents/Publications/AnnualReports/AnnualReport_08_2009.pdf [accessed 26 November 2010].

Tribunals Service (2010), *Annual Report and Accounts 2009–10*, HC239 (London: TSO).

Vehmas, S. (2010), 'Special needs: a philosophical analysis', *International Journal of Inclusive Education*, 14(1), 87–96.

Vernon, S. (2008), 'A flight from formality', *Tribunals*, Spring, 18–24.

Warnock, M.H. (1978), *Special Educational Needs. Report of the Committee of Enquiry into the Education of Handicapped Children and Young People*, Cmnd 7212 (London: HMSO).

Wilkin, A., Archer, T., Ridley, K., Fletcher-Campbell, F. and Kinder, K. (2005), *Admissions and Exclusions of Pupils with Special Educational Needs*, RB608 (London: DfES).

Wolfendale, S. (1994), 'Policy and provision for children with special educational needs in the early years', in S. Riddell and S. Brown (eds), *Special Educational Needs Policy in the 1990s* (London: Routledge), pp. 51–73.

Scottish research

s chapter uses a range of Scottish data drawn from the ESRC project on dispute olution in the field of special and additional support needs. In Scotland, the research n analysed policy documents and official statistics, conducted interviews with 28 informants, administered surveys to all 32 Scottish local authorities, carried out rvey of Scottish parents of children with additional support needs and finally pleted 24 case studies of families in three local authorities. There was an 80 per response rate to the local authority survey and a 24 per cent response rate to parents' survey. Further details of the methods used in the project are provided iddell and Weedon (2009); Weedon and Riddell (2009); Riddell et al. (2010).

ents' rights in the field of additional support needs in Scotland

of the central aims of the Education (Additional Support for Learning) otland) Act 2004 was to enhance parents' and children's rights in education. ore discussing the new arrangements for resolving disagreements, we provide ief account of the status quo with regard to parents' and children's rights in ttish education.

n the immediate post-war period in Scotland, parents had very little say over education of their children with special educational needs. They were compelled ring their children into clinics for assessment by medical officers, who would equently decide, in conjunction with education officers, on the appropriate form lucational provision (see Riddell 2006 for further discussion). From the 1970s ards, with the advent of child centred education, it was increasingly recognised parents played a very important role in their children's educational development, in the Warnock report (DES 1978) they were granted partnership status in sion making. The Conservative Government's educational reforms of the 1980s parents not just as partners, but as drivers of the market, in that their choices, eory if not in practice, would determine what type of educational provision ld flourish or dwindle (Tomlinson 2001). Within managerialist and consumerist ourses, which gained growing currency in the 1990s, parents also occupied an rtant position, with rights to information on performance and targets set out in a e of charters which employed the rhetoric of safeguarding consumers' interests ist the vested interests of service providers. From a very different philosophical ion, the growth of the disability movement from the 1980s onwards established course of rights, which recast disabled children as having the same rights to ation as their non-disabled peers, with parents acting as their proxies, using s of redress to ensure that rights were enforceable.

s noted in chapter 2, the citizen-consumer has featured prominently in New ur's social policy and Clarke et al. (2007) discuss the implications of this enation, pointing out the complexity and contested nature of both terms. In on to citizenship, as noted by Lister (2003), there continue to be disagreements

Chapter 4

Resolving Additional Suppor Disputes in Scotland: Cont Professionalism and Rig

Sheila Riddell and Elisabet Weedon

Introduction

As discussed in earlier chapters, the UK Government has s of years, to move away from the resolution of civil dis and tribunals, which are seen as expensive, inefficient 2004). A much greater emphasis is being placed on medi cost-effective and user-friendly way of resolving disagr citizen and the state. A review of the administrative justic (Consumer Focus Scotland, 2009) started from the prem a right to expect high quality public services and in orde and learn from mistakes, effective redress systems are re problems with the existing system were identified, inclu access barriers; unnecessary levels of complexity; and p advice, assistance and representation. Drawing on Scottish study, this chapter discusses the way in which disputes in support needs have been dealt with over recent years north briefly outlined the research methods used in Scotland, we of the additional support needs legislation which provid approaches to dispute resolution. We explore the use of diff resolution procedures (informal negotiation, formal med and tribunal) and the way in which each was perceived by parents. Finally, we present case studies illustrating Scottis of different types of dispute resolution. The conclusion dis balance of power between local authorities, parents and been brought about as a result of the new legislation. Th contrasts are drawn with the situation south of the Border, able to illuminate ongoing debates about whether devoluti convergence or divergence between England and Scotland over the areas of life in which the rights and entitlements of citizenship should hold sway, and who should be counted as a citizen. For example, in the field of education, it is evident that parents are accorded greater rights than children, even though, as argued by Harris (2005), these rights tend to be weak. Similarly, the consumer has been viewed through a variety of lenses (Trentmann 2006), sometimes regarded critically as an individualist seeking to capture scarce or valued resources, or alternatively as a champion of collective mobilisation against the vested interests of goods and service producers such as the food or automobile industry, or the providers of public services such as health and education. Direct payments, for example, were promoted by the disability movement on the grounds that the social services which were ostensibly meeting the needs of disabled people were, in reality, geared towards protecting the interests of public sector workers.

As argued elsewhere (Riddell et al., 2000, 2002, 2003; Riddell, 2006) and illustrated in the previous chapter, in the field of special educational needs parents in England have had greater power to challenge local authority decisions compared with their Scottish counterparts. Under the terms of the 1993 Education Act, a Code of Practice was instituted in England which specified the procedures which professionals must follow in order to comply with legislative requirements. This legislation also established the Special Educational Needs Tribunal, which gave parents access to a quasi-judicial system of appeal. At about the same time, parent partnership services were established in each local authority, with a remit to work with parents of children with special educational needs to try to minimise the possibility of conflict. As discussed in later sections of this chapter, similar, although not identical, measures were put in place a decade later in Scotland, indicating a time lag between developments north and south of the Border. A major focus of this chapter is the extent to which the new dispute resolution mechanisms have succeeded in enhancing parents' rights.

Children's rights in the field of additional support needs in Scotland

In the previous chapter, in relation to England, Harris and Smith discuss the assumptions which have traditionally governed the relationship between parents and children/young people in the field of education (see also chapter 1). Educational rights have been conferred on parents, rather than children, on the basis that the parent is able to determine the child's best interests and act accordingly. Children, particularly those with special or additional support needs, are assumed either to lack capacity or to have insufficient understanding of the wider implications of their choices.

In Scotland, very similar assumptions have been made with regard to the subordination of children's rights to those of their parents. For example, for more than two decades Scottish parents have had rights to choice of schools, to contribute their views within assessment procedures and to be involved in school boards, but children under the age of 16 did not enjoy similar rights. However, more recently efforts have been made to boost children's rights. Section 1 of the Standards in

Scotland's Schools etc. Act 2000 gave every child of school age a right to school education in a local authority school. Section 2 of the Act stated that such education must be directed towards developing the 'personalities, talents and mental and physical abilities of the child or young person to their fullest potential'. These sections were added to the Bill as it made its way through the Scottish Parliament, at least partially due to lobbying pressure to create more inclusive legislation as a counterpoint to the focus on raising standards (see Tisdall and Riddell, 2006).

These provisions not only promoted an inclusive approach for all children but they also introduced children's rights into education legislation. Previous education legislation required local authorities to provide education, and parents to ensure that their child received education, but children themselves did not have the right to education. Section 1 of the 2000 Act adds this third element. Furthermore, section 2 of the 2000 Act stated that children's views should be given due regard in all significant decisions in relation to their education. Those children under the age of 16 who are considered legally competent can now appeal their school exclusion themselves; before, only those with parental responsibilities and rights could do so on their children's behalf. Despite these changes, in the field of additional support needs, children continue to have weaker rights than their parents. Whilst young people between the ages of 16 and 18 who are competent have the same rights as their parents to make a reference to the tribunal or request 'adjudication' or mediation, children still do not have independent rights of appeal. The Supporting Children's Learning: Code of Practice (Scottish Government, 2010) emphasises the duty on local authorities and schools to take account of children's and young people's views, but, as illustrated below, children and young people still appear to play a very small role in the more formal aspects of dispute resolution.

The additional support needs legislative framework

The Education (Additional Support for Learning) (Scotland) Act 2004, amended in 2009, made major changes to the legislative framework in Scotland. The legislation replaced the term 'special educational needs' with a new term 'additional support needs', which was significantly broader. Additional support needs are defined[1] with reference to a child's need for whatever reason for additional support in order to be able to benefit from school education. Additional support for this purpose is defined in similar terms to special educational provision in England, namely provision which is 'additional to, or otherwise different from, the educational provision made generally for children' in the area.[2] The Scottish Executive's Code of Practice (Scottish Executive, 2005; Scottish Government, 2010) suggested that a wide range of factors might give rise to additional support needs. Within the classroom, inflexible curricular arrangements or inappropriate approaches to

1 Education (Additional Support for Learning) (Scotland) Act 2004, s. 1.

2 Ibid., s. 1(3).

learning and teaching might be problematic for children with learning difficulties, more able children and those for whom English is an additional language. Additional support needs might also arise as a result of family circumstances, such as homelessness or parental drug or alcohol abuse. In addition, family difficulties might lead to additional support needs, particularly for children who are looked after by the local authority or who are carers of other family members. Finally, disabilities and health needs, as well as social and emotional factors, might underlie additional support needs. Overall, whereas it is argued in the English Green Paper (DfE, 2011) that fewer children should be identified as having special educational needs, in Scotland an expansive approach to additional support needs was adopted.

A critical change in the legislation was the replacement of the record of need with a new statutory document, the co-ordinated support plan (CSP). A child whose additional support needs last more than a year and arise from one or more complex factors or multiple factors and whose needs require significant additional support may be the subject of a CSP (see section 2 of the 2004 Act). Furthermore, in order to qualify for a CSP, significant additional support must be required from education as well as at least one of: social work services (or another, non-education, council function); a health board; and/or another local authority. Thus, whereas a record of needs was for those children with the most severe and complex difficulties, eligibility for a CSP depends not so much on the severity or complexity of the needs but on the sources of support required to meet those needs. Since health boards have very different working practices with regard, for example, to the provision of speech and language therapy for children in school, a great deal of regional variation has emerged in relation to the proportion of children eligible for a CSP (Riddell et al., 2010). When developing the legislation, the Scottish Executive worked on the planning assumption that about 1 per cent of the pupils would receive a CSP, about half the proportion in receipt of a record of needs. In the event, less than 0.5 per cent of children have been given a CSP. Since the CSP acts as a passport for accessing the tribunal, these tight criteria have had a major limiting effect on access to redress (see further below).

The new legislation and rights of redress

Prior to the additional support for learning legislation, if dissatisfied with local authority or school provision, Scottish parents had weaker legal rights compared with their English counterparts. If a parent believed that the local authority was failing to make adequate educational provision, they could make a formal complaint to Scottish Ministers, who would pass the case to Her Majesty's Inspectorate for review. If the parent remained dissatisfied following this process, a case could be taken to the Sheriff Court. Following the legislation, new routes of redress (tribunal, 'adjudication' and formal mediation) were established, each with different access criteria. Whereas any parent of a child with additional support needs may request formal mediation or adjudication, as explained above, access to the tribunal is restricted to cases pertaining to children and young people deemed to qualify for

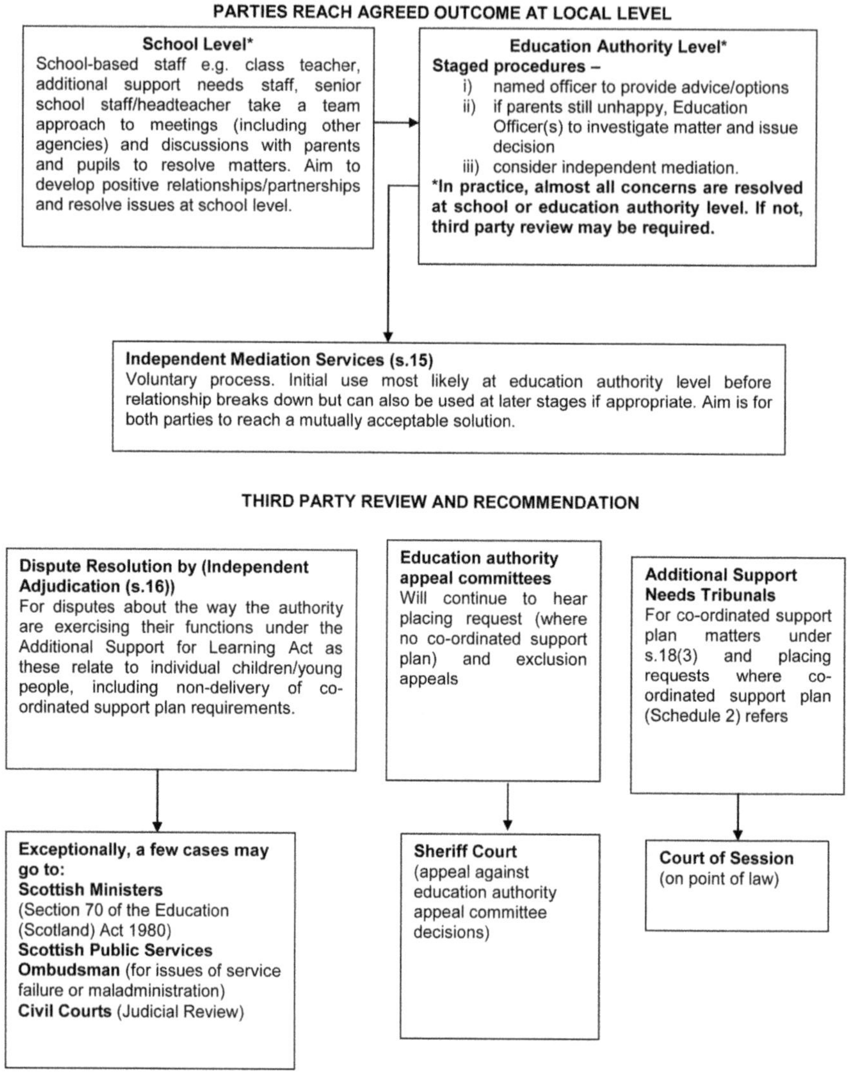

Source: Scottish Executive (2005).

Figure 4.1 Framework for resolving disagreements concerning ASN in Scotland

a CSP. Methods of dispute resolution are summarised in Figure 4.1 and each is discussed in more detail below.

The Tribunal

The Additional Support Needs Tribunals for Scotland (ASNTS) (referred to as the tribunal) were established under the 2004 Act. The Scottish tribunal's jurisdiction is narrower than that of the HESC First-tier Tribunal in England (described in chapter 3). Parents or (unless they lack capacity) young persons may (subject to certain qualifications) make a reference to the tribunal over a range of matters concerned with CSPs (s. 18), including whether a CSP is required; whether a time limit for preparing it was breached; the content of a CSP; whether a CSP should be reviewed; and where a placing request, relating to the school where the child or young person with a CSP is to be placed, has been refused. The tribunal also deals with all placing request appeals relating to special schools, regardless of whether the child has a CSP. The amending Act (the Education (Additional Support for Learning) (Scotland) Act 2009) extends the jurisdiction to include references concerning failures to obtain information or elicit parents'/children's/young people's views regarding post-school transitions.

Under the terms of the Disability Discrimination Act 1995, cases of disability discrimination involving schools were dealt with by the Sheriff Court in Scotland. Following the implementation of the Equality Act 2010, responsibility for dealing with such cases shifted to the Additional Support Needs Tribunals for Scotland. A disability discrimination claim may be made to the tribunal by either the parent or the young person, where they have capacity. Either party may appeal on a point of law to the Court of Session.

Local authorities and parents are discouraged from using legal representation at the tribunal, although, as discussed further below, there is a growing trend for local authorities to use advocates, whereas parents generally only have access to lay representation. Recognising this inequality, the 2009 Act placed a duty on Scottish Ministers to provide advocacy services to be available on request and free of charge to a parent or young person using the tribunal. A contract to provide advocacy services was awarded in 2010 to the Scottish Child Law Centre and Barnardos, two organisations which specialise in supporting children and their families.

'Adjudication'

In cases where there is no CSP and the dispute is not over CSP entitlement, the parent or young person does not have a right of appeal to the tribunal. In place of that right of appeal, the parent or young person may make an application to 'independent adjudication' in relation to a dispute concerning whether a child has additional support needs and the type of needs which are identified; a refusal by the local authority to determine whether a child has additional support needs; a decision by the local authority as to how, or by whom, an assessment or examination should be carried out; a failure by the local authority to provide the additional support required by the child or young person; or a failure by the local authority to make a statutory request for help from another agency (e.g. the Health Board) in relation to a child's additional support needs. There is no formal time limit to making a referral to the local authority, but the local authority need only accept a referral if it is reasonable.

The application is made to the local authority and within ten working days the local authority must provide confirmation of the acceptance of the application. At the same time, the local authority must send a request to the Scottish ministers to nominate an independent adjudicator. The local authority must then appoint the nominated adjudicator and meet his or her fees for the adjudication. Within 25 days of receiving the application, the local authority must send to the adjudicator the application, the authority's response, any further observations from either side and any further information requested. The adjudicator reports back to the local authority and the applicant within a period of 15 working days, providing recommendations as to how the dispute should be resolved. The local authority then has 10 working days to issue its decision as to what course of action it intends to take in light of the recommendations. This decision is communicated to the applicant, but not to the adjudicator, who has no power to order the local authority to carry out its stated course of action, a possible weakness in the operation of adjudication.

Mediation

Recognising that there were likely to be disagreements about the operation of the new legislation and, more widely, the allocation of resources to children with additional support needs, arrangements were put in place for mediation. As discussed in chapter 2 (and see also chapter 3), mediation is a means of conflict resolution aimed at helping people involved in a disagreement to find a mutually acceptable solution, with the help of an independent third party. The Education (Additional Support for Learning) (Scotland) Act 2004 requires that every local authority has in place arrangements for mediation, involving independent mediators, to try and resolve disputes between parents and the authority and/or school regarding a child with additional support needs. A key principle of mediation is that it is voluntary for both parties and the process is confidential. The cost of mediation is borne by the local authority and referring a matter to mediation does not affect a parent or young person's right of appeal.

The proportion and characteristics of children identified as having additional support needs in Scotland

One of the key aims of the legislation was to recognise the additional support needs of a much larger and more diverse group of children, thus allowing a larger section of the population to challenge local authority and school decisions. In practice, however, there was only a small increase in the proportion of children identified as having additional support needs (6 per cent in 2009) compared with those identified

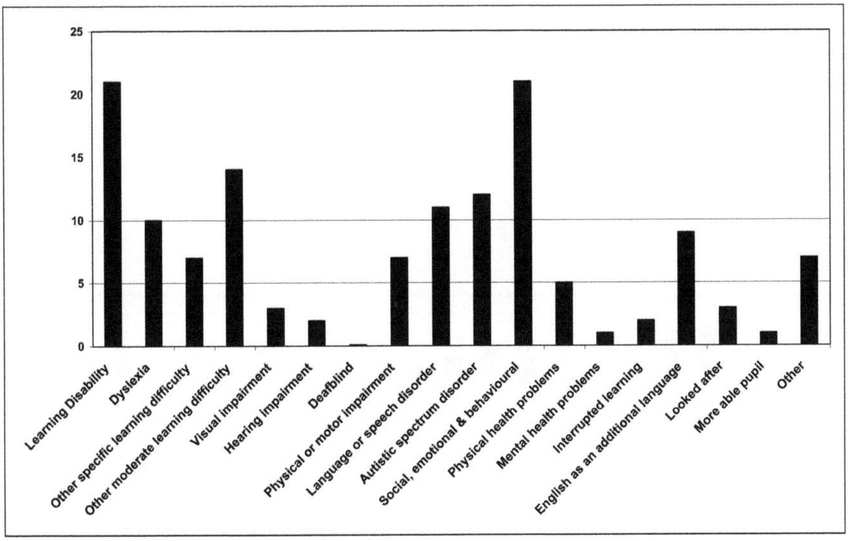

Source: Scottish Government 2008.

Figure 4.2 Pupils in Scotland with particular types of difficulty as a percentage of all pupils with additional support needs

as having special educational needs (4.5 per cent in 2003). In addition, whereas about 2 per cent of the pupil population received a record of needs under the old system, under the new system less than 0.5 per cent of children received a CSP. As a result of this, only a tiny minority of Scottish parents have been able to use the full range of dispute resolution routes.

Furthermore, the types of needs identified under the new legislation are very similar to those identified under the previous system. Figure 4.2 shows that the vast majority of children identified as having additional support needs have learning difficulties or social, emotional and behavioural difficulties, with a smaller proportion identified as having physical or sensory impairment. The new categories, including looked after and more able children, are being used extremely sparsely. In recognition of this problem, the 2009 legislation placed a duty on local authorities to assess all children looked after by the local authority to determine whether they required additional support. If local authorities and schools were to change their practice in response to the new legislation, this might lead to a channelling of resources towards extremely disadvantaged children and young people. However, at a time of massive reduction in public sector funding, local authorities are likely to be seeking to reduce, rather than expand, the additional support needs population, and are unlikely to welcome an opening up of the appeals system to new groups.

Analysis by Riddell et al. (2010) shows that there is a very strong association between living in an area of social deprivation as measured by the Scottish Index of Multiple Deprivation and being identified as having additional support

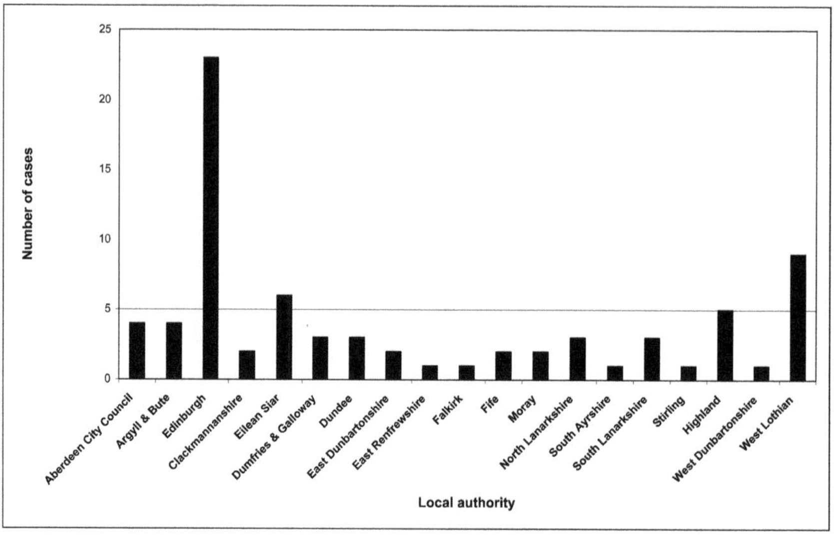

Source: Additional Support Needs Tribunals for Scotland, Annual Report, 2008.

Figure 4.3 Reference to the Additional Support Needs Tribunals for Scotland (ASNTS) by local authority, 2007–2008

needs. The association is particularly strong in relation to social, emotional and behavioural difficulties and learning disability, where children living in the most deprived areas are three times as likely to be identified with these difficulties as children living in the least deprived areas. However, children living in the most socially deprived areas of Scotland are only half as likely to have a CSP compared with those living in the least deprived areas. The discrepancy has consequences for social justice, since the CSP confers stronger rights on parents to challenge local authority decisions, acting as a passport to the tribunal. Furthermore, the majority of references to the tribunal concern children with autistic spectrum disorder, a category which is only weakly associated with social deprivation, occurring more evenly across the social spectrum (ASNTS 2008).

Use of the different routes to redress in Scotland

Since its inception in 2005, use of the tribunal in Scotland has been much lower than expected. Seventy six references were made to the tribunal during the period April 2007–March 2008, and these were concentrated in a small number of local authorities (see Figure 4.3). By way of comparison, during the same period, 3,392 references were made to the tribunal in England. Bearing in mind the relative size of the population in each country, this suggests that there were approximately ten times more appeals in England than Scotland, per head of population.

Seventeen of the references to the tribunal in Scotland were placing requests and 59 related to co-ordinated support plans. The majority of parents were represented at the tribunal by one voluntary organisation (ISEA, Independent Special Education Advice), with a much smaller proportion having legal representation. Just over half of the cases represented by ISEA at reference were withdrawn, 12 led to a hearing and a further six were awaiting a hearing when the statistics were gathered. Whilst the number of cases where parents had legal representation was low, a relatively smaller proportion of these were withdrawn. References made by parents without any representation were about as likely to be withdrawn as those represented by ISEA. In just over half of the appeal hearings, Scottish local authorities were legally represented, although the numbers are very low. Of the ten cases with legal representation, six used in-house legal teams and four used counsel. The tribunal upheld the parent's reference in 15 cases (ten of these without an oral hearing) and the local authority's in seven of the references. There is quite a wide regional variation in the number of references to the tribunal, but 13 authorities have not been subject to a single reference and this includes Glasgow City Council in spite of having the largest pupil population and a high proportion of children living in poverty. Eilean Siar (the Western Isles), with one of the smallest pupil populations, has a relatively high number of references. Since its inception, the number of references to the tribunal has been as follows: 2005–2006, 2 cases; 2007–2008, 76 cases; 2008–2009, 35 cases; and 2009–2010, 54 cases.

Parents whose children have additional support needs but who do not meet the criteria for a CSP (the majority) may request 'independent adjudication', described above. During the year in which our survey took place (2007–2008), approximately 12 adjudications were conducted throughout Scotland. To date, it appears that there have been very few requests for adjudication (Riddell and Weedon, 2009), although potentially, far greater use could be made of this route.

In addition, little use has been made of mediation services which local authorities are now obliged to provide. National data are not maintained on the use of mediation services, but in response to our questionnaire survey, three quarters of local authorities reported having fewer than five mediations each during the year 2007–2008 (see Table 4.1).

Table 4.1 Number of mediations reported by Scottish local authority officers, 2006–2007

Number of mediations	Frequency	%
None	5	18
5 or less	15	56
Between 6 and 10	6	22
Between 11 and 20	1	4
Between 21 and 30	0	0
Total	27	100

To summarise, Scotland lagged behind England in strengthening parents' rights to use a range of redress procedures in the field of additional support needs. As in England, relatively little use has been made of alternative dispute resolution routes, but whereas the number of appeals to the English tribunal far exceeded the anticipated demand, in Scotland the reverse was the case, with very few references. In the following sections, we explore local authority officers' and parents' views of the nature of disagreements and the various means of dispute resolution.

The nature and extent of disputes

Local authority officers' views

As shown in Table 4.2 (below), Scottish local authority officers believed that disagreements were rare, and when they arose, were likely to focus on access to classroom support and issues around opening and managing CSPs.

Table 4.2 Local authority officers' views of the nature and occurrence of disagreements between the local authority/school and parents in Scotland

Reason for disagreement	Frequent %	Sometimes %	Rarely %	Number	Missing
Local authority decision to place child in mainstream school	0	16.7	83.3	24	3
Local authority decision to place child in special school or a department of additional support	0	8.3	91.7	24	3
Particular school named regardless of sector	0	26.1	73.9	23	4
Decision of local authority not to open CSP	0	30.4	69.6	23	4
Resources specified in CSP	4.2	29.2	66.7	24	3
Failure to deliver resources specified in CSP/IEP	0	26.1	73.9	23	4
Decision of local authority not to open IEP	0	8.7	91.3	23	4
Content of IEP	0	13.0	87.0	23	4
Most appropriate teaching methods	0	20.0	80.0	25	2
Access to classroom assistant or other personnel	7.7	57.7	34.6	26	1

One respondent noted that there had been an increase in parental expectation of one to one classroom support and there were disagreements over what constituted 'significant input' from other agencies. A number of respondents felt that the additional support for learning legislation did not fully stress that problems and conflicts should be resolved at the local level wherever possible. The provision of a number of new routes of redress was believed to have contributed to a far more confrontational approach, damaging Scottish traditions of consensus and collectivism:

> This education authority has a history of having been able to resolve most disagreements at school level and having very few formal disputes such as referrals to Scottish Ministers. Disputes have escalated since the ASL Act came into force. Securing an active commitment to dispute reduction from advocacy organisations would help. (Local authority officer 5)

Scottish local authority officers were asked to comment on the actions they were taking to reduce the number of disputes. Some officers indicated that they had taken steps to improve communication with parents as the best means of preventing disputes arising in the first place:

> We always aim to have zero disputes as a target. The focus has been on building better partnerships with parents and other agencies e.g. through the use of Person Centred Planning. (Local authority officer 12)

There was clearly little sympathy with the idea that services might improve by listening to the voices of consumers:

> Parental guidance might place more emphasis on the fact that going to tribunal is a very poor way of seeking the best educational outcomes for their child. Parental guidance might discuss the possibility that CSPs actually change nothing if practice is already good. (Local authority officer 13)

To summarise, the predominant view amongst local authority officers was that parents had unrealistically high expectations of the level of support which could be funded by the local authority, particularly with regard to individual provision. They believed that disputes should be resolved at local level, and the new dispute resolution mechanisms were time-consuming, costly and unhelpful in terms of damaging relationships between parents and the authority. A minority view was that the new dispute resolution procedures might be helpful in forcing local authorities to pay greater attention to shortcomings in the services provided:

> This may sound like a paradox but I actually think that the existence of an effective appeals process has been helpful. I think the fact that there are clear processes in place and it's not on a grace and favour basis and parents have the right in law to request to proceed to [the tribunal], I think it has been helpful and

> I think probably locally it has been a factor in sharpening up our practice in this area. I would value that on reflection (Local authority officer 4).

Parents' views

Whereas local authority officers believed that disputes were rare and best dealt with through informal negotiation at school level, a large proportion of our sample (more than 80 per cent) had disagreed with the council at some point over educational provision for their child. The majority of disagreements focussed on additional educational support, followed by assessment of difficulties, teaching methods and the relationship with a staff member (see Table 4.3)

Table 4.3 Parents' accounts of nature of disagreement with school/local authority in Scotland

Subject	Yes	No/non-response
School placement	32%	68%
Additional education support	76%	24%
Additional support from health	25%	76%
Additional support from social work	12%	88%
Teaching methods	49%	51%
Assessment of difficulties by education staff	60%	40%
Assessment of difficulties by health staff	19%	81%
Assessment of difficulties by social work staff	7%	93%
Relationship with staff member	46%	54%

Parents who had been successful in obtaining support were broadly satisfied with what the council was providing. However, many reported that getting any support at all took considerable time and effort on their part. They often remained dissatisfied with the support which was finally provided and complained about lack of respect and poor communication on the part of the school:

> There has been no support whatsoever, even though he is starting P7 and was diagnosed in P2. The school has been unhelpful, even issuing a letter of exclusion. We have had to fight for basic rights. (Parent of child with ADHD, local authority 15)

Another parent became so frustrated by the poor level of support that she decided to educate her child at home:

> Niamh was supposed to have full-time help from an auxiliary helper. This is rarely the case because they were assigned to other children in the school. Not

> even in the same class! (Parent of child with autistic spectrum disorder, ADHD and dyslexic difficulties, home educated)

In general, local authority staff and parents differed in their assessment of levels of satisfaction with the system. Local authority officers believed that the council was providing high quality services, that disputes were rare and that the new dispute resolution mechanisms were responsible for 'stirring up trouble'. Of the parents we sampled, the majority were happy with the quality of services, but a significant minority were extremely dissatisfied and angry. In the following sections, we explore the extent to which different routes of redress have been used by parents to settle disputes with the local authority, before comparing perceptions and experiences of the different dispute resolution mechanisms from the point of view of parents and local authority officers.

Views of the tribunal

Local authority officers' views

Table 4.4 summarises Scottish local authority officers' level of satisfaction with the tribunal.

Table 4.4 Local authority officers' satisfaction with arrangements for mediation, adjudication and ASN Tribunal in Scotland

	Highly satisfactory %	Satisfactory %	No opinion %	Unsatisfactory %	Highly unsatisfactory %	No	Missing
Mediation	24.0	68.0	4.0	4.0	0	25	2
Adjudication	0	40.9	36.4	22.7	0	22	5
ASN Tribunal	0	39.1	4.3	47.8	8.7	23	4

Whilst the majority had no or little experience of the tribunal, they were nonetheless very critical, with 56 per cent regarding it as unsatisfactory or highly unsatisfactory. Interestingly, they were more critical of the tribunal than their English counterparts, who had far more experience of its operation. Comments from Scottish officers indicated that they saw the tribunal as unfairly weighted against them and in favour of parents, and there was an implicit defence of the discourse of professionalism, whereby benign professionals should be left to make decisions in the best interest of their clients:

> The tribunal process is adversarial. Assumption that local authority does not act in best interests of child. Assumption that parent knows what's best regardless of professional view/expertise. No emphasis on/recognition of the rights of the professional. No requirement that parent is able to show they have a case at point of referral. Where a further referral is made no requirement that parent can show that a change has occurred. Parent could, in theory, make an annual referral. (Local authority 23)

There was particular criticism of a voluntary organisation providing advocacy services, and a law centre offering legal support in a small number of cases:

> A less combative approach from independent organisations such as [advocacy organisation] and [law centre] might be more helpful in developing LEA practice/interpretation of the Act, and improving council/parent joint working. (Local authority 13)

> Our experience of the ASN Tribunal has led to no change in provision for the children. It has reinforced the power of [advocacy group] to unnecessarily challenge the authority – where resolution could have been made amicably between authority and parent. (Local authority 9)

Overall, local authority officers regarded the tribunal as an unnecessary and expensive institution, troubling the consensus on additional support needs provision which had previously remained unchallenged.

Parents' views of the tribunal

Parents were asked about how satisfied they were with the way in which their particular disagreement was dealt with by the tribunal. As shown in table 4.5 below, only a small number of parents had used the tribunal.

Of these, just over half were very satisfied or satisfied. As the comments below illustrate, they were frustrated by aspects of the experience, including the failure of the local authority to implement recommendations:

> Continual tribunal – council is untouchable and unaccountable. Council refused something the Tribunal ordered and the Tribunal could not do anything. (Parent of child with autistic spectrum disorder, local authority 12)

For one parent, the tribunal was a 'stressful nightmare':

> We have just received the Tribunal ruling. It was in our favour and quite critical of the local Education Authority and the Health Authority. Nevertheless, the Tribunal process was a stressful nightmare. It extended over 5 months (4 days sitting) and parents should not have to experience that. The Tribunal panel was

> fair in its conduct, but the actual process served to demonstrate that a quasi-judicial process like this is not family friendly and inquisitional, but adversarial and trial-like. How ministers and policy officials in SEED could think otherwise is beyond belief. (Parent of child with multiple impairments, local authority 1)

Whilst endorsing local authority officers' views that the tribunal tended to be very formal and somewhat intimidating in its operation, these parents did not support the view that it was unfairly weighted in their favour – rather the reverse.

Table 4.5 Parents' satisfaction with the way the disagreement was handled in Scotland

	Very satisfied	Satisfied	Not satisfied	Had not used that method
Negotiation with school	10 (8%)	27 (22%)	84 (69%)	18 (13%)
By information and advice provided by Enquire	41 (51%)	27 (34%)	12 (15%)	59 (42%)
By formal mediation provided by local authority	1 (3%)	15 (39%)	23 (59%)	100 (72%)
By independent adjudicator appointed by the Scottish Government	6 (40%)	3 (20%)	6 (40%)	124 (89%)
At Additional Support Needs Tribunal	5 (24%)	6 (29%)	10 (48%)	118 85%

Views of adjudication

Local authority officers' views

As discussed above, a system of adjudication was implemented in Scotland in order to provide a formal route of redress to parents whose children were deemed not to qualify for a CSP, but who nonetheless might have significant disagreements with the local authority with regard to additional support needs provision. At the time of the research, it appeared that adjudication was being little used. Local authority officers were unenthusiastic about adjudication, but, as indicated by Table 4.4, did not find it as threatening as the tribunal. Their main objections were that local authorities were likely to find the tight timescales difficult to adhere to, and the adjudicator might not have sufficient understanding of a particular local authority context. They believed that the written format might work to the advantage of local authorities rather than parents, and about half of respondents acknowledged that adjudication findings might help local authorities improve services.

Parents' views

Very few parents had used adjudication and, as shown by Table 4.5, of those who had, about 60 per cent were very satisfied or satisfied. As with the tribunal, there was a feeling amongst parents that enforcement procedures needed to be strengthened:

> We put in an application for independent adjudication but got no response (Parent of child with multiple impairments, local authority 16)

There were also some reports of victimisation following adjudication requests:

> We had a case at dispute resolution and the adjudicator's recommendations in Jan 2008 were agreed upon by the education authority. Since then they have refused to action a number of recommendations. He was to be immediately multi-agency assessed to identify needs. Health refused, totally dismissing the adjudicator's report. "Who was this person teaching them what to do?", said the manager in Health ... Since the dispute resolution case I am being personally attacked by school/authority. (Parent of child with ADHD)

Perhaps because of the fact that adjudication is based on the submission of written evidence rather than appearance in front of a panel or face to face negotiation, it is relatively popular with local authority staff and parents. However, comments from parents highlight some weaknesses in its operation, in particular the possibility that local authorities may simply ignore the adjudicator's recommendations.

Views of mediation

Local authority officers' views

As observed above, as in England, mediation has not been extensively used. Local authority officers approved of it in principle, believing that, compared with tribunal and adjudication, it was capable of resolving disputes quickly and with minimal stress for parents:

> [The largest mediation provider] is very approachable by parents and always communicates very effectively with all participants. Mediators are very well trained and mediation sessions very productive. Cases which are not suitable for mediation are recognised and alternatives suggested. (Local authority 23)

> If conducted appropriately, it will be fair, as will adjudication or tribunal. Less formal than a tribunal, less emphasis on rules and procedure. Generally it is more efficient in use of time and resources. It is also more conducive to consensus and compromise and supports positive and sustainable relationships. (Local authority 27)

In practice, however, they felt that it was an expensive system which was unlikely to be more effective than informal negotiation at school level:

> Mediation, like dispute resolution (adjudication) and the tribunal system appear to be a costly system established for little reason and less purpose ... the introduction of adversarial approaches into Scottish education was and remains unwanted and unnecessary. This Council, for example, spends £6,000 per annum as a retainer for mediation services which have never been used. (Local authority officer 25)

> Our experience to date is that mediation has not satisfied the parents who generally go on to seek redress/continue their complaint. (Local authority officer 7)

> As [Council X] has not yet had a mediation case, it is an expensive service to offer. (Local authority officer 4)

Parents' views

About 16 parents in our survey had used mediation and about 40 per cent were satisfied or very satisfied with the process (see Table 4.5). This is a lower satisfaction rate than was reported in relation to adjudication and tribunal, and may reflect the fact that the process of mediation involves compromise on both sides, which may be difficult for all parties once a dispute has become entrenched. Furthermore, the findings of a mediation report are not binding, so mediation may be used by parents as a step on the way to other forms of dispute resolution with more clear-cut outcomes. Finally, parents reported some difficulty in getting local authorities to engage with the mediation process:

> Part of the settlement (imposed by Council) was that we attend mediation which I feel would be beneficial. However, this has yet not taken place. (Parent of child with multiple impairments, Local authority 3)

Comparing local authority officers' and parents' views of different types of dispute resolution

Tables 4.4 and 4.5 suggest some interesting differences between parents and local authority officers' perspectives on dispute resolution, bearing in mind that parents were reporting on their experiences of particular routes, whereas local authority officers were not reporting on individual cases but on the general impact of each approach. More than half of parents in our sample had resolved their disagreement by seeking help from Enquire, the Scottish Government advice and information service for additional support needs. The vast majority (85 per cent) were satisfied with the service they received, suggesting that input from an external body was sufficient to help them resolve the problem with the local authority. By way of contrast, a high proportion of parents who tried to resolve the problem through negotiation with the school (72 per cent) were dissatisfied. This clearly has implications for local authority officers, who believed that this was by far the best way to resolve disputes.

There was also an interesting contrast in perceptions of adjudication. Sixty per cent of parents who had used this route were satisfied with their experience, whereas less than half (40 per cent) of local authority officers were satisfied. Just over half of parents (53 per cent) were satisfied with their experience of the tribunal, whilst only 30 per cent of local authority staff judged this to be a satisfactory way of resolving disputes. Taken together, these findings suggest something of a gulf between local authority officers, who believe that disagreements are rare and best dealt with through discussion with the school, and parents, who believe that disagreements are quite common and best dealt with through the involvement of an impartial outsider, if only as an advice provider. The parents in our sample are not necessarily typical of all parents of children with additional support needs. Nonetheless, the views reported in the survey point to a significant minority who are in dispute with the local authority over the quantity and quality of additional support, and far from satisfied with individual negotiation with the school. Of the new dispute resolution approaches, they are least satisfied with mediation and most satisfied with adjudication, probably because the latter ensures that their case is examined by a senior local authority officer and an adjudicator, who is charged with providing clear recommendations for action. The popularity of Enquire suggests that in many cases all that parents require is advice and information from a dispassionate external body, which is capable of clarifying the local authority's and school's responsibilities on the one hand and parents' rights on the other should the dispute fail to be resolved. In the following section, we present data from case studies of families in three Scottish local authorities to illuminate experiences of different types of dispute resolution processes, and their inter-connections.

Case studies

All names of individuals and local authorities in the case studies below are fictitious.

Raghid Daine – local negotiation at school level

Raghid was 15 years old at the time of the research and lived with his mother, a single parent, in a modern owner-occupied house in a small town in Coalshire. Located in central Scotland, the local authority was made up of both rural and urban areas and had very few formal disputes. Parents of children with additional support needs were not routinely informed of their rights of formal redress and were encouraged to resolve all difficulties through informal negotiation at local level. Mrs Daine, a Scottish woman of Asian origin, took the lead in managing her son's education. Her working life as a care assistant was extremely disrupted because her son was excluded from school on many occasions, and she was obliged to leave work without notice to look after him. At one point during his primary schooling, Raghid was out of school for a year because of the local authority's failure to suggest an appropriate placement. Mrs Daine resisted suggestions that he should be in a special unit on the grounds that he was clever and generally polite, though easily agitated, whilst pupils in the special unit had more significant cognitive and behavioural difficulties.

Raghid was identified at nursery as having severe behavioural difficulties, and the local child psychiatry service became involved at an early point. Doctors initially diagnosed 'attachment disorder', a diagnosis disputed by the consultant paediatrician who worked with Raghid over many years and believed from an early stage that he had classic Asperger's Syndrome symptoms. Mrs Daine believed that her son had been badly let down by the education service, which failed to act on the numerous plans which were drawn up. There was a particular failure to ensure that auxiliary staff had adequate knowledge and training, and as a result inappropriate confrontational tactics were often used, leading to further exclusions.

At the time of the research, Mrs Daine was beginning to lose patience with the local authority's failure to take responsibility for her son's education. She described a confrontation with the secondary schools' deputy head, who wanted her to take her son out of school:

> There was a situation where the deputy head had called me in, and we were sitting in a little interview room, and there had been a bit of a problem and he said 'I want you to take him home' … And I said, 'Sorry, but I have got a job to go to, got to be at my job, can't just take him home because there is a problem, how are you going to sort it? (Mrs Daine)

The consultant paediatrician concurred with Mrs Daine's perception that she was being blamed for her son's behaviour:

> I think it's fair comment that Mum had a lot of stuff coming in her direction implying … that there were other issues and causes for Raghid's presenting behaviour that she might be held responsible for in terms of her parenting, so it's a difficult time for her. To add insult to injury, I think it's fair to say that

> she was kind of left to push, as many parents are to be honest, left to stand up and say, 'No, that's something that doesn't suit me, that's not satisfactory, I want something different for my child that acknowledges his needs, there isn't a compromise'. (Consultant paediatrician)

Mrs Daine had finally decided that it would be necessary to use a more formal dispute resolution approach, probably the tribunal, to resolve the ongoing difficulties in her son's education. However, this was unlikely to achieve a positive outcome, since Raghid was nearing the end of compulsory schooling.

Ian Orr – local negotiation at school level

Ian Orr was 16 at the time of the research and had just completed his education at a special school in Glenside, a large rural local authority with a relatively high rate of tribunal and adjudication cases. Three cases had been brought to the Sheriff Court, on the grounds that the local authority was failing in its duty to provide 'adequate and efficient' education. Ian's parents owned their own home, but were financially tightly stretched; Mr Orr was unemployed and Mrs Orr worked for the local authority as a learning support assistant. In addition to Ian, there were two older children and a younger child who was being looked after by the family. Ian's difficulties began in the early stages of secondary school, when he was excluded from school for failing to turn up for detentions which his parents had not known about. He was subsequently excluded from school on such a regular basis that he was effectively not being educated at all. Mrs Orr felt that the systems put in place by the school to manage Ian's behaviour were stigmatising and counter-productive. For example, if he was feeling stressed in a class, he was meant to stand up holding a red card and ask to be excused, which he regarded as humiliating. Ian was not only excluded from school, but was also banned from school trips and the school dance, leading to increasing social isolation and distress:

> I had to take him to the doctor – he was covered in eczema, he had eaten the points of his fingers, drew blood … (Mrs Orr).

The health of the whole family was being adversely affected, and the family doctor eventually advised Mrs Orr to contact Enquire. Information from Enquire confirmed that the local authority was obliged to assess her son's difficulties under additional support for learning legislation. According to Mrs Orr, the school denied that Ian had additional support needs:

> I said, 'I beg your pardon, Ian does have additional needs …' 'Oh yes, you are right, but he has to be assessed'. And I said, 'Well, why hasn't he been assessed?' 'Oh, because we haven't got your permission'. I said, 'Well, you haven't asked for my permission, you have my permission, I want Ian assessed …' (Mrs Orr)

Despite requests for assessment reports, these were never received. By this time, all members of the family, including Ian, were under very high levels of stress and the offer of a place at a special unit for children with social, emotional and behavioural difficulties was accepted. In the event, Ian did very well in this structured environment and left with six Standard grades, which allowed him to start a vocational course in an FE (further education) college.

Graham Meikle – Formal mediation and adjudication

Graham Meikle was identified as having autistic spectrum disorder at three years of age, a diagnosis which was later modified to Asperger's Syndrome. His family, who lived in a pretty but isolated Glenside village, were middle class and his mother had direct knowledge of the local council through her work in family support. Although he was somewhat socially isolated, Graham's primary education was relatively successful. However, problems arose at secondary school where the demands of the curriculum were much greater. Mrs Meikle requested an IEP, but did not feel that the document was sufficiently detailed. She also felt that the support base was not meeting Graham's needs, since despite his social difficulties he was academically able. Having unsuccessfully attempted informal negotiation at school level on the advice of the educational psychologist, she requested independent mediation. The meeting took some time to arrange but, according to Mrs Meikle, 'It achieved nothing to be quite honest' because the council officials who attended were not budget holders.

Mrs Meikle subsequently requested adjudication, which was found in her favour with six recommendations being made to the council with regard to assessment, planning and provision. However, the subsequent meeting with the school was described as 'a farce' since she felt there was no intention of implementing the recommendations. Mrs Meikle was aware that making a reference to the tribunal was a possible option, but feared victimisation so decided not to pursue the dispute any further. Ultimately, Mrs Meikle believed that the system had laudable aspirations, but foundered on a lack of additional resources:

> As soon as you have a child with any additional need you are going to hit some kind of conflict because you obviously need additional funding to provide the additional need. And policy will state that children are entitled to be educated, you know, included and so on. And that's all well and good until it comes to needing an extra member of staff or extra room, extra resource, and then you are stumped really cause there's no money.

By way of contrast, local authority officials felt that Mrs Meikle was demanding too much of the system and, according to the educational psychologist, the case had 'used up a disproportionate amount of time'.

Paul Wilson – Formal mediation

Paul was diagnosed with autistic spectrum disorder and language difficulties at nursery school. The family lived in a small village outside Sea City and were owner occupiers. Mrs Wilson was a health worker and Mr Wilson stayed at home to look after the two children, both of whom were disabled. The Wilsons requested a placement in a language unit attached to a mainstream primary school, and were disconcerted to receive a standard letter from the council informing them that a decision had been made to place Paul in a special school which they did not believe was appropriate. They asked to know on what basis this decision had been made, and were upset when the council refused to provide any information about the decision-making process. They even wondered whether there had been some mistake and their child had been confused with another of the same name.

Frustrated at the lack of communication, the parents requested formal mediation, with little expectation that anything would be achieved:

> The council suggested us going to mediation but I just felt that at that point that mediation was just going to be in the same building, the council building, just going to help us see that we were taking it the wrong way round … But we had to do something, so we arranged a meeting with the mediator, and she was very good actually. (Mrs Wilson)

Before the full mediation meeting occurred, a place was offered in the language unit which the parents had initially requested.

The educational psychologist explained that he had provided a great deal of support throughout the process, and it was unreasonable to expect parents to navigate the system without assistance:

> I think the key thing is to have somebody guiding them through it. Explaining it in advance, letting them know who will be asked to provide a report and giving them advice about what they can put in their report … and sometimes we'll sit down and write it for them, scribe it for them and go through it so that their views are expressed. I think that is part of my job. (Educational psychologist)

The high level of support from the mediator and the educational psychologist was clearly instrumental in the parents' satisfaction with the outcome of this case, but as the other cases make clear, support of this type was the exception rather than the rule.

John Douglas – Tribunal

John Douglas lived in Sea City, a local authority with relatively high use of all types of dispute resolution. He was diagnosed with autistic spectrum disorder at the age of four. His father worked for a Scottish utilities firm and his mother worked at home looking after the children. The family lived in a middle class area on the east of the city. The family had insider knowledge of the educational system, for example, a close family member was a recently retired head teacher and a friend worked for a voluntary organisation providing advocacy services. Although Mrs Douglas said that she was not confident challenging the system, her husband said that he was used to managing formal meetings in his working life. The family had the economic resources to hire a lawyer and an advocate.

Problems arose in John's education when he refused to attend school at about seven years of age. Social work became involved, and Mrs Douglas believed that she was being blamed for poor parenting. The parents became very upset when a teacher queried the diagnosis of autistic spectrum disorder, and came to the view that John's difficulties were not being acknowledged or dealt with by the school. They requested a placement in a special school or unit, and a co-ordinated support plan. The response of the council was that John did not fully meet all of the criteria, in particular significant input from agencies outwith education. At this point the parents requested support from Enquire and ISEA, and decided to make a reference to the tribunal. They also hired a lawyer and an advocate to represent them. Just before the tribunal, a place in a language unit and a CSP were offered, and the case was therefore withdrawn before a hearing.

The parents were happy with the language unit, but felt that the CSP was totally inadequate. It was only two pages in length and contained many errors, including their name and address. Another reference was made to the tribunal to compel the council to compile a sufficiently detailed document. The tribunal found in their favour, but the parents still felt a lack of confidence in the system, believing there was collusion between the professionals involved to avoid resources being committed to individual children. Mrs. Douglas said that she might have used mediation had this been offered at an earlier point in the ongoing dispute, although the fact that this was run by the council might have acted as a deterrent. Both she and her husband felt that the tribunal did not have sufficient enforcement powers:

> Interviewer: So if I was to ask you if the new legislation has increased your rights, what would you say?
> Mr Douglas: Not at all, no rights.
> Interviewer: Even being able to go through the tribunal?
> Mrs Douglas: You go through the tribunal, they just ignore it.
> Mr Douglas: The council ignored this twice.
> Mrs Douglas: The tribunal is a joke because the council just ignored it.

Summary and conclusion

A major aim of the additional support needs legislation in Scotland was to strengthen parents' and children's rights in education. The new dispute resolution mechanisms were intended to play a major part in this, but, as the statistics reported earlier demonstrate, they have been used very sparsely. Local authority officers and parents clearly provide rather different explanations as to why this might be the case. According to the local authority officers, parents were generally happy with additional support needs provision, and any disagreements can be ironed out with minimal fuss at local level through informal negotiation. The new dispute resolution measures have simply given advocacy organisations the chance to stir up discontent where none previously existed. Given the cost to the public purse of providing these services, many local authority officers believed that the money would be better spent on improving educational provision.

By way of contrast, the majority of parents in our sample reported that they had been involved in a dispute with the council. Most had resolved this disagreement by contacting Enquire, funded by the government to provide advice and information services. There were high levels of satisfaction with this support, which was often sufficient to resolve the disagreement. Adjudication, mediation and the tribunal were seen as less helpful than Enquire, although parents rated them much more highly than local authority officers. Almost all parents had attempted to engage with the school in informal negotiation to sort out disagreements, but were very negative about their experiences, the majority reporting that this approach had simply not worked. This perception is clearly very different from the local authority view of the best way of proceeding.

The case studies provide some interesting insights into parents' experiences of different types of dispute resolution. The majority involved parents of children with some type of behavioural difficulty, a type of need which is more likely to be identified in children living in areas of deprivation (Riddell et al. 2010). Schools were often reluctant to recognise that children with behavioural difficulties had additional support needs, tending to regard such children as naughty and disruptive rather than in need of extra help. A frequent response was to send the child home, with the expectation that a parent, normally the mother, would leave work to look after the child. This clearly had an adverse impact on families who were already often struggling financially.

The socio-economic profile of families of children with additional support needs also goes some way to explain why dispute resolution routes have been little used. Our analysis suggested that children living in the most deprived areas of Scotland were much more likely to be identified as having additional support needs, but less likely to receive a statutory support plan. Case studies illustrated that parents with greater social, economic and cultural resources were much more likely to obtain the type of support they considered appropriate for their child, partly because they were able to deploy their social and cultural resources to engage the support of professionals. In addition, they were more adept in using the available dispute resolution mechanisms, including the tribunal, when negotiation was unsuccessful. Some local authority officers used this to argue that the new dispute resolution mechanisms were failing because they enabled middle class parents to secure an unfair share of limited resources. Conversely, it could be argued that local authorities were failing to assist parents from less advantaged backgrounds by informing them of their rights and the routes of redress available to support them. In addition, it was clear from our case studies that many parents from socially disadvantaged backgrounds lacked access to advocacy services which might have helped them challenge local authority resource allocation decisions. As public spending cuts are implemented, there is clearly a danger that the disadvantage experienced by poorer families in obtaining additional support for their children will intensify rather than diminish. Finally, it appears that efforts to engage children in the dispute resolution process have so far been unsuccessful, since disputes are almost always played out between parents and professionals. Whether children could or should be involved in formal processes remains a debatable point.

Acknowledgement: We would like to acknowledge the contribution of Dr Joan Stead and Kevin Wright who conducted some of the fieldwork on the ESRC project (Dispute Resolution and Avoidance in Education: A Study of SEN and ASN in England and Scotland, RES-062-23-0803).

References

Additional Support Needs Tribunals for Scotland (2008), *Annual Report* (Glasgow: ASNTS).

Arnott, M. (2005), 'Devolution, territorial politics and the politics of education', in Mooney, G. and G. Scott (eds), *Exploring Social Policy in the 'New' Scotland* (Bristol: Policy Press), 239–263.

Clarke, J., Newman, J., Smith, N., Vidler, E. and Westmarland, L. (2007), *Creating Citizen-Consumers* (London: Sage).

Consumer Focus Scotland (2009), *Administrative Justice in Scotland – The Way Forward: The Final Report of the Administrative Justice Steering Group* (Glasgow: Consumer Focus Scotland).

Department of Constitutional Affairs (DCA) (2004), *Transforming Public Services: Complaints, Redress and Tribunals* (London: TSO).

Department of Education and Science (1978), *Special Educational Needs* (The Warnock Report) (London: HMSO).

DfE (Department for Education) (2011) *Support and Aspiration: A New Approach to Special Educational Needs and Disability. A Consultation* Cm 8027 (Norwich: TSO).

Harris, N. (2005), 'Empowerment and state education: Rights of choice and participation', *The Modern Law Review,* vol. 98, no. 6, 925–927.

Lister, R. (2003), *Citizenship; Feminist Perspectives* (2nd edn) (Basingstoke: Palgrave).

Riddell, S. (2006) (2nd edition), *Special Educational Needs, Policy and Practice: Additional Support for Learning* (Edinburgh: Dunedin Academic Press).

Riddell, S., Adler, M., Farmakopoulou, N. and Mordaunt, E. (2000), 'Special needs and competing policy frameworks in England and Scotland', *Journal of Education Policy*, vol. 15, no. 6, 621–635.

Riddell, S.I., Mordaunt, E., Wilson, A. and Adler, M. (2002), 'Parents, professionals and SEN policy frameworks in England and Scotland', *Policy and Politics*, vol. 30, no. 3, 411–427.

Riddell, S., Adler, M., Mordaunt, E. and Wilson, A. (2003), 'Procedural justice and special educational needs assessments in England and Scotland', *International Journal of Inclusive Education*, vol. 7, no. 3, 201–222.

Riddell, S. and Weedon, E. (2009), 'Approaches to dispute resolution in additional support needs in Scotland' *European Journal of Special Needs Education*, vol. 24, no. 4, 355–369.

Riddell, S., Stead, J., Weedon, E. and Wright, K. (2010), 'Additional support needs reform and social justice in Scotland' *International Studies in Sociology of Education*, vol. 20, .no 3, 179–199.

Scottish Executive (2005), *Supporting Children's Learning: Code of Practice* (Edinburgh: Scottish Executive).

Scottish Government (2010), *Supporting Children's Learning: Code of Practice (revised edition)* (Edinburgh: Scottish Executive).

Tisdall, E.K.M. and Riddell, S. (2006), 'Policies on special needs education: competing strategies and discourses', *European Journal of Special Needs Education*, vol. 21, no. 4, 363–379.

Tomlinson, S. (2001), *Education in a Post-Welfare Society* (Buckingham: Open University Press).

Trentmann, F. (ed.) (2006), *The Making of the Consumer: Knowledge, Power and Identity in the Modern World* (Oxford: Berg).

Weedon, E. and Riddell, S. (2009), 'Additional support needs and approaches to dispute resolution: the perspectives of Scottish parents', *Scottish Educational Review*, vol. 41, no. 2, 62–81.

Chapter 5

Rights and Interests in the Balance: Special Educational Needs and Disputes in the Netherlands

Paul Zoontjens

Introduction

For most people in the Netherlands, including educationalists, special education is *terra incognito*. The arrangements, which are somewhat immune to reform under the Dutch system, are complicated, diffuse and above all seem to have too low a profile to become a key issue in discussions about education. Nevertheless, special education is governed by important principles concerning its organisation and the rights of individuals. This chapter begins by explaining the constitutional framework governing special education. It then provides a short history of the arrangements for special education in the Netherlands before explaining the current legal and institutional framework, including parental rights and equality legislation. It then concentrates on the mechanisms for resolving disputes about special education matters. The chapter aims to highlight the difficult balance between the rights of parents and the responsibilities of school authorities and to show how non-judicial dispute settlement plays an important role in resolving conflicts that arise.

Special education and the Dutch Constitution

The constitutional provisions are the foundation of a dual education system, in which – with the exception of university education – state (public law) institutions are outnumbered by non state (private law) ones. In 2010, the Dutch education system consisted of 6,910 schools for primary education and 660 for general secondary education. Additionally, 636 schools provided special education to a total of 110,000 pupils in the age range 4–20 years.[1] In the Netherlands a large number of the fully funded schools are in fact non state schools (see below).

---

1 From 4–12: special education at the primary level; 12–20: special education at the secondary level. It should be noted that many pupils that are identified as requiring a certain type of special education receive education in mainstream schools. Under certain conditions parents can choose a mainstream school: see below.

Two provisions of the Dutch Constitution are relevant to education for children with special needs. One concerns equality. Section 1 of the Constitution provides: 'All persons in the Netherlands shall be treated equally in equal circumstances. Discrimination on the grounds of religion, belief, political opinion, race, or sex or on any other grounds whatsoever shall not be permitted.' According to general professional and academic opinion, the phrase 'or on any other grounds whatsoever' entitles children with special needs to educational provision of the same level and quality as that which is given to other children. Thus the principle of equal treatment guarantees (publicly funded) education to children with special educational needs.[2] Furthermore this is the basis, as shall be shown, for the weighing of the individual interest against the school interest if it comes to a decision about the admission of a child with special needs to a mainstream school. Also relevant is section 23 of the Constitution, which guarantees the freedom to establish schools, without prior consent of government.[3] It also guarantees that non state schools providing compulsory education are eligible for government funding to the same extent as state schools if they meet the relevant legal requirements. Non state schools that provide education which is not covered by the Compulsory Education Act can receive public funding, according to conditions laid down in law.[4]

The Dutch constitution also provides, in Article 23 section 5, that non state (but fully funded) schools enjoy the freedom to provide education according to particular sets of religious or philosophical beliefs. This freedom gives room for these non state schools to express their own religious or philosophical views on all issues in the context of education (Vermeulen 1999, p. 51). As such, non state schools differ radically from state schools in their education, because they are allowed to develop and communicate singular visions concerning a way of life, while state schools, on the other hand, have to be neutral, that is to say neutral in an active way (Vermeulen 1999, p. 29). State schools must, in particular, pay attention to the religious, philosophical and societal values presented in Dutch society as a whole, with recognition of the meaning and range of these values.[5]

2 The term 'special educational needs' is used in this chapter in a generic sense as referring to all children with inherent problems of a physical or mental nature which affect their access to and experience of education.

3 Cf. section 23, subsection 2, Dutch Constitution: All persons shall be free to provide education, without prejudice to the authorities' right of supervision and, with regard to forms of education designated by law, their right to examine the competence and moral integrity of teachers, to be regulated by Act of Parliament.

4 Cf. section 23, subsection 7, Dutch Constitution: Non state primary schools that satisfy the conditions laid down by Act of Parliament shall be financed from public funds according to the same standards as state schools. The conditions under which non state secondary education and pre-university education shall receive contributions from public funds shall be laid down by Act of Parliament.

5 Primary Education Act, s. 46.

The freedom of non state schools includes in particular, as the Constitution indicates, the freedom to choose their teaching aids and to appoint teachers as they see fit. It is assumed however, that state schools are also to have these particular freedoms, because as a general (unwritten) principle it is forbidden for the state to involve itself directly in pedagogical matters. Unlike state schools, non state schools have also, as denominational institutions operating under private law, freedom, within limits, with regard to internal and external organisation and in the arrangements made for the admission of pupils.

With regard to the relationship between the national legal order and (written) international law, the Dutch system can be characterised as monistic. It is, however, a matter of conditional monism. When international treaties come into force they automatically become part of the Dutch legal order. As a consequence they are always binding on the State as norms of instruction, but whether they are also binding on the individual citizen, as a (set of) permissive or prohibitive norm(s), is dependent on the nature of the particular treaty provision in question. Section 94 of the Constitution determines that national legal prescripts are inapplicable if they conflict with international treaties of a generally binding nature. The meaning of the words 'generally binding nature' will be critical and will be a matter for judicial interpretation, in all courts (Kortmann 2008, p. 181; Alkema 1993, p. 264–265). The criteria conclusive to 'generally binding nature' are the nature, content and wording of the treaty's provisions and the parties' intentions.

The most important examples of treaties of a legally binding nature are the European Convention on Human Rights (ECHR) and the International Covenant on Civil and Political Rights (ICCPR). These treaties, to which the Netherlands is a signatory, do not, however, play an important role in the field of special educational needs. As far as the right to education under article 2 of the First Protocol to the ECHR is concerned, it does not lay down a blueprint for national education systems. In fact, the European Court and (the former) Commission show in their jurisprudence that they want to exercise utmost restraint towards the organisation and design of education systems, which are primarily considered to fall within the scope of national discretion. That means, for instance, that a Contracting State's citizen cannot draw from Article 2 of the First Protocol the right to demand from the public authorities the creation of a particular kind of educational institution,[6] such as for disabled children.[7] The right to education under the ECHR merely confers a right of access to the national educational institutions existing at a given time.[8] If the state has established or subsidises institutions for special education, or when the education given in such institutions is better suited for disabled children, government is not under an obligation to confer children with special needs or

6 ECHR 23 July 1968, Publ. ECHR, Series A, vol. 6 (*Belgian Linguistics*).

7 European Commission of Human Rights 14 July 1995, appl. nr. 25212/94 (*Klerks*).

8 ECHR 23 July 1968, Publ. ECHR, Series A, vol. 6 (*Belgian Linguistics*).

disabilities access to mainstream schools.[9] In this respect, the importance of the ECHR for special education is modest. In theory, however, the ECHR or ICCPR could be cited in support of appeals on equal treatment for disabled children in education.[10] It is to be expected that the Convention on the Rights of Persons with Disabilities,[11] to which the Netherlands is a contracting party, would not be regarded as having provisions binding on national courts. The same is true of the European Social Charter and the International Covenant on Economic, Social and Cultural Rights. So, the direct influence of international law with respect to the legal position of children with special educational needs in the Netherlands is limited (Zoontjens 2009, p. 148–152).

Probably more important than these international conventions is the European framework directive for the equal treatment in the field of labour and vocational training.[12] The implementation of this directive in the Dutch legal order has led to the establishment of non-judicial dispute settlement by the Dutch Equal Treatment Commission for all educational sectors, from primary up and to higher education. This is discussed below.

Brief history of special education in the Netherlands

The first institutions for special education were created in the middle of the nineteenth century. Around 1850 there were four institutions for blind and deaf children. In 1855 the first school for 'idiotic' children started in The Hague. The first school for children with a speech impediment was established in Utrecht in 1859 and the first school for mentally disadvantaged children opened in Amsterdam in 1899 (Graas 1996, p. 27–31). In those days the schools were a result of citizens' initiatives. It was not until 1900 that special education for particular groups of children entered the political sphere. It was clear though, that at that time the issue of education for blind, and deaf or mute children was not a controversial matter. However, after the first Act on compulsory education came into force in 1901, teachers in ordinary schools experienced many practical problems related to the inclusion of mentally and physically disabled children in their crowded classrooms. This, coupled with the increased social awareness of a number of

9 European Commission of Human Rights, 2 October 1989, nr. 14.135/88, Decisions and Reports 62, 292 (*P.D. and L.D. v United Kingdom*).

10 See, for example, the judgment concerning Roma children, although not relevant for this argument; ECHR 7 February 2006, appl. nr. 57325/00, (*D.H. and others v the Czech Republic*).

11 See Chapter 1.

12 Council Directive 2000/78/EC of 27 November 2000 establishing a general framework for equal treatment in employment and occupation, Official Journal L 303, 02/12/2000, pp. 0016–0022.

teachers and medical practitioners, contributed to a more urgent need to find a solution (Graas 1996, p. 35–36).

After some time, the Dutch government accepted the imperative of creating educational provisions covering children who, because of mental or physical impairments, were not able to follow 'ordinary' education (Graas 1996, p. 24). The Basic Education Act of 1920 laid a foundation for the existence and development of 'extraordinary education', the forerunner of special education. In a Royal Decree the same year[13] the first regulation on this matter appeared. After several modernisations, via new Royal Decrees of 1949 and 1967, by which the differentiation of school types grew and the conditions under which they had to act were extended, the first temporary Act on Special Education (ISOVSO) came into force, in 1985.[14] Over the years, special education had become an important matter: in the period 1928–1967 the number of pupils receiving it grew from 8,000 to 70,000 (Van Rijswijk and Kool 2002, p. 102). As already mentioned, there are now some 110,000 pupils attending Dutch schools for special education.

The issue of inclusion in mainstream schools has remained a contentious subject. Around the time of the 1967 Decree there was widespread agreement that separate schools for special education could help children with special educational needs much better than mainstream schools. But only a few years later, with the growth of special education, debate on this and other aspects of special education increased. Gradually, the following difficulties were identified:

a. a danger that disabled children in separate schools would have an increasingly isolated position: this isolation could hamper their social integration;
b. the problem, however, that mainstream schools do not have the means to help children with special educational needs adequately, such as sufficient experience and training among the teachers and adequate facilities;
c. A lack of uniformity in the criteria for referral and admission. As a result, children with more or less equal problems would be referred to different types of special education;
d. Lack of co-operation between schools providing mainstream and special education (Van Rijswijk and Kool 2002, p. 103).

Of these matters, the first three are still prevalent.

From the lively discussions that were going on in the preceding decade, one could conclude by the beginning of the 1980s that the special education system needed to change. But with regard to the nature and the implementation of change, consensus was lacking. Therefore, when it became necessary to adopt new

13 Royal Decree of 31 December 1920, Stb. 1920, 948. Stb. is an abbreviation of 'Staatsblad', the official Dutch bulletin of acts, orders and decrees.

14 Interim-wet op het speciaal en voortgezet speciaal onderwijs (Temporary Act on Special and Secondary Special Education), Act of 15 December 1982, Stb. 1982, 730.

legislation in the first half of the 1980s, it was understandable that the legislator opted for a temporary act, intended to run for ten years. This was ISOVSO, noted above. In the year in which this act came into force, 1985, serious criticism arose about the extent of differentiation in school types in special education. Not long afterwards, however, the political climate changed. A majority of the Dutch Parliament appeared to be against the practice of dividing children at a young age into one group that is suitable for mainstream education and another that is dependent exclusively on special education. Many politicians also had problems with the financial consequences of the growth of special education. So, from the middle of the decade onwards there was political consensus around the general importance of checking the growth of special education (Van Rijswijk and Kool 2002, p. 107). It was the beginning of a long term policy by which the differences between special and mainstream education gradually were reduced, with respect to children with learning difficulties or behavioural problems.

Since then, the most important legislative changes have occurred at the end of the 1990s and the turn of the current century. These measures have shaped the current system, in which the right of disabled pupils to go to a mainstream school has been improved. But the current situation is considered to be far from ideal. There are government plans to change the legislation in a rather radical way, noted below. It is expected that these government plans will meet the needs and rights of pupils and their parents in a much better way than occurs at present.

The organisational framework under the current legislation on special education

An important principle concerning the participation of disabled children in the official education system is laid down in the Compulsory Education Act of 1969.[15] According to this Act, persons entrusted with the legal custody of a child (or with the actual care for him or her)[16] must ensure that the child is enrolled at a school and that he or she attends the school regularly. This legal obligation does not apply, however, if the child is not fit, on physical or mental grounds, to attend the school. The unfitness of the child has to be assessed by an independent and qualified doctor, psychologist or educationalist and can only be considered to present a legal exemption if the assessment is requested by the parents. That means that, when parents of disabled children do not ask for a legal exemption, the children must receive, and have a right to receive, education in an official (government funded or recognised) school. Compulsory education starts at the age of 5 and ends in the year when the age of 16 has been reached. For persons who are not adequately qualified at the age of 16, compulsory education can extend to the age of 18. Someone is only qualified adequately when he or she has gained a diploma

15 Leerplichtwet 1969, Stb. 1968, 303.

16 For brevity, we use the term 'parents' in this context.

of preparatory higher education (after 5 or 6 years in general secondary education) or a diploma of basic vocational training on the middle level of tertiary education.

Since 1998 the legislation on special education has been modernised. The ISOVSO, which it will be recalled was a temporary measure, ended that year. At the same time a new Act on special education,[17] a new Act on primary education[18] and changes to the Act on secondary education[19] came into force. In 2002, new rules were introduced concerning the relationship between mainstream education and the new system of special education.[20] The result was that the chances of parents being able to place their disabled children at a mainstream school have increased. On the other hand, a pattern of rather scattered services and procedures developed, which has come to be regarded as a labyrinth. It is not possible to describe these reforms in a detailed manner here, but the following are the key elements of the new structure.

Responsible authorities

Special education is within the remit of the national authorities, the legislator (in the Netherlands this is the government and Parliament together) and the Minister of Education, Culture and Science who is responsible for reform and for giving effect to existing legislation. The Minister is, in particular, responsible for the planning of new schools, the funding of schools and the quality of education. Traditionally, at least since the beginning of the nineteenth century, municipalities and provinces have played a very small role in education provision. They do not have any legal powers in that area. However, for some time local authorities have been active in the field of deliberation, coordination and specific financial support for schools, including special schools, but for the success of their policies they are dependent on the role of the school boards. As shown below, a new kind of administrative layer is filling the gap that exists between the Minister on the one hand and the individual school boards on the other. It involves co-operation between schools, regional cooperative bodies and regional (semi) governmental units. The process is still new, but it is clear that the autonomy and power of the individual school has been diminished and will remain so in the near future.

Schools

Under the ISOVSO a division was made between (among others) two categories of special schools: those for children with standard learning difficulties or behavioural problems and those for children with 'severe' learning difficulties or behavioural problems. Since 1998, the first category of schools has been classified, under the

17 Wet op de expertisecentra (Act on centres of expertise), Stb. 1998, 228.

18 Wet op het primair onderwijs (Act on primary education), Stb. 1998, 228.

19 Stb. 1998, 337.

20 Stb. 2002, 631; changed afterwards by Stb. 2007, 445.

legal regime for mainstream schools for primary education,[21] as 'special schools for basic education', while the second category comprises 'special schools' per se (see Table 5.1). The first category, attended by about three per cent of children in primary education in the Netherlands (Ruijs et al. 2010, p. 355), comprises schools in which primary education is intended for children who require a predominant orthopedagogical and orthodidactical approach in teaching such that, at least for a temporary period, placement at such a school is necessary. These schools do not belong to the statutory system of special education but are a (special) version of mainstream primary education, despite their designation as 'special school for basic education'.

Table 5.1 Special schools in the Netherlands: types and legislative basis

'Special school for basic education'	'Special school'
Primary education sector	*Special education sector*
Intended for children for whom it is regarded as certain that a predominant orthopedagogical and orthodidactical approach in teaching is appropriate such that, at least for a temporary period, placement at such a school is necessary.	Intended for children for whom it is regarded as certain that a predominant orthopedagogical and orthodidactical approach in teaching is appropriate.
Legislation: Primary Education Act	Legislation: Special Education Act (Act on centres of expertise [special education])

Boards of mainstream and 'special schools for basic education', regardless of whether they are state or non state schools, receive in principle the same amount of government aid for their schools. They are legally obliged to work together in regional cooperative bodies in order to arrange adequate facilities for pupils who experience problems in school. In the Netherlands there are 234 regional cooperative bodies of this kind. The board of the regional cooperative body, which has to represent a minimum of 2,000 children across the schools, must adopt (by majority decision) a plan on a yearly basis, in which the extra care for pupils is coordinated. This extra care can, for example, go to individual children within the mainstream school for primary education. It also can mean that children are admitted to a 'special school for basic education' for which the cooperative body is responsible. In the latter case, every child has to be assessed for admission to the school by a 'permanent committee on pupils' care' that has been established by

21 The Primary Education Act.

the board within the regional cooperative body. It decides on the basis of criteria fixed by the board.

The funding of both state and non state schools is on the same basis. The budget will vary from a couple of hundred Euros to some thousands of Euros – dependent on the special educational needs concerned. It is intended to fund extra hours for an assistant or a remedial teacher to support the child or various forms of specialist support or resources. For the purpose of coordinating extra care, the regional bodies receive governmental aid. This money is meant to enable the appointment of extra personnel for mainstream and/or special schools for basic education. The amount to be allocated by the regional body is based on the normative assumption that the total number of pupils that need extra care in education does not exceed 2 per cent of the school population as a whole within the regional cooperative body. When the need of the schools exceeds 2 per cent, their boards have to make up the difference out of their own budget. It is clear that this arrangement is designed to keep control over government spending. In 2009, the average government expenditure per pupil in the mainstream school for primary education was 4,900 Euros and in special schools for primary and secondary education it was 9,900 Euros (Ministry of Education 2010, p. 82). The equalisation of mainstream and special schools for basic education also has the consequence of improving the freedom of choice of pupils and their parents between the different schools. This is discussed further below.

Also in 1998 the new Special Education Act appeared. This covers 'special schools', defined as schools for special education. Section 2 of this Act provides a rather broad definition of special education: that is, education at the primary and secondary level, intended for children for whom it is regarded as certain that a predominant orthopedagogical and orthodidactical approach in teaching is appropriate. The phrasing is oriented towards every child that has educational difficulties. Nevertheless, the target group of special education is explicitly limited by virtue of the way that the Act distinguishes ten different kinds of special schools, divided over four clusters. *Cluster 1*: education for the visually disabled; *cluster 2*: education for the deaf, for pupils with hearing impediments or communicative impairments, and for pupils with severe speech disorders; *cluster 3*: education for the physically, mentally and multiply disabled and for chronically ill children with disability; *cluster 4*: education for the chronically ill and severely maladjusted children, for pupils with behavioural disorders and for pupils in paedological institutes. Approximately 2 per cent of the children in primary education in the Netherlands attend a special school (Ruijs et al. 2010, p. 355).

The average expenditure per pupil for special education at a 'special school' was, in 2009, a sum of 21,600 Euro (Ministry of Education 2010, p. 82). That means that average expenditure per pupil for special education is over four times greater than in respect of mainstream primary education. Special education is regionally organised in so called centres of expertise. Every centre of expertise covers all kinds of special schools of a certain cluster in the relevant geographical area. This sort of regionalisation is completely different from that of the regional cooperative bodies, mentioned earlier. There are some 40 regional centres of expertise. Among other things, they are responsible for the arrangement and management of an assessment committee, the coordination of ambulant care in the mainstream schools and the support of parents – when they have expressed their explicit wish – in connection with completing a request for assessment or with their search for a mainstream or special school place.

A pupil can only be admitted to a 'special school' after he or she has been assessed by an independent committee of the centre of expertise, which decides on the basis of national criteria. When assessed positively the child may not be refused admission to the special school, unless – in the case of a non state school – the child's parents are not willing to accept the religious values of the school. Since 2002, the parents of a child who is assessed positively for admission to a special school can select instead – under certain conditions – a mainstream school. In that case they receive a person-related budget, which has to be spent to professionally determined, pupil-specific requirements. As to the way that the person-related budget for education is applied, the parents have to make an agreement with the staff of the mainstream school. The conditions under which pupils (or their parents) can select a mainstream school instead of a special school are discussed below.

Pre-vocational secondary training and practical education

Since 1998, the final two or three years of general secondary education have consisted of either preparatory higher education or pre-vocational secondary training. The latter is divided into four programmatic tracks that differ with respect to their orientation. First there is the 'theoretical track' *(theoretische leerweg),* which is designed to prepare for middle management, vocational training at the middle level of tertiary education and pre higher education. Then there are two vocational tracks, the basic vocational track *(basisberoepsgerichte leerweg)* and the 'middle management-oriented track' *(kaderberoepsgerichte leerweg)* that is concerned with advanced vocational training at the middle level of tertiary education. There is also a 'mixed track' *(gemengde leerweg)* which is an intermediate form in between the theoretical and one of these two vocational tracks. Pupils in all these tracks have the possibility of receiving 'track supporting education' *(leerweg ondersteunend onderwijs),* especially intended for those who have educational or behavioural problems and who are considered to be capable of obtaining a diploma in one of the tracks. Teaching of these pupils will be undertaken by specialised teachers and it will take place in small classes. Track supporting education is therefore supplementary to the existing tracks. Pupils can only qualify for track supporting education following assessment by the 'regional reference committee' on the basis of a request from the board of the school at which they have been enrolled. The 'regional reference committee' is an independent assessment body, established by law, that decides on the basis of uniform criteria, fixed by Royal Decree.

There is also 'practical education' *(praktijkonderwijs)* – a part of general secondary education – consisting mainly of vocational training. It is meant for pupils who would otherwise not obtain a diploma in one of the tracks of pre-vocational secondary training, because of their limited abilities. After obtaining a diploma, 'practical education' pupils can enter the lower segments of the job market without further training. As is the case with track supporting education, pupils can only qualify for practical education via an assessment by the 'regional reference committee' (see above) on the basis of a request by the board of the school at which they have been enrolled.

The role of the Equal Treatment Commission in education

A final element within the organisational structure is the role of the Equal Treatment Commission (*Commissie Gelijke Behandeling*), which, as discussed below, has made an important contribution to the resolution of some disputes concerning education. The Commission is an independent complaints committee, established in 1994 by the General Equal Treatment Act,[22] which gives decisions, so called opinions, but also provides advice and information about the standards that apply. Three years after the European Framework Directive for equal treatment in employment and occupation took effect the Dutch Equal Treatment Disability and Chronic Illness Act (*Wet gelijke behandeling op grond van handicap of chronische ziekte*) came into force as a consequence of it.[23] According to this Act, discrimination is prohibited in, among other things, 'allowing people to attend education and training during and prior to an employment relationship'. More precisely, discrimination is prohibited in 'granting access to, offering, examining and concluding education aimed at entry to and performance in the labour market'. From the beginning, vocational education at the secondary and tertiary level, including university education, has been considered to be covered by the legal definition. As from 1 August 2009 primary and general secondary education form part of the Act.[24] In the first instance, the Equal Treatment Commission is responsible for the application and maintenance of this Act.[25]

The rights and obligations of school boards, parents and children

In this section, rights concerning the attendance of a child with special educational needs at a mainstream school or a school of special education will be discussed,

---

22 Algemene wet gelijke behandeling, Stb. 1994, 230.

23 Act of 23 April 2003, Stb. 2003, 206. We use the unofficial translation of this Act, published on http://www.cgb.nl/artikel/equal-treatment-disability-and-chronic-illness-act.

24 Stb. 2009, 101.

25 See for information about the Commission: www.cgb.nl. The Commission sets standards for a broad range of Acts concerning equal treatment.

rights which in both cases are mirrored by obligations placed on the board of the educational institution. The discussion will focus on the two key areas of admission and exclusion.

As previously stated, generally speaking the opportunities for parents to place their children with special educational needs in a mainstream school have increased over the past decade. However, the picture is diverse, because there is not one overall system of special education and the procedures for school admission differ substantially, depending on the specific type of educational service. The possibility of admission to a mainstream school as an alternative to some types of school of special education is restricted by the arrangements created by the Primary Education Act (governing mainstream schools and special school for basic education) and the Special Education Act relating to centres of expertise (governing special schools and the person-related budget for visiting mainstream schools) (noted above). Often, parents who request the admission of their child experience difficulties from the school. Special arrangements for mediation are made to help parents in connection with them, and there is the jurisprudence of the Equal Treatment Commission and the judiciary governing the question of to what extent and under what conditions the mainstream school is obliged to admit children with special educational needs (see below).

Various questions are covered, to some extent, by the rights laid down by law. For example, has a child who is assessed for admission to a special school or to education in a special setting the enforceable right to go to that school or to that type of education? There is a right covering this, but as discussed below, a place in any type of special education is a scarce resource, for which the limits are determined by financial, spatial, labour, social or expertise factors. Is the use of a waiting list for entrance acceptable? How should children who have behavioural problems be accommodated? These issues are explored under the following themes.

Freedom of access

Dependent on the type of special education in question, parents of children who are assessed as having special needs can choose a mainstream school. Attention must, however, be paid to the differences between the regimes of the Primary Education Act and the Special Education Act (on centres of expertise), respectively. Although the former Act does not provide an explicit right of access to a mainstream school for parents of children who would be eligible for entrance to a 'special school for basic education', there is a presumption that such a right exists. An essential starting point is the provision covering the assessment by the 'permanent commission on pupils' care'. According to this provision parents alone are entitled to file an application with the commission. The law seems to imply that all parents actually start to enrol their child at a mainstream school and from there may consider transferring the child to a special school for basic education within the regional cooperative body. Therefore, it is fair to conclude that the right of access to a mainstream school does not relate to any mainstream school but only the school of first choice under the remit of the regional cooperative body. The right of access includes a limited right to choose. When parents do not file an application for access to a special school for basic education, the child stays at the mainstream school.

In the Special Education Act there is not a clear provision concerning freedom of access to mainstream schools. Nevertheless, parents can choose with the support of a person-related budget a mainstream school instead of a special school. Here, however, it would be going too far to speak of an absolute right of access. Access to a mainstream school is in fact dependent on the nature of the child's disability, having regard to the suitability of the school (Nijkamp 2002, p. 275–280). Parents can opt for a mainstream school and the school board can only prevent admission if it is able to show plausible reasons and grounds for its refusal. Thus there is a reversal of the normal burden of proof, as it is not the case that the parents who want a provision that deviates from the normal pattern have the burden of establishing their claim, but that the board of the mainstream school, confronted with the application, has to provide sufficient argument as to why the parents are not eligible for admission of their child. (This reversed burden of proof counts, of course, for the exclusion of a pupil who initially has been admitted.) However, choice is limited by the fact that admission is dependent on the policy and appropriateness of the mainstream school. The implications of this reversed burden of proof concerning admission to a mainstream school are discussed more fully below. Note that if the school is private, not state funded, the above obligation concerning admission does not apply.

The filing of an application for assessment of the child for a 'special school for basic education' or for a 'special school' is a matter of free will; the board or principal of the school must not put intolerable pressure on the parents to do so.[26] Nor is the board of the school entitled to exclude the child without the consent of the parents, when there is reason to think that the child is better off in a school of special education of some type. The school board does not have the competence to assess the child for education in a special setting, unlike the relevant assessment body.[27] But when the child has been officially assessed (per decision of the assessment body) and has been considered to be suitable for access to a 'special school for basic education' or a 'special school', the situation may be different. Then the board is allowed to exclude the child from the mainstream school, if it can make a reasonable case for not being able to meet the special educational needs of the child.[28]

---

26 Rechtbank Almelo (Court Almelo) 27 August 2004, LJN: AQ8307.

27 Voorzieningenrechter Rechtbank Haarlem (President Court Haarlem) 18 March 2004, J.O. 2004, nr. 23. Rechtbank Haarlem (Court Haarlem) 13 June 2005, LJN: AT9498.

28 Rechtbank Almelo (Court Almelo) 27 August 2004, LJN: AQ8307. Voorzieningenrechter Rb. Rotterdam (President Court Rotterdam) 24 January 2005, LJN: AS4379; J.O. 2005, nr. 5.

In the case of a *non state school*, a child that has been assessed for access to a 'special school for basic education' or a 'special school' cannot be refused admission, unless his or her parents are not willing to pay respect to the denomination of the school.[29] Where the school is a 'special school for basic education' there are further limitations regarding access, as the assessment is only valid for schools within the regional cooperative body. It does not count for schools outside the region.[30]

A question that has arisen concerns the use of waiting lists for admission to a 'special school for basic education', because of, for instance, financial reasons or oversubscription. It is considered to be unacceptable as far as state school education is concerned,[31] but sometimes reality is stronger than the rule. In 2000, the Court of Alkmaar found that the regional cooperative body, which covered the state special school for basic education in question, could have chosen such a financial arrangement that admittance to the state school should have been possible.[32] Therefore, using a waiting list was considered to be unlawful. But two years later the jurisprudence turned: a waiting list would be acceptable, for a maximum of three months.[33] Later this norm was laid down in section 40 of the Primary Education Act. The problem of waiting lists in special education is in fact cyclical. In the light of imminent large governmental budget cuts in special education from the start of 2011, it may be expected that, at least in some regions, especially cluster 4 schools[34] (which are the most densely populated schools) will be confronted with limits in their capacity to admit new pupils.

In principle, the board of a mainstream school or 'special school for basic education' has the right to exclude a child with special educational needs, when the child by its behaviour causes serious problems for the direct environment and

---

29 Section 40, subsection 4, Act on Primary Education; section 40, subsection 4, Act on centres of expertise.

30 Section 40, subsection 4, Act on Primary Education.

31 Voorzieningenrechter Afdeling rechtspraak van de Raad van State (President Administrative Law Judicial Division of the Council of State) 10 May 1989, NTOR 1989, p. 147–157, KG 1989, 200 with respect to special education. Voorzieningenrechter Rechtbank Alkmaar (President Court Alkmaar) 25 August 2000, LJN: AA7145, Rechtspraak Onderwijsrecht 2000–2002, SDU Uitgevers, Den Haag 2002, nr. 11, with respect to special schools for basic education.

32 Voorzieningenrechter Rechtbank Alkmaar (President Court Alkmaar) 25 August 2000, LJN: AA7145, Rechtspraak Onderwijsrecht 2000-2002, SDU Uitgevers, Den Haag 2002, nr. 11, m.nt. BPV.

33 President Rechtbank Den Bosch (President Court Den Bosch) 12 March 2002, J.O. 2002, nr. 34.

34 Cluster 4: education for the chronically ill (not by handicap) and severely maladjusted children, for pupils with behavioural disorders and for pupils in paedological institutes (see above).

for other children in the school.[35] However, in practice it seems very important, if possible, to draw a clear line between behaviour that causes problems for safety and order within the school and behaviour that the school does not know how to deal with in the pedagogical, didactical or logistical sense. After all, the requirements covering decision making about the second category of behaviour are stricter for the school board.

The burden of proof resting with the board of a mainstream school in the case of admission was outlined above. So far as the grounds for refusal of admission are concerned, one would not expect that the simple argument that the school staff would not be able to handle a new pupil with special educational needs or that school policy is against the admission of the pupil in question, would be acceptable. During the years of its existence, from 2002–2009, the 'Advisory Commission on Admission and Guidance' (Adviescommissie Toelating en Begeleiding, ACTB), the direct forerunner of the Equal Treatment Commission in these cases, developed a framework for reviewing the adequate use of the burden of proof. This framework consists of four questions that need to be answered: (i) what is necessary for the adequate functioning of the pupil in the school? (ii) what financial means has the school board for this pupil at its disposal (either person-related budget or other means)? (iii) what can be achieved on the basis of these means? (iv) why would the school not be able to offer appropriate education that meets the pupil's special educational needs, despite the use of the financial means?

On the basis of this framework the school board cannot refer to general opinions or criteria. In every case, individual testing is required. Therefore, a school board cannot refer to its policy of having a maximum number of places available in the school.[36] Neither can a refusal of admission be legitimated by the argument that democratically it has been decided that children with behavioural problems or with a psychiatric disorder are not welcome in the school.[37] Furthermore, the mere argument that the pedagogical climate and the lack of an adequate framework for meeting special educational needs in the school militate against admission is not tenable.[38] Finally, arguments that refer to a shortage of expertise among the staff, to social arguments or to limits of space within the school are not acceptable. The decisive factor must be that the school board should, in the case in question, have made inquiries or should have consulted experts.[39]

---

35 Voorzieningenrechter Rechtbank Haarlem (President Court Haarlem) 18 March 2004, J.O. 2004, nr. 23. Voorzieningenrechter Rechtbank Zwolle (President Court Zwolle) 3 July 2003, J.O. 2004, nr. 2. Voorzieningenrechter Rechtbank Zwolle-Lelystad (President Court Zwolle-Lelystad) 6 November 2007, LJN: BB7200. Voorzieningenrechter Rechtbank Arnhem (President Court Arnhem) 18 February 2010, LJN: BL4396.

36 ACTB 2004/9.

37 ACTB 2004/1, 2.

38 ACTB 2004/1, 2.

39 ACTB 2004/8.

Only in one judgment does the judiciary refer directly to this framework for review of the Advisory Commission on Admission and Guidance.[40] The administrative courts use a more general standard of judicial review, although the results do not seem to differ seriously from the jurisprudence of the Advisory Commission. A typical phrase in a judgment of the Administrative Law Judicial Division of the Council of State, which is the highest administrative court in most cases of education law, is the following:

> 'the standard of judicial review is not the judgment of this [Division] about the admittance of T (a girl with serious physical and mental disabilities) to one of the (mainstream) schools, but the question whether there is a reasonable ground for the judgment that the school board could refuse T admission to these schools.'

The Administrative Law division found that the school board had made a convincing case that an unconditional admittance of T could overburden the school and the teachers, who had no experience with children with disabilities and were not properly trained in teaching them. Moreover, it was not clear whether the amount of the person-related budget could cover the necessary and desirable physical and educational adaptations for having the child within the school.[41] In general, it appears that the judiciary considers a requirement for a careful testing of the individual case to be of the utmost importance.[42] In several cases the explicit judgment of experts has been required to underpin the decision of the school board.[43]

Disability and educational targets

Another important question is whether, if a pupil meets all the legal requirements for access, the school board of a mainstream school for secondary education may refuse admission on the ground that the pupil, because of his or her disabilities, will not benefit sufficiently from education that could normally lead to a diploma. The general line in the case law is confirmative of this ground. According to the

---

40 Voorzieningenrechter Rechtbank Zwolle-Lelystad (President Court Zwolle-Lelystad) 19 May 2005, Reg.nrs: AWB 05/324 en AWB 05/942.

41 Afdeling Bestuursrechtspraak Raad van State (Administrative Law Judicial Division of the Council of State) 16 November 2005, LJN: AU6238.

42 Among other things: Voorzieningenrechter Rechtbank Zwolle-Lelystad (President Court Zwolle-Lelystad) 19 May 2005, Reg.nrs: AWB 05/324 and AWB 05/942, and Voorzieningenrechter Rechtbank Rotterdam (President Court Rotterdam) 24 January 2005, LJN: AS4379, J.O. 2005, nr. 5.

43 Voorzieningenrechter Rechtbank Zutphen (President Court Zutphen) 17 November 2003, J.O. 2004, nr. 1; Hof Arnhem (Court of Appeal Arnhem) 1 June 2004, LJN: AR3579; Rechtbank Almelo (Court Almelo) 27 August 2004, LJN: AQ8307; Voorzieningenrechter Rechtbank Zwolle (President Court Zwolle) 3 July 2003, J.O. 2004, nr. 2; Equal Treatment Commission 20 July 2004, Oordeel (Opinion) 2004–94, J.O. 2004, nr. 33.

jurisprudence of the Equal Treatment Commission (ETC), the question of the actual suitability of a person to follow the desired education – in terms of academic competence, practical ability and capacity for access – is a preliminary issue with regard to whether the person has been discriminated against on the ground of disability and/or chronic illness by the school board. If the actual suitability of the pupil to pursue the education is disputed, an inquiry into the matter will be needed. The information must be carefully gathered and published to the parents and/or the child[44] and must be adequate and objective.[45] If it is established with certainty that the person involved is unsuitable for following the desired education a complaint about discrimination will be declared inadmissible.[46] The judiciary has confirmed that actual unsuitability leads to such an impediment to admission:

> 'the educational limitations of the daughter are such, that they cannot be neutralized with the help of a person-related budget … The school board could therefore understand that the nature and weight of the daughter's disability will lead to objections of a pedagogical-didactical character that oppose her admittance. The court has considered correctly that the school board could refuse the admittance of the daughter.'[47]

Effective adjustments

For pupils and students in all spheres of education (from basic up and to higher education) the Equal Treatment (Disability and Chronic Illness) Act offers to purported victims of unjustified discrimination on the grounds of their disability or chronic illness[48] two ways of enforcing their right to equal treatment. First they can ask the Equal Treatment Commission for an opinion. Alternatively, although this practice is very rarely invoked in this context, they can apply to a court. Dependant on the question of whether the act of discrimination can be qualified as an order

---

44 Equal Treatment Commission (ETC) 13 May 2008, opinion 2008–51.

45 Equal Treatment Commission (ETC) 20 July 2004, opinion 2004–94.

46 Equal Treatment Commission (ETC) 25 October 2004, opinion 2004–139, ETC 9 February 2005, opinion 2005–18, ETC 13 May 2008, opinion, 2008–51.

47 ABRvS (Administrative Law Judicial Division of the Council of State), 16 May 2007, LJN: BA5240 and various sentences of other administrative and civil courts.

48 The terms are not defined in the Act nor in the European Framework Directive that is at the basis of the Act. The only relevant and reasonable lead that may bring us further is section 1 of the Convention on the Rights of Persons with Disabilities: "persons with disabilities include those who have long-term physical, mental, intellectual or sensory impairments which in interaction with various barriers may hinder their full and effective participation in society on an equal basis with others." However, until now the ETC had had no need of a clear definition. If it is undisputed between parties that the person involved is disabled or has a chronic illness, and that has until now always been the case, the competence of the ETC is established.

according to public law or not (see for more details below), one can go to an administrative or to a civil court.

Under the Act, section 10(1), a reversed burden of proof exists, meaning that the onus is on the person against whom the complaint of discrimination lies to show that he has not acted unlawfully:

> 'If a person who believes that he is or will be discriminated against to his disadvantage as described in this Act produces facts in court which can give grounds for suspecting that such discrimination exists, the counterparty must prove that they have not acted contrary to the law'.

The Act includes a duty to make reasonable adjustments in order to prevent the discrimination. Section 2 of the Act states that '[t]he prohibition on discrimination also means that the persons on whom this prohibition is imposed are obliged to make effective modifications according to need, unless this would impose a disproportionate burden on them'. The complainant can ask the ETC or the judge to declare that the prohibited discrimination can be removed by making effective adjustments for the benefit of the disabled or chronically ill person. Again there is a reversed burden of proof:

> 'If a person who believes that he has been disadvantaged by acts contrary to section 2 produces facts in court which can give grounds for suspecting that there has been a failure to make effective modifications, the counterparty must prove that they have not acted contrary to this provision.'

In a number of opinions the ETC has dealt with the issue of how far the obligation to make effective adjustments goes. Generally, adjustments are considered to be effective when they enable persons with disabilities or a chronic illness to participate in society on an equal footing with others.[49] In the ETC's interpretation, an adjustment is effective if it is directed towards the removal of barriers to equal participation in education.[50] Therefore a request for an adjustment will not be upheld if it is for the benefit of personal care and other daily necessities, and has no relationship with 'the organisation, design or other aspects of regulation of education'. A request for assistance when going to the toilet within the school, for example, will not be included: that is a daily necessity and does not refer to a mere responsibility of the school.[51] The prospect of a request for adjustment being successful is also poor if as a result of the adjustment the actual disadvantage of the person involved would not be removed or decreased sufficiently. A university does not, for example, need to allow an extension to the duration of a written exam

49 Kamerstukken II (Parliamentary proceedings) 2001/02, 28 169, nr. 3, p. 8.

50 ETC 29 June 2006, opinion 2006–132, ETC 6 April 2006, opinion 2006–59, ETC 6 April 2006, opinion 2006–60.

51 ETC 6 April 2006, opinion 2006–59, ETC 6 April 2006, opinion 2006–60.

for a dyslexic student, if it has learned from experience that an extension does not affect that student's chances of passing or the marks likely to be awarded.[52]

The proposal to make effective adjustments has to come from the disabled or chronically ill person.[53] If, however, the request is too unspecified the board of the educational institution cannot be reproached for doing nothing.[54] But the board has to make reasonable efforts in response to a request and in making any adjustments that need to be made.[55] The costs of the adjustments made may not, however, be placed on the disabled or chronically ill person.[56] Whether an adjustment is necessary is not dependent on the wishes of the applicant, but needs to be assessed on the basis of objective criteria.[57] In this respect the board of the institution has a duty to inquire and to inform, meaning that the pupil or student has to be informed about the institution's policy and that the institution contacts actively the student or pupil about the adjustments to be made.[58]

Resolving disputes between parents and schools

Education counsellors

As stated above, children who are (by independent assessment) found fit to go to a school of special education cannot be refused admission to the school, unless – in the case of a denominational non state school – the parents are unwilling to respect the denomination of the school. In practice, this means that access to such a school tends not to be limited. The whole debate is instead concentrated on problems in selecting mainstream education as an alternative to special education. Indeed, the legal provisions concerning disputes about admission are exclusively directed towards the relation between parents and mainstream schools.

Parents of children who are eligible for special education, as well as the boards of mainstream schools (state and non state alike), can summon the help of independent education counsellors (*onderwijsconsulenten*). The network of education counsellors was founded in 2002. It is funded by the government and consists of persons experienced in education. The service provided and the procedures are informal. Since 2002 the counsellors have assisted thousands of parents and children.[59] The counsellors provide advice and support to the persons involved, and mediate between them, in cases where the board of the mainstream

52 ETC 27 May 2004, opinion 2004–59.
53 ETC 1 May 2006, opinion 2006–81.
54 ETC 29 May 2008, opinion 2008–56.
55 ETC 31 January 2005, opinion 2005–11.
56 ETC 26 October 2004, opinion 2004–140.
57 ETC 10 July 2007, opinion 2007–128.
58 ETC 9 February 2005, opinion 2005–18.
59 See http://www.onderwijsconsulenten.nl/onderwijsconsulenten/.

school refuses to admit the pupil or wishes to exclude him or her. Moreover, they can advise and mediate when the mainstream school and the parents cannot reach an agreement about the use of the person-related budget in education. In both cases there is some scope for negotiated settlements via mediation.

Matters of admission to and exclusion from state and non state schools fall within the discretionary powers of the school board. However, as the law concerning secondary education prohibits conditional admission of pupils to the first school year,[60] which means that school boards are not competent to admit a child for a trial period, the room for negotiation is limited. That is not the case with regard to exclusion. In this field fine-tuned agreements are possible, as seems also the case with matters of admission (and exclusion) in relation to primary education. Although there is jurisprudence which has broadened the prohibition of conditional admission in respect of primary education,[61] the situation with respect to children with disabilities seems to be more balanced. In one judgment the administrative court of Haarlem accepted that the board of a state mainstream school of basic education and the parents can agree on the admission of a child to that school under a condition that the parents will accept the placement of the child in a special school if it becomes clear that the child's placement in this mainstream school was not successful. The parents had also agreed that the school officials would eventually decide on whether the child's stay was successful or not. According to the court this agreement was legally valid.[62] Note that for children who have been granted a person-related budget and who have been admitted to a mainstream school, the school board has to make a supportive treatment plan in consultation with the parents.[63] The law does not prescribe content for this plan, but it is clear that the agreement is about the use of the person-related budget in education.

If the dispute about placement/admission cannot be resolved, the counsellors look for alternative places for the child in other mainstream schools or in special schools. Parents who want to pursue a legal remedy to their problem, by going to the Equal Treatment Commission (ETC) (above), can receive help and information from officers who are regionally organised in the Anti Discrimination Bureaux (ADBx). These ADBx are legal entities under private law, subsidised by central and local authorities. Depending on the nature of the complaint they can help individuals through mediation or by initiating a procedure at the ETC. ADBx can act independently in the procedure before the ETC. That is because ADBx are legal persons which, in accordance with their constitution or statutes, represent

60 Section 27 subsection 1, Act on Secondary Education (Wet op het voortgezet onderwijs), juncto section 3 of the Organisation Decree Act on secondary education (Inrichtingsbesluit Wvo).

61 See for instance ABRvS (Administrative Law Judicial Division of the Council of State) 4 May 1990, JO 1991, 33 and Voorzieningenrechter Rechtbank Amsterdam (President Court Amsterdam) 14 September 2006, LJN AY9480.

62 Rb. Haarlem (Court Haarlem) 13 juni 2005, LJN AT9498.

63 Section 40a Act on Primary Education, section 26 Act on Secondary Education.

the interests of those whose protection is the objective of the Equal Treatment Disability and Chronic Illness Act.

The role of the courts

Earlier, in the discussion on the constitutional background, the 'dual' character of the Dutch education system was noted: state (public law) institutions and non state (private law) institutions are brought together in one system on an equal footing. This duality leads to direct consequences for the character of judicial legal protection. Parents, pupils and students can challenge decisions of a school board concerning admission or exclusion through court action. Decisions of boards of *non state* educational institutions in this field are private law acts, so appeals would need to be lodged with a civil court. A similar decision of state schools and other public law educational institutions, however, is considered to comprise an 'order', as defined in section 1(3) of the General Administrative Law Act (GALA):[64] 'a written decision of an administrative authority constituting a public law act'. Appeals in such a case must be lodged with an administrative court. Parents also have the right to challenge a decision of the assessment commission with respect to the question whether placement of the pupil in a special school for basic education[65] or in a special school[66] is necessary or admissible. In both cases this decision is considered to be an order according to the GALA, so that parents can lodge their appeal with an administrative court.

What remedy can the judiciary provide? If the administrative court rules the appeal well-founded, it will annul all or part of the disputed order. Then it may direct the administrative authority to make a new order or to perform another act in accordance with its judgment, or it may determine that its judgment shall take the place of the annulled order or the annulled part thereof. It also may, at the request of a party and if there are grounds for doing so, order compensation to be paid for the damage suffered by that party.[67] Turning to the civil court, according to tort law, the court may order the party charged to pay compensation. Furthermore, any claimant with sufficient interest in the matter can obtain from the civil court a declaratory judgment establishing the unlawfulness of the act of discrimination. He or she may also seek an injunction, imposed with damages in case of non-compliance, forbidding future unlawful conduct or ordering the carrying out of some action, if there has been an unlawful omission. Such injunctions are also possible to prevent an unlawful act.[68]

While the civil courts form a part of the judicial system, the administrative courts are separate and are legally charged with the administration of justice in

64 In Dutch: *Algemene wet bestuursrecht*.

65 Section 23(6), Act on Primary Education.

66 Section 28c(1), Act on Centres of Expertise.

67 Sections 8:72 and 8:73 GALA.

68 Sections 6:106, 3:302, 3:303 and 3:296 Civil Code respectively.

administrative matters. When a certain act – being an order – opens the possibility of appeal to an administrative court, one cannot appeal to a civil court, and vice versa. Administrative and civil justice are opposites that exclude each other in this respect. Of course, this situation requires explicit attention to be paid to the precise understanding of the term 'order'. Needless to say, it takes up a great proportion of the texts on Dutch administrative law. An order is *not*: an act emanating from something other than an administrative authority, an unwritten order, an act according to private law and an act that cannot be defined as a legal act. For the parties to a dispute the administrative court procedure holds certain advantages[69] over that before a civil court. Unlike the latter, the administrative court procedure makes no reference to mandatory legal representation and orders for costs. Also the procedures involve less formality and are not as complicated. Therefore, under modern education law, the administrative court procedure is imposed in cases where the legislator finds that the interests of persons seeking justice outweigh those of institutions (Vermeulen/Zoontjens 2000, p. 145–149). In practice, the different courts try to attune their jurisprudence to each other. There is, however, no legal provision that deals with conflicts between administrative and civil courts. To one and another they form separate pillars that possess complete autonomy with respect to their own jurisprudential policy.

In most education cases before civil and administrative courts parents use lawyers. The number of lawyers, specialised in matters of education law, has quadrupled over the last six years. The national association of education lawyers now has some 150 members. Every year, between approximately 50 and 100 education cases are heard in the civil or administrative courts in the Netherlands.

Non-judicial dispute resolution

Dutch education law has a long tradition of non-judicial dispute settlement. In general there are two reasons for that (Vermeulen and Zoontjens, p. 144–145). First, it is a reflection of the fact that the majority of the decisions that really affect pupils and parents are taken at the decentralised level of the school (board). As a consequence of the dominant political perception of the constitutionally guaranteed freedom of education in the recent decades, the steering principles behind legislation and central government policy have always been directed towards more school autonomy with respect to personnel management, general management and finances. Secondly, there has been a longstanding aim of balancing the legal differences between state and non state education. Recently this aim has led to a process of reducing the legal differences between public law (state education) and private law (non state education). Thus the same procedure and instance of non-judicial dispute settlement is prescribed for state and non state school affairs. In general, effective non-judicial dispute settlement is seen as an

69 The term 'advantage' in this respect had been used by Hoge Raad (High Court) 26 January 1990, AB 1990, 408 (Windmill).

important means of avoiding or minimising recourse to the courts. As such – at least in the field of education – it seems to work. The 50–100 courts cases per annum in education law (noted above) do not exceed the numbers of cases brought before complaints committees and other (legally prescribed or not prescribed) non-judicial authorities. Exact numbers are not known, however. Moreover, outside the examples given in the discussion of education counsellors above, parents and pupils are not officially encouraged to reach negotiated agreements to disputes. What follows is a short deliberation on the most important forms of non-judicial dispute settlement.

In most cases a person who has the right of appeal against an order to an *administrative court* has an obligation to make an objection against the order before lodging that appeal.[70] 'Making an objection' means 'making use of a statutorily conferred power to seek redress against an order from the administrative authority which made the order'.[71] The objection must be lodged with the board of a state school against the decision concerning admission or exclusion. When the appeal is made to the administrative court, it is an appeal against the decision (order) on the objection.[72] The 'objection' gives rise to a process of reconsideration and possible alteration of the decision: 'If the objection is admissible, the disputed order shall be reviewed on the basis thereof. In so far as the review provides grounds for so doing, the administrative authority shall rescind the disputed order and, in so far as necessary, make a new order replacing it'.[73] Education law has also imposed a procedure of objection before a person applies to a *civil court*, which as noted above is the route that would need to be taken in a case where the decision has been made by the board of a non state school. Objectors do make use of lawyers in these procedures in relation to education matters, but only in a minority of cases.

What is the effectiveness of the objection? From the beginning it has been claimed that the procedure of objection would temper the need for an appeal to the court, and indeed – although exact facts and figures are not available – in many cases the procedure ends after the decision on objection. There is still room for improvement, however. The common practice of objection applied by most administrative authorities and a minority of the schools is still quite formal: the objection has to be made in written form, the authority sends a confirmation receipt and sometime after that a notice of the hearing. The hearing, which can be conducted by the authority itself or by an independent commission, is followed by the decision. Some 18 per cent of the municipalities and a small number of different administrative authorities have in fact found ways of making the procedure of objection less formal, by adopting mediation-like methods. Straight after the objection is received a civil servant of the administrative authority calls the objector to find out what has occurred and discover the objector's perspective

70 The most important exemption to this general rule is where the order already 'has been made in respect of an objection or an administrative appeal': Section 7:1, GALA.

71 Section 1:5 GALA.

72 Section 7:1 GALA.

73 Section 7:11(1), GALA.

on the problem. There is room for feelings and explanations to be expressed on both sides. Then the civil servant enters into consultation with the objector to reach a suitable solution which is agreeable for both parties, within the limits of the law and general policy. Research has shown that some 30–50 per cent of the objections can be concluded successfully, dependent on the nature of the disputed order or decision (Schwartz 2010, pp. 113–120; De Koning and Brouwer 2008, pp. 61–63).

Reference was also made earlier to the role of the Equal Treatment Commission as an important non-judicial dispute resolution mechanism in cases of discrimination on the grounds of disability or chronic illness by and in institutions across all educational sectors. The role and importance of this Commission in matters of admission, exclusion and other forms of treatment in education, noted above, is in fact growing. This cannot however be deduced from facts and figures concerning case load, but may be derived from the fact that since August 2009 all sectors of education are brought under the competence of the Commission.[74] Everyone in the Netherlands can ask the Commission for a decision/opinion about his or her specific situation concerning unequal treatment, free of charge. In the period from 2003 to 2009 the Commission published 1,364 opinions in total. Some 3 per cent of them were about disability and chronic illness, and just a minor segment of it concerned educational matters. The total number of requests for an opinion is estimated to be 2,000 per year (CGB 2007, p. 2). Being a complaints committee, the opinions of the Commission do not have legally binding force. That means that the Commission's authority has to be gained from the quality of its jurisprudence on the equality duties.

According to an evaluation study that was initiated by the Commission about the reception and acceptance of its opinions over the years 1999–2004, 60 per cent of the persons interviewed that had dealt with the Commission as a former complaining party, defending party or proxy, found the final opinion of the Commission in their case 'convincing'. A quarter, however, did not. Also, three-quarters found that the procedure before the Commission had been careful, and according to two-thirds the Commission proved to be objective during the session. It needs to be noted, however, that only half of the defending parties and their proxies found the Commission objective (CGB 2005, p. 89–91). Compared to an evaluation carried out in 1999, similar groups of persons were more critical of the work and attitude of the Commission. After 2001, some opinions of the Commission that concerned manifestations of the multicultural society also drew strong negative political attention. But on the whole it cannot be said that the Commission and its activities are considered to be controversial (Havinga 2007, p. 259). Until now there is no indication that the opinions in the field of disability and chronic illness evoke negative social reactions.

74 The last sectors, of primary and secondary education, were included by Stb. 2009, 101.

Complainants who have obtained a Commission's opinion seldom challenge it before a judge. During the period January 2000 to June 2004 the courts reviewed 5.5 per cent of the cases. From an analysis of court decisions it has been observed that judges take account of the Commission's opinion. That does not mean of course that they always follow the opinion, but it is fair to conclude that judicial scrutiny of the Commission has not undermined its authority or credibility (Wentholt 2007, p. 290).

Conclusion

Do parents and pupils have an enforceable right to choose mainstream education instead of special education? The answer is negative. Once the pupil has been assessed for admission to a special school, the board of the mainstream school to which the pupil was initially allocated can weigh the interests of its school against the individual interests of the pupil in determining the question whether the pupil can be admitted to the special school or can stay under its umbrella. The 'freedom' parents have in the Dutch system is therefore that of *not* applying for an assessment of their child's educational needs. The jurisprudence is quite clear about the fact that parents cannot be forced to do so. One can expect that this right of parents creates problems affecting the legitimate interests of the school, which schools may try to defend, for instance by removing children because of perceived behavioural problems or by putting these children in settings that stand apart from the regular classroom. We do not have clear information concerning such practices, but we do know that the numbers of children entering special schools for behavioural problems are growing.

The most important objection one can make against the current system is that it forms a bureaucratic labyrinth in which parents and pupils may lose their way and leave empty-handed. Special education provisions and procedures in the Dutch context create, as a whole, a diffuse image. Due to the differences between assessment procedures and admission criteria at the different levels there is a possibility that parents of certain 'difficult' children may have to follow more than one process, could be denied their rights in every new procedure they follow because the criteria differ with respect to aim and substance, and may realise after a long and difficult route that their child cannot be placed. As a reaction to this state of affairs new plans for '*passend onderwijs*' (suitable education) are in preparation (Zoontjens 2009, pp. 187–193). The heart of the plans will be formed by a so-called, general duty of care provision in the law which, roughly speaking, will appear as follows: 'Every school board is responsible for the supply of a combined education-care arrangement to any pupil who applies for a school of that school board or has been admitted to a school of that school board.' The practical implications of such a duty with regard to care provision may be great. Every child that knocks on the door of a certain school must be allowed in. The school board has subsequently the choice of retaining the child or finding a suitable place for him or her in another (mainstream or special) school. The latter implies that different schools in a region have to co-operate intensively to create a network for the effective education of children with special needs. Criteria for the assessment of these children have to be unified and one uniform procedure has to be introduced in place of the existing ones. The elaboration of the plan is complicated. There is much concern about the estimated change in the 'streaming' of government money to the schools and regions. Some regions rank behind others, and the unification of criteria for access to all kinds of special education is still going to take a great deal of thought. There seems to be consensus about the importance of redesigning the often medically orientated criteria into benchmarks on the basis of behavioural features, but concrete results have yet to be achieved. It is to be expected that also in the future the role of the Equal Treatment Commission will be increasingly important. As now, individual equal treatment will be an issue at the heart of special educational needs. The prospects for these plans concerning 'suitable education' that lean heavily on the initiative and readiness of schools in the field are unclear. The former government introduced severe budget cuts in the sphere of special education. The new government has not reversed them. That means that the pressure on mainstream schools to fill the gap will increase.

So far as dispute resolution is concerned, non-judicial dispute settlement plays an important role in the sphere of special education in the Netherlands. Being a part in this respect of a long and widespread tradition, it mirrors the situation in other parts of the education system. The work of the educational counsellors and the Equal Treatment Commission in particular has considerable practical importance. Furthermore, the fact that, contrary the GALA, the route to the administrative courts is sometimes also available in cases in which decisions of private law schools and institutions are in dispute reveals an acknowledgement by the education legislator of the interests and position of persons seeking justice. As we have seen, the administrative court procedure holds certain advantages in comparison with that before a civil court and can offer parents and pupils a more accessible remedy to an otherwise unresolvable dispute.

References

Alkema, E.A. (1993), Constitutional Law, in: J. Chorus, P.H. Gerver, E. Hondius and A. Koekkoek (eds), *Introduction to Dutch law for foreign lawyers* (2[d] revised edition) (Deventer-Boston: Kluwer), pp. 241–278.

CGB (2007), *De toegankelijkheid van het beroepsonderwijs voor gehandicapten en chronisch zieken* (The accessibilty of vocational education for persons with disabilities and chronic illness) (Utrecht: CBG).

CGB (2005), *Het verschil gemaakt* (Difference made) (Utrecht: CGB).

Graas, D (1996), *Zorgenkinderen op school; geschiedenis van het speciaal onderwijs in Nederland, 1900–1945* (Children with special educational needs on school; history of special education in the Netherlands 1900–1945) (Leuven/Apeldoorn: Garant).

Havinga, T. (2007), *Werkt de Algemene wet gelijke behandeling? Twee evaluatieonderzoeken besproken* (Does the General Equal Treatment Act work? Two evaluation studies discussed), in: J.H. Gerards, B.P. Vermeulen and P.J.J. Zoontjens (eds), *Gelijke behandeling: oordelen en commentaar 2006* (equal treatment: opinions and comment 2006) (Nijmegen: Wolf Legal Publishers), pp. 243–262.

Koning, A.M. de and Brouwer J. (2008), *Methode Overijssel: bouwen aan vertrouwen. De inzet van vaardigheden en mediation door overheden* (Overijssel method: building on trust. The input of skills and mediation by public authorities) (Rotterdam: NMI).

Kortmann, C.A.J.M. (2008), *Constitutioneel recht* (Constitutional law), 6ᵉ druk (Deventer: Kluwer).

Ministerie OCW (2010), *Kerncijfers 2005–2009* (Ministry of Education, Statistical figures education 2005–2010), Den Haag: Ministry of Education.

Nijkamp, H.J. (2002), 'De rugzakleerling komt er eindelijk aan' (The pupil with a personal budget is coming!), *School en Wet*, nr. 8, November, pp. 275–280.

Rijswijk, C.M. van and Kool, E. (2002), 'Speciaal onderwijs met zevenmijlslaarzen' (Special education with seven-league boots), in: J.D. van de Ploeg (ed.), *Orthopedagogische werkvelden in Nederland* (Orthopedagogic work fields in the Netherlands) (2d ed) (Leuven/Apeldoorn: Garant), pp. 101–115.

Ruijs, N.M., Van der Veen, I. and Peetsma, T.T.D. (2010), 'Inclusive education and students without special educational needs', *Educational Research,* 52, 4, 351–390.

Schwartz, A. (2010), De adviescommissie in bezwaar. Inrichting van de bezwaarprocedure bij gemeenten (The advisory committee in obejection. The design of the procedure of objection at municipalities) (Den Haag: Boom Juridische Uitgevers).

Vermeulen, B.P. (1999), Constitutioneel onderwijsrecht (Constitutional education law) (Elsevier: Den Haag).

Vermeulen, B.P. and Zoontjens P.J.J. (2000), 'Het "algemene" bestuursrecht en het "bijzondere" onderwijsrecht' ('General' administrative law and 'specific' educational law), preadvies VAR-Vereniging voor Bestuursrecht, in: C.A.J.M. Kortmann, B.P. Vermeulen and P.J.J. Zoontjens, *De Awb en de bijzondere wetgeving,* Den Haag, pp. 45–186.

Wentholt, K. (2007), *De door – en wisselwerking van CGB-oordelen in c.q. met rechterlijke uitspraken* (About Commission opinions: their continued effect on and interaction with court sentences), in: J.H. Gerards, B.P. Vermeulen and P.J.J. Zoontjens (eds), *Gelijke behandeling: oordelen en commentaar 2006* (equal treatment: opinions and comment 2006) (Nijmegen: Wolf Legal Publishers), pp. 279–290.

Zoontjens, P. (2009), 'Toelating en verwijdering van zorgleerlingen' (Selection of pupils with special educational needs), in: P.W.A. Huisman and P.J.J. Zoontjens (eds), *Selectie bij toegang tot het onderwijs* (Selection at the entrance of education) (Deventer: Kluwer), pp. 145–193.

Chapter 6
Where the Buck Stops: Special Education and Dispute Resolution in the United States

Charles J. Russo and Allan G. Osborne, Jr.

Introduction

Prior to the mid-1970s, the United States federal government did not require states to provide special education services for students with disabilities. Although some jurisdictions enacted laws providing special education for children with special needs, they were in the minority. However, in the wake of the civil rights movement that the landmark case of *Brown v Board of Education*[1] (*Brown*) spawned, the federal government assumed a major role in ensuring equal educational opportunities for children who needed special education. In fact, once Congress enacted the two most significant federal statutes on the rights of students with disabilities,[2] Section 504 of the Rehabilitation Act of 1973 (Section 504)[3] and the Individuals with Disabilities Education Act (IDEA)[4] in 1975, their status improved dramatically. Section 504 requires education officials to provide reasonable accommodations for students who are otherwise qualified to participate in programmes that receive federal financial aid, unless doing so would result in financial burdens on schools, require significant alterations in the nature of programmes, or create health or safety risks for members of school communities. Insofar as Section 504 does not provide a precise definition of the conditions covered by its provisions, not referring to them as disabilities, nor afford parents and students as extensive due process, including dispute resolution provisions, it is not as valuable a tool in ensuring equal educational opportunities for students with disabilities as the IDEA. The far more extensive provisions of the IDEA require school officials to provide a free appropriate public education in the least restrictive environment for all students between the ages of three and 21 who have specifically identified disabilities; hence the term 'students with disabilities' is used when referring to children who are protected by the IDEA. The most recent comprehensive federal

1 347 U.S. 483 (1954). See below.

2 A third statute, the Americans with Disabilities Act, 42 U.S.C. §§ 12101 *et seq.*, which extends similar protections to individuals in the private sector but has limited implications for public schools, is beyond the scope of this chapter.

3 29 U.S.C. § 794(a).

4 20 U.S.C. §§ 1400 *et seq*. For more detail, see Russo and Osborne Jr. (2008).

data, available for the 2007–2008 school year, reveal that the 6,606,000 students with disabilities, representing 13.4 per cent of all American students,[5] received services under the IDEA.

Against this background, this chapter reviews the key elements of these two main statutes protecting the educational rights of students with disabilities along with the role that their parents play in the process, paying particular regard to the processes of dispute resolution. The 2002 report of the *Presidential Commission on Excellence in Special Education*, cognizant of the need to improve the process of providing special education for students with disabilities suggested that the 'IDEA should encourage states – perhaps through financial incentives – to develop early processes for conflict avoidance'.[6] In re-authorising the IDEA two years later, Congress specified that '[p]arents and schools should be given expanded opportunities to resolve their disagreements in positive and constructive ways'.[7] As such, this chapter pays particular attention to the closely related issues of due process, dispute resolution, and remedies. The chapter focuses on dispute resolution because although the IDEA always addressed the right of parents, and to a much more limited extent, students themselves, to challenge the actions of school officials via alternative methods of dispute resolution such as mediation and due process hearings before seeking judicial review, it was only over time that the courts and Congress, in a symbiotic relationship, expanded the reach of the Act. In fact, the IDEA did not initially allow parents to be reimbursed for attorney fees in the event that they successfully challenged boards over issues relating to the placements of their children, essentially putting themselves in the position they would have been in had educators made the correct decision initially. Further, the IDEA still does not allow parents to be reimbursed for the cost of expert witness fees where they needed such assistance to prevail. Both of these topics are discussed below.

The majority of the disputes in due process hearings and court proceedings involve parental claims that school officials have not followed all of the procedures mandated by the IDEA or challenges to recommended placements. In this respect hearing officers and judges are asked to decide whether the placements offered were developed in a procedurally correct manner and will provide the free appropriate public education (FAPE) called for in the Act. When hearing officers or judges determine that school boards failed to live up to their responsibilities legal actions often arise over the remedies required to compensate the students

5 Fast Facts, National Center for Educational Statistics, United States Department of Education, Institute for Education Sciences, available at http://nces.ed.gov/fastfacts/display.asp?id=64 (last accessed October 1, 2010). This table also identifies numbers and percentages of children by specific disabilities, aged 3–21, for selected years between 1977 and 2007–2008.

6 At p.40. Available at http://www2.ed.gov/inits/commissionsboards/whspecialeducation/index.html

7 20 U.S.C. §§ 1400(c)(8)–(9).

for that failure. Parents generally seek either reimbursement for their out-of-pocket costs in unilaterally ensuring that services are provided while disputes are ongoing, or awards of compensatory educational services. A fair number of disputes also arise over the IDEA's disciplinary provisions and its requirement the school boards provide related, or supportive, services when needed for students to receive FAPEs.[8] The Supreme Court has held, in a case from Ohio, *Winkelman v Parma City School District*,[9] that since non-attorney parents have rights separate and apart from those of their children, they can in fact initiate *pro se*[10] judicial actions challenging their child's 'Individualised Education Program' (IEP), a judgement which may result in confusion since divorced parents can each have their own attorneys along with those representing students who are old enough to act on their own behalf and those of school boards. Many legal actions also arise on behalf of students with disabilities under Section 504 of the Rehabilitation Act and the Americans with Disabilities Act as well as the IDEA. The plaintiffs in these actions by and large allege that students were subjected to discriminatory treatment on the basis of their disabilities or that school boards failed to provide reasonable accommodations for their disabilities.

At the outset it is important to note that, with literally thousands of suits having been filed on the rights of students with disabilities in federal and state courts, it is probably safe to say that there are more cases on special education in one year in the United States than at least a decade or longer elsewhere. Thus, although the footnotes in this chapter often identify just one suit, in most instances they could be replaced with multiple case citations.

This chapter begins with a brief review of the legal background leading up to the enactment of federal disability laws in order to contextualise the legal-

8 For cases supporting the rights of parents to act pro se, see *Maroni v Pemi-Baker Reg'l Sch. Dist.*, 346 F.3d 247 (1st Cir. 2003); *Collinsgru v Palmyra Bd. of Educ.*, 161 F.3d 225 (3d Cir. 1998); *Devine v Indian River County Sch. Bd.*, 121 F.3d 576 (11th Cir. 1997). For cases refusing to allow parents to act pro se, *see, e.g.*, *Fauconier v Committee on Special Educ.*, 2003 WL 21345549 (S.D.N.Y. 2003), *aff'd*, 112 Fed.Appx. 85 (2d Cir. 2004); *Cavanaugh ex rel. Cavanaugh v Cardinal Local Sch. Dist.*, 409 F.3d 753 (6th Cir. 2005).

9 550 U.S. 516 (2007). For a commentary on this case, see Charles J. Russo, 'The Rights of Non-Attorney Parents Under the IDEA: *Winkelman v Parma City School District*', 221 *Educ. L. Rep.* 1 (2007). The case follows lines of conflicting decisions. For cases supporting the rights of parents to act pro se, *Maroni v Pemi-Baker Reg'l Sch. Dist.*, 346 F.3d 247 (1st Cir. 2003); *Collinsgru v Palmyra Bd. of Educ.*, 161 F.3d 225 (3d Cir. 1998); *Devine v Indian River County Sch. Bd.*, 121 F.3d 576 (11th Cir. 1997). For cases refusing to allow parents to act pro se, see, e.g., *Fauconier v Committee on Special Educ.*, 2003 WL 21345549 (S.D.N.Y. 2003), *aff'd*, 112 Fed.Appx. 85 (2d Cir. 2004); *Cavanaugh ex rel. Cavanaugh v Cardinal Local Sch. Dist.*, 409 F.3d 753 (6th Cir. 2005).

10 Literally, 'to appear on one's own behalf'.

historical background to a metamorphosis in American public schools in response to the enactment of federal disability statutes.[11]

Legal Background

The impetus for ensuring equal educational opportunities for all American children can be traced to *Brown*, cited above.[12] In this case children of African-American origin from Delaware, Kansas, South Carolina and Virginia challenged segregated schooling on the grounds of race. A unanimous Supreme Court held that separate facilities were intrinsically unequal and thus unconstitutional and set the tone for later developments, including those leading to the provision of equal educational opportunities for all students, including females[13] and those with disabilities. In the immediate aftermath of *Brown*, though, the rights of individuals with disabilities continued to be overlooked. Throughout the 1950s, more than half of American states had laws calling for the sterilisation of individuals with disabilities while others limited such basic rights, such as voting, marrying, and obtaining drivers' licenses (Burgdorf and Burgdorf, 1975, pp. 861–868). By the 1960s, the percentage of children with disabilities who attended public schools began to increase; from 12 per cent in 1948 to 21 per cent in 1963 and 38 per cent in 1968 (Zettel and Ballard, 1982). As of 1 July, 1974, the date of the last report available to Congress prior to the enactment of the IDEA,[14] data from the federal Bureau for the Education of the Handicapped indicated that 78.5 per cent of America's children with disabilities received some form of public education. Of these students, 47.8 per cent received special education and related services, 30.7 per cent received no related services, and the remaining 21.5 per cent received no educational services at all.[15]

A major push for the legislative development of special education came as a result of judicial actions. Rather than trace the full history of this litigation, this brief

11 Since the rules applying to religiously-affiliated non-public schools are significantly different this chapter focuses on students in public schools. See Russo, Osborne, Massucci and Cattaro (2009).

12 347 U.S. 483 (1954). See note 1 above.

13 A review of the extensive litigation that has emerged under Title IX of the Education Amendments of 1972 (Title IX), a statute that was initially enacted to ensure gender equity in intercollegiate sports, is beyond the scope of this chapter. Even so, it is worth noting that under the relevant portion on Title IX, '[n]o person in the United States shall, on the basis of sex, be excluded from participation in, be denied the benefits of, or be subjected to discrimination under any education program or activity receiving Federal financial assistance ...' 20 U.S.C. § 1681.

14 Although what is now known as the IDEA was named the Education for All Handicapped Children Act when it was enacted in 1975, this chapter refers to it as the IDEA throughout both to avoid confusion and to ensure consistency.

15 House Report No. 332, 94th Congress (1975).

review focuses on the two most significant cases that contributed to developments aimed at protecting the rights of students with disabilities. These cases, although decided in federal trial courts, as opposed to appellate proceedings, are considered landmarks insofar as they helped to provide the impetus for Congress to pass sweeping legislation to safeguard the rights of students with disabilities.

Pennsylvania Association for Retarded Children v Pennsylvania[16] *(PARC)* provided the conceptual bases for what developed into the IDEA. In *PARC*, advocates filed suit in a federal trial court in Pennsylvania on behalf of all individuals between the ages of six and 21 who had intellectual disabilities and were excluded from public schools. Officials sought to justify the exclusions by relying on four laws that:

i. relieved local school boards of their duties to educate children whom school psychologists certified as uneducable and untrainable, terminology that is no longer employed;
ii. allowed educators to postpone the admission of children who had not attained a mental age of five;
iii. excused children from compulsory attendance if they were unable to profit from school; and
iv. defined compulsory school age as eight to 17 but used these limits to exclude children who had intellectual disabilities and were not between those ages.

The plaintiffs challenged the constitutionality of the statutes while seeking to enjoin their enforcement. The case was resolved via a consent decree, meaning that the parties essentially reached a settlement on their own that the court later approved. Pursuant to the decree, no children who were intellectually disabled, or who were thought to have been so, could have been assigned to or excluded from special education programmes without due process. More specifically, the court explained that placements in regular school classrooms were preferable to those in more restrictive settings for children with disabilities and that such children could not be denied admission to public schools or subjected to changes in educational placements unless they, through their parents, received procedural due process. The court added not only that *all* children have a right to go to school but also that Pennsylvania was obligated to provide students who were mentally 'retarded' with a free appropriate public education and training programme appropriate to their capacities.

In similar fashion to *PARC*, in *Mills v Board of Education of the District of Columbia*,[17] the parents of seven exceptional children filed a class action suit in the federal trial court against the school board in the Nation's Capitol on behalf

16 *Pennsylvania Ass'n for Retarded Children v Pennsylvania* 334 F. Supp. 1257 (E.D. Pa. 1971), 343 F. Supp. 279 (E.D. Pa. 1972).

17 348 F. Supp. 866 (D.D.C. 1972).

of perhaps as many as 18,000 students with disabilities who were not receiving special educational programmes. Most of the children, who were minorities, were classified as having behaviour problems or being mentally 'retarded', emotionally disturbed and/or hyperactive. The plaintiffs sought a declaration of their rights and an order directing the board to provide a publicly supported education to students with disabilities. The court rejected the board's claims that since it lacked the resources for all of its students, it could deny services to children with disabilities. Unlike *PARC,* which was a consent decree, *Mills* was a decision on the record, meaning that the court reached its judgment after a trial on the merits of the dispute. The court ruled that the United States Constitution, coupled with law and regulations from the District of Columbia, required school officials to provide a publicly supported education to all children, including those with disabilities. The court held that the school board had to expend its funds equitably so that all students would receive an education consistent with their needs and abilities. If sufficient funds were unavailable, the court ordered officials to distribute resources in such a manner that no child would be entirely excluded and the inadequacies would not be allowed to bear more heavily on one class of students. In addition, the court ordered the board to provide due process safeguards before any children were excluded from the public schools, reassigned, or had their special education services terminated. The court also outlined elaborate due process procedures that helped to form the foundation for the safeguards that were included in the IDEA.

Insofar as *Mills* originated in Washington, D.C., it was undoubtedly among the more significant influences moving Congress to ensure adequate protection for children with disabilities. In the wake of *PARC* and *Mills,* Congress enacted the two most significant federal statutes on the rights of children with disabilities, Section 504 and the IDEA.

Section 504 of the Rehabilitation Act of 1973

Section 504, which traces its origins to the aftermath of the First World War and vocational rehabilitation for veterans who were injured and disabled,[18] was re-authorised partially in response to *PARC* and *Mills* as the first federal statute to address the needs of disabled people. According to Section 504:

> '[n]o otherwise qualified individual with a disability in the United States … shall, solely by reason of her or his disability, be excluded from the participation in, be denied the benefits of, or be subjected to discrimination under any program or activity receiving [f]ederal financial assistance'.[19]

18 For the history of the law generally, see Scotch (2001). See also Russo and Osborne (2009).

19 29 U.S.C. § 794(a).

Since this last phrase, 'federal financial assistance', is interpreted broadly,[20] most courts agree that it applies to virtually all schools. Although Section 504, unlike the IDEA, also covers employees in and visitors to schools, this chapter focuses on the rights of children.

Pursuant to Section 504, an individual with a disability is one 'who (i) has a physical or mental impairment which substantially limits one or more of such person's major life activities, (ii) has a record of such an impairment, or (iii) is regarded as having such an impairment'.[21] In order to have a record of impairment, individuals must have histories of, or been identified as having, mental or physical impairments that substantially limit one or more major life activities, 'such as caring for one's self, performing manual tasks, walking, seeing, hearing, speaking, breathing, learning, and working'.[22] Once students are identified as being disabled, the next step is to evaluate whether they are 'otherwise qualified'. In order to be 'otherwise qualified', children must be:

> '(i) of an age during which nonhandicapped persons are provided such services,
> (ii) of any age during which it is mandatory under state law to provide such services to handicapped persons, or
> (iii) [a student] to whom a state is required to provide a free appropriate public education [under the IDEA]'.[23]

Students who are 'otherwise qualified', meaning that they are eligible to participate in programmes or activities despite the existence of impairments, must be permitted to take part in them as long they can do so by means of a 'reasonable accommodation'. Reasonable accommodations may involve minor adjustments such as allowing a child to bring a service dog to school,[24] modifying

---

20 See *Bob Jones Univ v United States*, 461 U.S. 574 (1983) (upholding the revocation of tax exempt status on the ground that it constitutes federal financial assistance).

21 29 U.S.C. § 706(7)(B). The regulations define physical or mental impairments as including:

> (A) any physiological disorder or condition, cosmetic disfigurement, or anatomical loss affecting one or more of the following body systems: neurological; musculoskeletal; special sense organs; respiratory, including speech organs; cardiovascular; reproductive, digestive, genito-urinary; hemic and lymphatic; skin; and endocrine; or
> (B) any mental or psychological disorder, such as mental retardation, organic brain syndrome, emotional or mental illness, and specific learning disorders. 34 C.F.R. § 104(j)(2)(I).
> A note accompanying this list indicates that it merely provides examples of the types of impairments that are covered; it is not meant to be exhaustive.

22 34 C.F.R. § 104.3(j)(2)(I).

23 34 C.F.R. § 104.3(l)(2).

24 See, e.g., *Sullivan v Vallejo City Unified Sch. Dist.*, 731 F. Supp. 947 (E.D. Cal 1990); *Gaudiello v Delaware County Intermediate Unit*, 796 F. Supp. 849 (E.D. Pa. 1992).

a behaviour policy as applied to a disruptive student with an autoimmune disease,[25] or acquiring a hearing interpreter for a student.[26] Academic modifications may include permitting students more time to complete assignments or examinations, using tutors, having teachers distribute outlines in advance, and/or permitting students to use laptop computers to record answers on examinations. In modifying facilities, school officials do not have to make every classroom and/or area of buildings accessible. When making modifications, it may be enough for educators to bring services to students such as offering keyboards for musical instruction instead of moving entire music rooms for students who wish to take piano classes.

Even if children appear to be 'otherwise qualified', educators can rely on one of three defenses to avoid being charged with noncompliance with Section 504, a major difference between it and the IDEA, which operates under a 'zero reject policy', under which no children can be excluded from special education.[27] First, school officials can be excused from making accommodations that would result in 'a fundamental alteration in the nature of [a] program'.[28] The second defence allows officials to avoid compliance if a modification imposes 'undue financial burden[s]'.[29] The third defence is that otherwise qualified students can be excluded from programmes if their presence creates a substantial risk of injury to themselves or others.[30] A determination of what constitutes undue financial burdens on school boards is not set in stone but is decided on a case-by-case basis. While boards may be required under Section 504 to provide aides to assist students with physical challenges and navigate school buildings, courts are unlikely to require boards to install elevators in older pre-existing schools that were built before federal barrier free statutes came into effect, because of the extensive cost that this would impose.

Once identified, qualified students are entitled to receive an appropriate public education, regardless of the nature or severity of their disabilities. In order to guarantee that an appropriate education is made available to all students, Section 504's regulations include due process requirements for evaluation that are similar to, but are not as extensive as, those under the IDEA. Among these requirements, Section 504 directs school officials to take various measures. They must file assurances of compliance that their programmes are nondiscriminatory[31] and

---

25 *Thomas v Davidson Acad.*, 662 F. Supp. 376 (M.D. Tenn. 1994).

26 *Jones v Illinois Dep't of Rehab. Servs.*, 689 F.2d 724 (7th Cir. 1982).

27 The seminal case on this point is *Timothy W. v Rochester, N.H., Sch. Dist.*, 875 F.2d 954 (1st Cir. 1989), *cert. denied*, 493 U.S. 983 (1989).

28 *Southeastern Community College v Davis*, 442 U.S. 397, 410 (1979) (upholding a nursing programme's refusal to admit a student with a learning disability). See also *Alexander v Choate*, 469 U.S. 287 (1985) (ruling that Section 504 only requires reasonable modification and not substantial changes).

29 *Davis,* ibid. at 412.

30 See *School Bd. of Nassau County v Arline*, 480 U.S. 273, 287–88 (1987) (establishing criteria for evaluating whether, under Section 504, a teacher with tuberculosis posed a significant health risk to the school community).

31 34 C.F.R. § 104.5.

take voluntary remedial actions if they have violated the law so as to overcome the effects of conditions that resulted in limiting the participation of individuals with disabilities.[32] They must also complete self-evaluations to ensure that they comply with Section 504,[33] designate a staff member as compliance coordinator,[34] and adopt grievance procedures[35] even though neither the law nor an accompanying regulation specify what steps such a process should follow. Section 504 also requires recipients of federal financial aid to provide notice to students, parents, employees, and others that they do not discriminate on the basis of disability.[36]

Parties who are dissatisfied with regard to the delivery of educational services under Section 504[37] can file complaints with the Office of Civil Rights, which is responsible for enforcing the law, within 180 days[38] of when alleged infractions occurred. In another difference with the IDEA, Section 504's regulations do not require aggrieved parties to exhaust administrative remedies via due process hearing before filing suit. Even so, since the IDEA is the more comprehensive statute when it comes to providing special education services, litigants have been required to exhaust administrative remedies under the IDEA when that process could provide the relief they sought. Due to the limited nature of relief available under Section 504, most suits alleging that students with disabilities have not been given necessary services are filed under both laws.

The Individuals with Disabilities Act (IDEA)

Background

Initially enacted in 1975 as the Education for All Handicapped Children Act, and still occasionally identified as Public Law (or PL) 94–142,[39] its name was changed to the IDEA in 1990 to focus on students rather than their disabilities. The law was revised in 1986, 1990, 1997 and 2004. In order to receive federal funds,[40] the IDEA and its regulations require states, through local educational agencies or school boards, to identify, assess, and serve all children with disabilities, including those

32 34 C.F.R. § 104.6(a)(b).

33 34 C.F.R. § 104.6(c).

34 34 C.F.R. § 104.7(a).

35 34 C.F.R. § 104.7(b).

36 34 C.F.R. § 104.8.

37 7 C.F.R. § 2.300(a)(1)(vi).

38 34 C.F.R. § 100.7(b).

39 This refers to the fact that it was the 142nd piece of legislation introduced during the 94th Congress.

40 Although federal funds are inadequate under the IDEA, courts have been unreceptive to calls for relief. See, e.g., *City of Worcester v The Governor*, 625 N.E.2d 1337 (Mass. 1994); *Nashua Sch. Dist. v State,* 667 A.2d 1036 (N.H. 1995) (rejecting a claim that. the IDEA was an unfunded federal mandate).

in non-public schools,[41] regardless of the severity of their needs. A young person is entitled to receive IDEA services if they meet four requirements. First, they must be between the ages of three and 21[42] (they are treated as being 21 until the end of the academic year in which they reach the upper age limit). Second, they must have specifically identified disabilities.[43] Third, they must be in need of special education,[44] meaning that they need a 'free appropriate public education'[45] (FAPE) in the least restrictive environments (LRE) that are directed by the contents of their IEPs.[46] Fourth, they must be in need of related services.[47]

As one of its unique features, the IDEA includes extensive due process protections, discussed below, safeguarding the rights of children[48] and their parents.[49] Among these protections, the IDEA and its regulations,[50] in addition to the Family Educational Rights and Privacy Act and its regulations,[51] protect the privacy of data used in the evaluation, placement, and education of students

---

41 34 C.F.R. § 300.129. See Russo et al. (2009), generally, for a discussion of the rights of students in non-public schools.

42 20 U.S.C. § 1412(a)(1)(A).

43 20 U.S.C. § 1401(3)(A)(I):

The term 'child with a disability' means a child—

(I) with mental retardation, hearing impairments (including deafness), speech or language impairments, visual impairments (including blindness), serious emotional disturbance (referred to in this chapter as 'emotional disturbance'), orthopedic impairments, autism, traumatic brain injury, other health impairments, or specific learning disabilities ...

44 20 U.S.C. § 1401(3)(A)(ii).

45 U.S.C. § 1401(9).

46 20 U.S.C. §§ 1401(11), 1414(d).

47 The IDEA, 20 U.S.C. § 1401(26)(A), defines related services as:

'transportation, and such developmental, corrective, and other supportive services (including speech-language pathology and audiology services, interpreting services, psychological services, physical and occupational therapy, recreation, including therapeutic recreation, social work services, school nurse services designed to enable a child with a disability to receive a free appropriate public education as described in the individualised education program of the child, counselling services, including rehabilitation counselling, orientation and mobility services, and medical services, except that such medical services shall be for diagnostic and evaluation purposes only) as may be required to assist a child with a disability to benefit from special education, and includes the early identification and assessment of disabling conditions in children.'

There is an exception: 'The term does not include a medical device that is surgically implanted, or the replacement of such device.'

48 20 U.S.C. § 1415.

49 The IDEA defines a parent as natural, adoptive, or foster parents, guardians, and individuals acting in the place of natural or adoptive parents (including grandparents, step-parents, or other relatives) with whom children live, or individuals who are legally responsible for a child's welfare. 20 U.S.C. § 1401(23).

50 20 U.S.C. § 1417(c); 34 C.F.R. §§ 300.610–627.

51 29 U.S.C. § 1232g; 34 C.F.R. §§ 99.1–99.8.

with disabilities. In addition, parents must be informed before consenting to initial evaluations, which must occur within 60 days of when educational officials received consent to conduct them, and/or placements of their children; and parents have the right to take part in developing IEPs that direct the education of their children.[52] A recent addition in the IDEA, although not addressing dispute resolution directly, requires state officials to develop policies and procedures to prevent the over-identification or disproportionate representation of students by race and ethnicity.[53] It is clear that this issue is on the minds of lawmakers, but data are as yet unavailable since the statistics, discussed below,[54] are gathered by state and aggregated to national totals but not by such categories as gender, race, and/or ethnicity.

Identification and Assessment of Students with Disabilities

The IDEA requires states to create procedures to identify and evaluate all students with disabilities.[55] Testing and evaluation materials as well as procedures must be selected and administered in a manner that is not racially, linguistically, or culturally biased.[56] Further, students whose language or other mode of communication is not English need to be evaluated in their native language or other mode of communication.[57] When evaluating students with disabilities, educators must employ multidisciplinary measures and cannot allow a single examination to serve as the basis for determining whether students are entitled to IDEA services.[58] Assessments, which must be valid and reliable, are to be administered by trained personnel in conformity with the instructions provided by their producers.[59] Decisions as to whether children are eligible to receive special education services must be made by teams of qualified professionals in conjunction with the parents of children who were assessed.[60] School officials must complete annual reevaluations for all children with disabilities and full evaluations at least every three years.[61] Evaluations can take place earlier than these time frames if officials think that they are warranted or if parents or teachers make such requests.[62] As noted, school officials must complete all evaluations of students suspected of having disabilities

52 20 U.S.C. § 1414(a)(1)(D)(i)(I); § 1414(a)(1)(C)(i)(I); § 1414(a)(1)(D)(I); and §§ 1414(d)(1)(B)(i).

53 20 U.S.C.A. §§ 1412 (a)(24), 1418 (d)(1)(A)(B).

54 See below, notes 130–131, and accompanying data.

55 20 U.S.C. § 1412(a)(3).

56 20 U.S.C. §§ 1412(a)(6)(B), 1414(b)(3)(A)(i).

57 20 U.S.C. §§ 1412(a)(6)(B), 1414(b)(3)(A)(ii).

58 20 U.S.C. § 1414(b)(2)(B).

59 20 U.S.C. §§ 1414(b)(3)(A)(iii)–(v).

60 20 U.S.C. § 1414(b)(4)(A).

61 20 U.S.C. § 1414(a)(2)(B)(ii).

62 20 U.S.C. § 1414(a)(2)(A).

within 60 days of receiving parental consent for the evaluations.[63] If state laws mandate different time frames for completing evaluations than those called for in federal law, then the parties must follow the state requirements. Depending on state laws, educators may have to conduct evaluations over summer breaks if necessary to complete them within the statutory time limits.[64] The 60-day rule does not apply if 'the parent of a child repeatedly fails or refuses to produce the child for the evaluation'.[65] If parents refuse to respond to requests consenting to initial evaluations or to services, educational officials may continue with evaluations as long as they follow the procedures outlined in the IDEA's due process provisions.[66]

Parents have the right to obtain independent evaluations of their children if they disagree with the assessments completed by their school boards[67] or if officials fail either to evaluate their children entirely[68] or in a timely manner.[69] These independent evaluations are at public expense if it can be shown that assessments conducted by board personnel were inappropriate. Parents cannot obtain independent evaluations at public expense simply to get another opinion. While parents who succeed in challenging the assessments of their children can be reimbursed for the costs of doing so, if hearing officers or courts find that board evaluations were appropriate, parents are not entitled to further testing at public expense.[70] When parents obtain independent evaluations, regardless of whether they or their boards pay for them, school personnel must consider, but are not bound by, the results of these assessments.[71]

When assessments are completed, educators must convene IEP meetings within 30 calendar days to evaluate whether children are entitled to special education services.[72] IEP teams encompass an array of individuals. Teams must include parents, in the light of their right to participate actively in the development of IEPs for their children; at least one of the student's regular education teachers if the child is, or will participate, in regular education; at least one special education teacher or, if appropriate, one special education provider; a school board representative who can provide, or supervise, the delivery of special education, knowledgeable about

---

63 20 U.S.C. § 1414(a)(1)(C)(i)(I).

64 For such a case, *see Gerstmyer v Howard County Pub. Schs*, 850 F. Supp. 361 (D. Md. 1994) (mandating an evaluation over the summer vacation).

65 20 U.S.C. § 1414(a)(1)(C)(ii)(II).

66 20 U.S.C. §§ 1414(a)(1)(D)(ii)(I),(II).

67 20 U.S.C. § 1415(b)(1); 34 C.F.R. § 300.502(b).

68 *N.B. v Hellgate Elementary Sch. Dist., ex rel. Bd. of Directors, Missoula County, Mont.*, 541 F.3d 1202 (9th Cir. 2008).

69 *Idea Public Charter Sch. v District of Columbia*, 374 F. Supp.2d 158 (D.D.C. 2005).

70 34 C.F.R. § 300.502(b).

71 34 C.F.R. § 300.502(c)(1); *James and Lee Anne D. ex rel. Sarah D. v Board of Educ. of Aptakisic-Tripp Community Consol. Sch. Dist. No. 102*, 642 F. Supp.2d 804 (N.D. Ill. 2009).

72 34 C.F.R. § 300.323(c)(1).

general education, the board's resources, and evaluation procedures; an individual who can interpret the instructional implications of evaluation results; others, at the discretion of parents or boards, who are knowledgeable or have special expertise concerning the child; and, when appropriate, in light of age and intellectual ability, the child.[73]

IEPs must describe students' current levels of educational performance, annual goals and short-term objectives, the specific services that they will receive, the extent to which they can take part in general education, the date services are to begin and how long they will be offered, and criteria to evaluate whether they are achieving their goals.[74] IEPs must also discuss how students' disabilities affect their ability to be involved in and progress in inclusive settings and necessary modifications to allow them to take part in the general curriculum. In addition, IEPs must detail related services that students need to benefit from their IEPs. Once developed, school officials must implement IEPs '[a]s soon as possible'.[75]

Placement of Special Education Students

The IDEA requires school boards to provide a range of alternative placements for students with disabilities. The continuum of seven steps ranges from (i) full inclusion in regular education classrooms, to: (ii) inclusion with help of personal aides; (iii) partial inclusion with the help of a classroom aid and partial time in a resource room placement; (iv) individualised placements in resource rooms; (v) special day schools; (vi) hospital or homebound instruction; and (vii) residential placements.[76] If parents have insurance, they can be asked to file claims to help defray costs associated with the education of their children with special needs. Even so, educators cannot refuse to provide services if parents are unwilling, or unable, to place claims with their insurance companies.[77]

As important as the 'appropriate' component of FAPE is, the IDEA offers little guidance in defining this term beyond declaring that an appropriate education consists of special education and related services that is provided in conformance with an IEP.[78] Since a precise definition of 'appropriate' is lacking in the IDEA

73 20 U.S.C. § 1414(d)(1)(B); 34 C.F.R. § 300.321(a).

74 20 U.S.C. § 1414(d)(1)(A).

75 34 C.F.R. § 300.323(c)(2).

76 34 C.F.R. §§ 300.154(d)–(g). For a breakdown on the types of environments where students with disabilities aged 6–21 were placed as of Fall 2007, covering regular schools (with breakdowns for students who spent less than 21 per cent, 21–60 per cent, and more than 60 per cent outside of general classes), separate schools, separate residential facilities, parentally placed in private schools, homebound/hospital placements, and correctional facilities, see Fast Facts, National Center for Educational Statistics, United States Department of Education, Institute for Education Sciences, available at http://nces.ed.gov/fastfacts/display.asp?id=59 (last accessed October 1, 2010).

77 34 C.F.R. §§ 300.154(d)–(g).

78 20 U.S.C. §§ 1402 (14), 1414 (d).

and its regulations, one must turn to judicial interpretation for further guidance on FAPE. *Board of Education of the Hendrick Hudson Central School District v Rowley* (*Rowley*),[79] was the Supreme Court's first case interpreting the rights of students with disabilities. *Rowley* was filed by the parents of a kindergarten student in New York who had a dispute with their school board over whether their daughter was entitled to a sign-language interpreter. Lower federal courts ordered the board to provide the interpreter on the basis that an appropriate education was one that would have allowed the child to achieve at a level commensurate with that of her peers who were not disabled. The Supreme Court, acknowledging that the child was earning passing grades and advancing from one class to the next without a sign-language interpreter, reversed in favour of the school board. The Court ruled that a FAPE was one that was formulated in accordance with all of the IDEA's procedures and was 'sufficient to confer some educational benefit'[80] on a child with a disability. Insofar as the child in *Rowley* received some educational benefit without the sign-language interpreter, the Court thought that educators were not required to provide her with one even though she might have achieved at a higher level with the services. *Rowley* establishes a minimum standard of what constitutes a FAPE under federal law. Since states are free to establish higher requirements, though, courts apply these more stringent standards in litigation. Courts have refined the *Rowley* standard by interpreting 'some educational benefit' as requiring more than just minimal or trivial benefits.[81] Other courts have expanded the criteria by deciding that an educational benefit must be meaningful[82] or appreciable.[83] In fact, the Eleventh Circuit went so far as to maintain that student gains must be measurable to meet the *Rowley* standard.[84] Regardless of which criteria educators apply, case law has made it clear that under the IDEA's 'zero-reject' approach, all children with disabilities must be served, regardless of cost.[85]

At the same time, the IDEA, calls for students with disabilities to be educated in the least restrictive environment (LRE),[86] creating a conflict over whether LRE or a FAPE is more important. Starting in the late 1980s, federal appellate courts increasingly directed school boards to place students with disabilities in regular settings rather than segregated special education classrooms, ordering them to consider a variety of factors when formulating IEPs. In *Oberti v Board of*

79 458 U.S. 176 (1982).

80 Ibid. at 200.

81 See, e.g., *Hall v Vance County Bd. of Educ.*, 774 F.2d 629 (4th Cir. 1985); *Carter v Florence County Sch. Dist. Four*, 950 F.2d 156 (4th Cir. 1991), *aff'd on other grounds*, 510 U.S. 7 (1993).

82 See, e.g., *Board of Educ. of E. Windsor Reg'l Sch. Dist. v Diamond*, 808 F.2d 987 (3d Cir. 1986); Polk v Susquehanna Intermediate Unit 16, 853 F.2d 171 (3d Cir. 1988).

83 See, e.g., *Chris C. v Gwinnett County Sch. Dist.*, 780 F. Supp. 804 (N.D. Ga. 1991).

84 *J.S.K. v Hendry County Sch. Bd.*, 941 F.2d 1563 (11th Cir. 1991).

85 *See Timothy W. v Rochester, N.H., Sch. Dist., supra* note 22.

86 20 U.S.C. §§ 1406(b)(2), 1412(a)(5).

Education of the Borough of Clementon School District,[87] a case from New Jersey, the Third Circuit adopted a two-part test for assessing compliance with the LRE requirement.[88] The first element of the test is whether education in the regular classroom, with the use of supplementary aids and services, can be achieved satisfactorily. The second part of the test adds that if students must be placed outside of regular classrooms, educators must consider whether they were mainstreamed, now referred to as full inclusion, to the maximum extent appropriate. According to the Ninth Circuit in *Sacramento City Unified School District Board of Education v Rachel H.*,[89] a case from California, educators must address four factors in making placements. These elements examine the educational benefits of placing children with disabilities in regular classrooms; the non-academic benefits of such placements; the effect that the presence of students with disabilities would have on teacher and other children in classes; and the costs of inclusionary placements.

Case law on LRE is premised on the notion that educators must make reasonable efforts to place students with disabilities in fully inclusive settings by providing them with extra aids and services to ensure their success. Even with the focus on inclusion, and in a point that many educators and parents fail to grasp, the IDEA does not mandate that full inclusion. Instead, inclusion is a goal rather than a right for children with disabilities. Courts have thus approved more restrictive placements when educators have demonstrated that students with disabilities could not function in regular classrooms or would not benefit in such settings, even with extra help.[90]

Discipline

One of the most challenging issues for educators who deal with students with disabilities is discipline.[91] Surprisingly, Congress did not add specific provisions on discipline for students with disabilities until 1997.[92] Earlier, courts generally applied the IDEA's overall procedural protections to the disciplinary process. Yet, the Supreme Court went so far as to declare that special education students could not be expelled for disciplinary reasons where their transgressions were manifestations of, or caused by, their disabilities.[93] The IDEA allows educators to transfer students with disabilities to interim alternative settings for up to 45 days for possession of weapons or for knowing possession of drugs or infliction of

87 995 F.2d 1204 (3d Cir. 1993).

88 An earlier version of this test emerged in *Daniel R.R. v State Bd. of Educ.*, 874 F.2d 1036 (5th Cir. 1989).

89 14 F.3d 1398 (9th Cir. 1994).

90 See, e.g., *Clyde K. v Puyallup Sch. Dist.* No. 3, 35 F.3d 1396 (9th Cir. 1994).

91 For more detail, see Osborne and Russo (2009a).

92 20 U.S.C. § 1415(k).

93 *Honig v Doe*, 484 U.S. 305 (1988).

serious bodily injury.[94] The IDEA also makes it clear that educational services must continue during exclusions.[95] Further, the IDEA directs school officials to conduct functional behavioural assessments and develop behaviour intervention plans whenever disciplinary sanctions may result in a loss of educational opportunities.[96] All the same, the Supreme Court and the IDEA have not left educators without recourse when students with disabilities misbehave. Students with disabilities may be suspended temporarily and are subject to other normal disciplinary sanctions that do not result in changes in their placements. If necessary, educators may seek relief from hearing officers or the courts pending completion of due process hearings if they can show that students are dangerous and that educators cannot reach agreements with their parents over proper changes in placements.

The IDEA forbids school officials from excluding students with disabilities from school for ten or more days if their misconduct is a manifestation of, or caused by, their disabilities. Before changing the placements of students with disabilities for disciplinary reasons, educators must meet with IEP teams, including parents, to consider whether the (mis)behaviour was a manifestation of, or caused by, their disabilities.[97] The IDEA defines a manifestation as conduct that was caused by, or had a direct and substantial relationship to, the child's disability or was the direct result of the local educational agency's failure to implement the IEP.[98] In making manifestation determinations, teams must weigh all relevant information, including evaluations and diagnostic results as well as student observations.[99] If IEP teams agree that (mis)behaviours were not manifestations of students' disabilities, the students may be disciplined in the same manner as peers who are not disabled, except that the delivery of a FAPE may not be terminated.[100] If teams interpret misconduct as a manifestation of disability or as result of an improperly implemented IEP, the child may not be expelled or suspended for more than ten days without having their current placements reconsidered.[101]

Dispute Resolution and Procedural Due Process

Perhaps the most unique aspect of the IDEA is its extensive due process provisions that afford parents who disagree with school board actions regarding the placements of their children with an array of procedures to raise challenges in timely fashion. In this regard, the federal trial court in New Mexico has pointed out that '[t]he

94 20 U.S.C. § 1415(k)(1)(G).
95 20 U.S.C. § 1415(k)(1)(D).
96 20 U.S.C. § 1415(k)(1)(D),(E).
97 20 U.S.C. § 1415(k)(1)(E)(I).
98 20 U.S.C. § 1415(k)(1)(E)(I).
99 20 U.S.C. § 1415(k)(1)(E)(I).
100 20 U.S.C. § 1415(k)(1)(C), 20 U.S.C. § 1412(a)(1)(A).
101 20 U.S.C. § 1415(k)(1)(C).

IDEA favors prompt resolution of disputes'[102] involving the educational rights of students with disabilities. Insofar as the education of students with disabilities hangs in the balance, as noted, Congress itself also recognised the need to resolve disputes quickly. In fact, the IDEA now declares that '[p]arents and schools should be given expanded opportunities to resolve their disagreements in positive and constructive ways', and that '[t]eachers, schools, local educational agencies, and States should be relieved of irrelevant and unnecessary paperwork burdens that do not lead to improved educational outcomes'.[103] To this end, parents who disagree with the actions of school boards, IEP teams, administrators, or teachers who work with their children may invoke the IDEA's dispute resolution process, which begins with voluntary mediation[104] before potentially progressing to resolution sessions, due process hearings, and litigation (below). However, according to a survey by the National Association of State Directors of Special Education (NASDSE) in association with the Consortium for Appropriate Dispute Resolution in Special Education (CADRE), states have also been seeking the resolution of disputes via non-IDEA-required alternative mechanisms, such as special meetings and non-IDEA mediation (Henderson 2008). There is in any event evidence that a majority of disputes are resolved prior to a hearing and irrespective of the involvement of mediation (Reimann et al. 2007).[105] It has been noted that parents chose to pursue more than one route to redress in over one third of special education disputes (Schrag and Schrag 2004).

IDEA mediation

In providing parents with alternative remedies in disputes over the placements of their children, the IDEA and its accompanying regulations[106] direct states and local school boards to begin by offering mediation at public expense[107] when due process hearings are possible.[108] Official data, which may not, however, be complete, indicate that in 2007/2008 across the 50 states there were 2,621

102 *Sanders v Santa Fe Pub. Schs.*, 383 F. Supp.2d 1305, 1311 (D.N.M. 2004).

103 20 U.S.C. §§ 1400(c)(8)–(9).

104 20 U.S.C. § 1415(e). For a discussion of mediation and resolution sessions, see Osborne and Russo (2007).

105 For example, national statistics reporting that 11,392 disputes were resolved without hearings, a total that increases to 11,398 by including American Samoa, Guam, the Northern Marianas Islands, and the Virgin Islands: *Number of hearings (fully adjudicated) through dispute resolution procedures for children ages 3 through 21 served under IDEA, Part B, by case status and state: 2007–2008*. https://www.ideadata.org/arc_toc10.asp [accessed 5 November 2010].

106 20 U.S.C. § 1415(e)(1); 34 C.F.R. § 300.506(a).

107 20 U.S.C. § 1415(e)(2)(D).

108 To date, these provisions have been subject to little litigation. See *Spencer v District of Columbia*, 416 F. Supp.2d 5 (D.D.C. 2006) (holding that resolution sessions can be waived only with the consent of both parties).

mediations held relating to due process and 3,046 not related to it.[109] The IDEA specifies that mediation must be voluntary on the part of the parties; cannot be used to deny or delay parental rights to due process hearings or to deny any other rights under the IDEA; and must be conducted by trained, qualified, impartial mediators[110] whose names are on state-maintained lists of qualified mediators in special education.[111] According to the IDEA's regulations, mediators cannot be employees of states, school boards, or other agencies that provide direct services to students who are subject to the mediation process, nor can they have personal or professional conflicts of interest.[112] Consistent with general legal principles in the United States, those who otherwise qualify as mediators are not considered employees of states or boards solely by virtue of being paid to serve as mediators.[113]

Mediation sessions must be scheduled in a timely manner in locations convenient to the parties.[114] There seems to be no imperative to involve children, who do not attend the sessions (Frank 2003, p. 118). Agreements that the parties reach as a result of mediation must be formalised in writing.[115] Discussions that occur during mediation must be kept confidential and cannot be used as evidence in later due process hearings or civil proceedings; the parties may also be required to sign confidentiality pledges prior to initiating mediation.[116] The results of mediation agreements can, however, be enforced in federal or state courts.[117] Even though mediation is intended to be a non-adversarial process, nothing in the IDEA or its regulations prohibits the participation of attorneys.[118] Indeed, lawyers have become active in mediation sessions on behalf of parents in some states (Russell 2003, p. 22).

If parents choose not to participate in mediation, states may establish procedures allowing the parties to meet at convenient times and locations with disinterested third parties who are under contract with parent training and information centres, community parent resource centres, or appropriate alternative dispute resolution entities to encourage the use of, and explain the benefits of, the process.[119] The success that some commentators have had with mediation notwithstanding (Fitz 2008), to the extent that the process is totally voluntary and occurs only after relations between parents and the relevant authorities have already soured, it remains to be seen whether this approach is successful in the long run. One study

109 https://www.ideadata.org/arc_toc10.asp [accessed 5 November 2010].

110 20 U.S.C. § 1415(e)(2)(A)(iii); 34 C.F.R. § 300.506(b)(1).

111 20 U.S.C. § 1415(e)(2)(C).

112 34 C.F.R. § 300.506(c)(1).

113 34 C.F.R. § 300.506(c)(2)).

114 20 U.S.C. § 1415(e)(2)(E).

115 20 U.S.C. § 1415(e)(2)(F).

116 20 U.S.C. § 1415(e)(2)(G).

117 34 C.F.R. § 300.506(b)(7).

118 Although the federal government has started gathering data on the number of mediation sessions that are taking place, it does not provide information on who is present.

119 20 U.S.C. § 1415(e)(2)(B).

indicated a 51 per cent success rate for mediations in forging an agreement (Schrag and Schrag 2004). Whether this is a good rate of success is open to debate.

Resolution sessions

As part of the dispute resolution process, educators must convene meetings, known as resolution sessions, between parents and relevant members of the IEP teams for their children[120] within 15 days of parental requests for due process hearings, in an attempt to resolve placement disputes.[121] If officials fail to convene resolution sessions within 15 days, parents can seek the intervention of hearing officers to begin that process.[122] Resolution sessions must include a school board representative with decision-making authority on the board's behalf[123] but may not involve a board attorney unless parents are also accompanied by counsel.[124] However, if school officials are unable to get parents to participate in resolution sessions and can document their reasonable efforts in this regard within 30 days, hearing officers can dismiss complaints.[125] The parties need not attend resolution sessions if they agree, in writing, to waive their meetings or instead agree to mediation.[126]

If parties are unable to resolve their disputes within 30 days, they should schedule due process hearings.[127] If the parties do resolve their differences at resolution sessions, they must execute and sign legally binding agreements.[128] Settlement agreements are enforceable in state or federal courts, but either party may void them within three business days.[129]

Due process hearings

As reflected by a comprehensive longitudinal study which reported that there were 37,069 special education hearings in the United States between 1991 and 2005 (Zirkel and Gischlar 2008),[130] and official data which (subject to the above

120 34 C.F.R. § 300.510(a)(4).

121 20 U.S.C. § 1415(f)(1)(B)(i); 34 C.F.R. § 300.510(a).

122 20 U.S.C. § 1415(f)(1)(B)(i); 34 C.F.R. § 300.510(a).

123 34 C.F.R. § 300.510(a)(i).

124 34 C.F.R. § 300.510(a)(ii).

125 34 C.F.R. § 300.510(b)(4).

126 34 C.F.R. § 300.510(a)(3).

127 20 U.S.C. § 1415(f)(1)(B)(ii); 34 C.F.R. § 300.510(b).

128 20 U.S.C. § 1415(f)(1)(B)(iii); 34 C.F.R. § 300.510(c).

129 20 U.S.C. § 1415(f)(1)(B)(iv); 34 C.F.R. § 300.510(d).

130 For previous studies of this type, see Schrag and Schrag (2003). See also Dispute Resolution Activities: State Data Collection, National Association of State Directors of Special Education (July 1999), available at http://www.directionservice.org/cadre/qta-3a.cfm

caveat as to reliability) indicate that in 2007/2008 across the 50 states there were 3,217 full adjudicated due process hearings under IDEA (part B),[131] it is readily apparent that this a relatively common means by which parents and school boards engage in alternative dispute resolution in order to resolve differences over the education of students with disabilities. In theory, since due process hearings are quasi-judicial proceedings, an alternative method of dispute resolution in lieu of litigation in which the rules of evidence and procedure are relaxed, Congress had hoped that this more informal setting would help to ease the tensions that can arise between parents and school boards. However, as reflected in the amount of ensuing litigation, it seems that as noble as the hope to avoid legal actions was, it was not entirely successful.

Either parents or school board officials can request due process hearings to resolve disputes over placement of students with disabilities. Examples of when courts granted parental requests for due process hearings include when educators refused to assess whether a child had a disability;[132] when parents disagreed with a recommendation that officials offered;[133] and when parents were dissatisfied with the content or implementation of an IEP.[134] If parents refuse to consent to evaluations, boards may request due process hearings compelling them to cooperate.[135] In a key preliminary matter, the Supreme Court clarified the issue of burden of proof in challenges to the contents of IEPs in due process hearings. In *Schaffer ex rel. Schaffer v Weast*,[136] the Court affirmed an order of the Fourth Circuit placing the burden of proof on the parties challenging IEPs.[137] In rejecting

131 Washington, E.C., and Puerto Rico a total that increases to 3,218 by including American Samoa, Guam, the Northern Marianas Islands, and the Virgin Islands: 'Number of hearings (fully adjudicated) through dispute resolution procedures for children ages 3 through 21 served under IDEA, Part B, by case status and state: 2007–08'. https://www.ideadata.org/arc_toc10.asp.

132 *Hacienda La Puente Unified School Dist.* of Los Angeles v Honig, 976 F.2d 487 (9th Cir. 1992).

133 *Dong v Board of Educ.*, 197 F.3d 793 (6th Cir. 1999).

134 *Kuszewski v Chippewa Valley Schools*, 117 F. Supp.2d 646 (E.D. Mich. 2000).

135 *Yates v Charles County Bd. of Educ.*, 212 F. Supp.2d 470(D. Md. 2002).

136 546 U.S. 49 (2005). For the earlier case, *see Weast v Schaffer*, 377 F.3d 449 (4th Cir. 2004), *affirmed sub nom. Schaffer v Weast*, 546 U.S. 49 (2005). For a discussion of this case, see Russo and Osborne, Jr. (2006).

137 For cases agreeing with the Fourth Circuit, see, e.g., *Alamo Heights Independent School District v State Board of Education*, 790 F.2d 1153 (5th Cir. 1986) and *Johnson v Independent School District No. 4*, 921 F.2d 1022 (10th Cir. 1990), *cert. denied*, 500 U.S. 905 (1991). For cases placing the burden on school boards, see, e.g., *Grim v Rhinebeck Central School District*, 346 F.3d 377 (2d Cir. 2003) and *Seattle School District No. 1 v B.S.*, 82 F.3d 1493 (9th Cir. 1996).

the claim that parents who questioned their son's IEP were at a disadvantage due to a lack of knowledge, the Court found that they had significant due process protections available to make sure that this was not so. The Court emphasised that while the question was not before it, states could have, as several already had, overridden what it described as the default position by placing this burden of proof on school boards.

The IDEA specifies that hearing officers, who are selected pursuant to state law, must be fair and impartial third-party decision makers,[138] meaning that they cannot be employees of the states or school boards involved in educating students or have personal or professional interests in the outcomes.[139] Public agencies must keep lists of qualified hearing officers along with explanations of their qualifications.[140] As to the actual dispute resolution process, depending on state law, either state or local school boards may conduct due process hearings.[141] In states with two-tiered systems, if local boards conduct initial hearings, either party can appeal to the state.[142] Prior to the start of hearings, both parties must make full disclosures of all evaluations that have been completed by that date and recommendations that they intend to rely on at least five business days in advance.[143] If parties fail to provide this information, hearing officers can prevent them from introducing the relevant evaluations or recommendations at hearings without the consent of the other parties.[144] The reason why parties must reveal all of this information stems from the fact that insofar as the goal of these due process hearings is to arrive at placements that best suit the needs of students with disabilities rather than have one side 'win' outright, Congress wrote the law in such a fashion that hearing officers, and the parties, should have all of the information available at their disposal in reaching their decisions. Whether hearings are open to the public is a parental choice.[145] Both parties have the right to be accompanied and advised by counsel and by individuals with special knowledge or training with respect to the problems of children with disabilities;[146] the right to present evidence and confront, cross-examine, and compel the attendance of witnesses;[147] the right to written, or, at the option of the parents, electronic verbatim records of such hearings;[148]and the right to written, or, at the option of the parents, electronic findings of fact and final adjudications.[149] Although nothing in IDEA addresses the question, nothing

138 20 U.S.C. § 1415(e)(2)(B).
139 34 C.F.R. § 300.511(c)(3).
140 34 C.F.R. § 300.511(c)(3).
141 *Van Duyn v Baker School Dist.*, 502 F.3d 811 (9th Cir. 2007).
142 20 U.S.C. § 1415(g).
143 20 U.S.C. § 1415(f)(2)(A).
144 20 U.S.C. § 1415(f)(2)(B).
145 34 C.F.R. § 300.512(c)(2).
146 20 U.S.C. § 1415(h)(1).
147 20 U.S.C. § 1415(h)(2).
148 20 U.S.C. § 1415(h)(3).
149 20 U.S.C. § 1415(h)(4).

prevents students from being present at and participating in due process hearings. However, to the extent that children under the age of 18 have limited rights in this regard,[150] the reality is that parents, rather than students, tend to drive the process.

Hearing officers must render final decisions based on the record,[151] indicating that they can rely only on evidence that was before them, within 45 days from the expiration of the 30-day period,[152] but can grant extensions at the request of either party.[153] The orders of hearing officers are final, and binding on all parties, unless one of the parties appeals.[154] In jurisdictions with two-tiered due process hearing systems, officials must ensure that final judgments are reached within 30 days of when requests for reviews are made.[155] Parties who are displeased with the results of administrative proceedings may appeal to state or federal courts within 90 days[156] or the appropriate state time limitations[157] once they exhaust administrative remedies unless it is futile to do so. While administrative or judicial actions are pending, the IDEA's stay-put provisions dictate that unless school officials and parents agree or officials obtain orders from hearing officers or judicial decrees granting them permission to change their placements, students must remain in their then current settings.[158]

In its most recent revision, the IDEA added a two-year limitations period during which parties can request due process hearings.[159] If state laws set different limitations periods, then those periods prevail. Moreover, the IDEA stipulates that the federal statute of limitations is to be stayed if parents can show that school officials misrepresented that they resolved a disagreement or if they withheld pertinent information from the parents.[160] Once litigation has started, courts can review the record of administrative proceedings, hear additional evidence and grant such relief as they deem appropriate based on the preponderance of evidence standard.[161]

As extensive as it is, the IDEA is not the exclusive avenue through which parents can enforce the rights of their children. According to the IDEA, none of its provisions can be interpreted as restricting or limiting the rights, procedures, and remedies available under the Federal Constitution, Section 504, or other federal laws protecting the rights of students with disabilities.[162]

---

150 See, e.g., the Family Education Rights and Privacy Act, 29 U.S.C. § 1232g, under which students do not control access over their records until they reach the age of 18.

151 20 U.S.C. § 1415(f)(3)(E)(i)(ii).

152 20 U.S.C. § 1415(i).

153 34 C.F.R. § 300.515(C).

154 20 U.S.C. § 1415(i)(1)(A).

155 34 C.F.R. § 300.515(b).

156 20 U.S.C. § 1415(i)(2)(B).

157 20 U.S.C. § 1415(i)(2)(B).

158 20 U.S.C. § 1415(j); 20 U.S.C. § 1415(k)(2); *Honig v Doe*, 484 U.S. 305 (1988).

159 20 U.S.C. § 1415(f)(3)(C).

160 20 U.S.C. § 1415(f)(3)(D).

161 20 U.S.C. § 1415(i)(2)(C)(iii).

162 20 U.S.C. § 1415(l).

Judicial action and remedies

As indicated, once parents take school boards to court in disputes over the placements of their children, the judiciary has the power to provide the relief that it deems appropriate.[163] In a manner similar to the law of breach of contracts, keeping in mind that IEPs are essentially contracts between parents and school systems, or negligence, courts have awarded monetary damages, tuition reimbursement, compensatory services, and attorney fees in attempts to put parents in the position that they would have been in had their children received the FAPEs to which they were entitled at the outset of the IDEA process. Insofar as parental receipt of such awards is integral to the IDEA's dispute resolution process, they require some discussion.

Courts generally have not imposed monetary damages on school officials in their individual[164] or official[165] capacities for failing to provide appropriate educational placements or services for students with disabilities, recognising that they are in positions wherein they must apply discretion, often times in very close cases. While courts do not ordinarily award general damages for 'pain and suffering',[166] in special education cases, recent, albeit scant, litigation suggests that this may be changing.[167]

The IDEA affords parents who disagree with the placements of their children the right to place their children in private schools and attempt to recover the costs of tuition.[168] In *School Committee of the Town of Burlington v Department of Education, Commonwealth of Massachusetts*,[169] the Supreme Court decided that parents are entitled to tuition reimbursement if they can show that officials failed to offer appropriate placements and if the parents' chosen placements are appropriate. The Court added that awarding reimbursement requires boards to pay retroactively for costs that they should have absorbed from the beginning. In another aspect of the issue, in *Florence County School District Four v Carter*,[170] the Court ruled that parents are entitled to tuition reimbursements even if their chosen placements are not in state-approved facilities, as long as they place their children in settings that are otherwise appropriate.

---

163 20 U.S.C. § 1415(i)(2)(C)(iii).

164 See, e.g., *L.M.P. ex rel. E.P. v School Bd. of Broward County*, 516 F. Supp.2d 1305 (S.D. Fla. 2007).

165 See, e.g., *Bradley v Arkansas Dep't of Educ.*, 301 F.3d 952 (8th Cir. 2002).

166 See, e.g., *Ft. Zumwalt School Dist. v Missouri State Bd. of Educ.*, 865 F. Supp. 604 (E.D. Mo. 1994).

167 *Mark H. v Lemahieu*, 513 F.3d 922 (9th Cir. 2008).

168 20 U.S.C. § 1412(a)(10)(C)(ii).

169 471 U.S. 359 (1985).

170 510 U.S. 7 (1993).

One issue that remained, particularly in the light of ambiguous language in the IDEA,[171] was whether parents whose children never received special education from public agencies were entitled to reimbursement when the parents enrolled those children in private facilities before availing themselves of the IDEA's procedures in public school settings. Since the federal courts disagreed over whether they did so at their own financial risk,[172] the Supreme Court intervened to resolve the difference. The Court ruled, in *Forest Grove School District v T.A.*,[173] that the IDEA did not prohibit parental reimbursements for the costs associated with private school placements when their children had not previously received special education and related services from public schools.

The courts have also observed that compensatory services, such as providing children with extra time in class, extended school year placements, or services beyond the ceiling age of 21, like tuition reimbursements, are designed to offer relief for the failure of school board officials to provide children with appropriate education.[174] The rationale for awards of compensatory services is that appropriate remedies should not be available only to students whose parents can afford to pay for alternate educational placements while litigation is pending. Compensatory services are ordinarily awarded for the time that children were denied services[175] even if they passed the IDEA's age limit.[176] As with tuition reimbursement, compensatory services can be awarded only if hearing officers or courts agree that school officials failed to provide appropriate placements.[177]

---

171 20 U.S.C. § 1412(a)(10)(C)(ii) provides that courts may award reimbursement to 'the parents of a child with a disability, who previously received special education and related services under the authority of a public agency' who had enrolled the child in a private school. As discussed below, some courts interpreted this to mean that reimbursement could not be awarded to the parents of students who had never received special education from a public agency.

172 For cases allowing reimbursement, see, e.g., *Greenland Sch. Dist. v Amy N.*, 358 F.3d 150 (1st Cir. 2004); *Marissa F. ex rel. Mark and Lavinia F. v William Penn Sch. Dist.*, 199 Fed. Appx. 151 (3d Cir. 2006). For cases not allowing reimbursement, see, e.g., *Frank G. v Board of Educ. of Hyde Park*, 459 F.3d 356 (2d Cir. 2006), *cert. denied*, 522 U.S. 985 (2007); *M.M. ex rel. C.M. v School Bd. of Miami-Dade County*, 437 F.3d 1085 (11th Cir. 2006).

173 129 S. Ct. 2484 (2009). For a more comprehensive treatment of this topic, see Osborne, Jr. and Russo (2009b).

174 See, e.g., *Burr by Burr v Ambach*, 888 F.2d 258 (2d Cir. 1989), cert. denied, 494 U.S. 1005 (1990).

175 See, e.g., *Todd D. by Robert D. v Andrews*, 933 F.2d 1576 (11th Cir. 1991).

176 See, e.g., *Pihl v Massachusetts Dep't of Educ.*, 9 F.3d 184 (1st Cir. 1993).

177 See, e.g., *Ms. M. ex rel. K.M. v Portland Sch. Comm.*, 360 F.3d 267 (1st Cir. 2004); *Z.W. ex rel. G. and J.W. v Smith*, 210 Fed. Appx. 282 (4th Cir. 2006); *M.M. ex rel. C.M. v School Bd. of Miami-Dade County*, 437 F.3d 1085 (11th Cir. 2006).

Turning next to legal costs, the IDEA did not, initially, include provisions permitting parents to be reimbursed for what can be sizeable attorney fees even if they prevail in disputes with their school boards over the placements of their children.[178] In fact, in *Smith v Robinson*,[179] the Supreme Court rejected the claim of parents of children with disabilities to recover legal expenses from their school boards even when they prevailed. Displeased with this outcome, Congress amended federal law, enacted the Handicapped Children's Protection Act in 1988,[180] and incorporated it into the IDEA. The IDEA now allows prevailing parents to recover attorney fees in IDEA litigation against their school boards, affording them the right to representation by attorney,[181] but not lay advocates,[182] undoubtedly to the chagrin of parent advocates.[183] Awards must be based on a variety of factors including the prevailing rates in the areas in which cases were litigated[184] and are subject to review to ensure that trial courts did not abuse their discretion.[185] However, the IDEA expressly authorises courts to deny parental requests for attorney fees where they rejected settlement offers and failed to obtain more favourable judicial relief.[186] In an attempt to limit costs of litigation, the IDEA now allows school boards to seek reimbursement of their legal expenses when parents file complaints that are later found to be frivolous, unreasonable, or without foundation or when litigation was continued after it clearly became frivolous, unreasonable, or without foundation.[187] Interestingly, boards can recover

178 See, e.g., *J.P. ex rel. Peterson v County Sch. Bd. of Hanover County, Va.*, 516 F.3d 254 (4th Cir. 2008) (noting that parents incurred attorney fees and costs in excess of $180,000).

179 468 U.S. 992 (1984).

180 20 U.S.C. §§ 1415(i)(3)(B)(C).

181 20 U.S.C. § 1415(h)(1).

182 *In re Arons*, 756 A.2d 867 (Del. 2000), *cert. denied sub nom. Arons v Office of Disciplinary Counsel of Sup. Ct. of Del.*, 532 U.S. 1065 (2001).

183 For a paper stressing the need to increase the role of parent advocates in special education disputes, see Nespor and Hicks (2010). Disappointingly, the article does not cite the only reported case in which parents were involved in seeking help from a non-attorney.

184 20 U.S.C.§ 1415(i)(3)(B).

185 See, e.g., *A.R. ex rel. R.V v New York City Dep't of Educ.*, 407 F.3d 65 (2d Cir. 2005).

186 20 U.S.C. § 1415(i)(3)(D)(I). Courts have refused to grant parental requests for attorney fees when they did not complete due process hearings (*P.O. ex rel. L.T. v Greenwich Bd. of Educ.*, 210 F. Supp.2d 76 (D. Conn. 2002) and when fees (*Holmes v Millcreek Township Sch. Dist.*, 205 F.3d 583 (3d Cir. 2000) or time billed for legal services was excessive (*Cavanaugh ex rel. Cavanaugh v Cardinal Local Sch. Dist.*, 409 F.3d 753 (6th Cir. 2005) or vague (*C.C. ex rel. Mrs. D. v Granby Bd. of Educ.*, 453 F. Supp.2d 569 (D. Conn. 2006). As to parents who are attorneys, some courts have allowed them to recover fees when they represent their own children (*Woodside v School Dist. of Philadelphia Bd. of Educ.*, 248 F.3d 129 (3d Cir. 2001) but others refuse to do so (*Pardini v Allegheny Intermediate Unit*, 524 F.3d 419 (3d Cir. 2008).

187 20 U.S.C. § 1415(i)(3)(B)(i)(II).

costs from attorneys who file suit on behalf of parents if the attorneys' actions are premised on improper purposes, cause unnecessary delays, or needlessly increase the cost of litigation,[188] not from their clients.

The status of attorney fees under the so-called catalyst theory, pursuant to which courts have awarded fees if litigation, or the threat of suits or administrative actions, motivated school officials to grant parental requests, is now uncertain in light of a non-school case, *Buckhannon Board & Care Home v West Virginia Department of Health and Human Resources* (*Buckhannon*).[189] In *Buckhannon*, the Supreme Court rejected the catalyst theory in acknowledging that prevailing parties must, in order to be awarded the cost of fees, succeed in court by obtaining judgments on the merits or in the form of consent decrees. Federal courts have since reached mixed results over this question as some courts have granted requests[190] while others have refused to grant[191] such awards.

A related question that emerged addressed whether parents may recover fees for expert witnesses who help them to prevail in actions under the IDEA. In response to a split between the Circuit Court for the District of Columbia which refused to award such fees to parents[192] and the Second Circuit, in a case of from New York that reached the opposite result, the Supreme Court agreed to intervene. In reviewing the latter case, *Arlington Central School District v Murphy*,[193] the Court refused to allow parents to recover fees for expert witnesses even if they prevailed, since they are unauthorised in the text of the IDEA. The Court reasoned that since it was not its job to amend the IDEA, any such changes had to have been made by Congress. In view of this and the fact that Congress has yet to amend the IDEA to this end, parents are left in a precarious financial situation. In other words, since the use of expert witnesses can be costly, it is unclear why Congress has yet to authorise such reimbursement awards in light of its having previously added

---

188 20 U.S.C. § 1415(i)(3)(B)(i)(III). See *Moser v Bret Harte Union High School Dist.*, 366 F. Supp.2d 944 (E.D. Cal. 2005) (imposing sanctions on a school board); *K.S. ex rel. P.S. v Fremont Unified School Dist.*, 545 F. Supp.2d 995 (N.D. Cal. 2008) (imposing sanctions on an attorney).

189 532 U.S. 598 (2001).

190 See, e.g., *Goldring v District of Columbia*, 416 F.3d 70 (D.C. Cir. 2005); *.M. ex rel. G.M. v Board of Educ., Center Moriches Union Free Sch. Dist.*, 296 F. Supp.2d 400 (E.D.N.Y. 2003).

191 See, e.g., *Doe v Boston Pub. Schs.*, 358 F.3d 20 (1st Cir. 2004); *J.C. v Regional Sch. Dist. 10, Bd. of Educ.*, 278 F.3d 119 (2d Cir. 2002); *.O. ex rel. C.O. v Orange Township Bd. of Educ.*, 287 F.3d 267 (3d Cir. 2002); *J.S. v Ramapo Cent. School Dist.*, 165 F. Supp.2d 570 (S.D.N.Y. 2001); *P.O. ex rel. L.T. v Greenwich Bd. of Educ.*, 210 F. Supp.2d 76 (D. Conn. 2002).

192 *Goldring v District of Columbia*, 416 F.3d 70 (D.C. Cir. 2005).

193 548 U.S.291 (2006). For a more detailed discussion of this case and related issues, see Allan G. Osborne, Jr. and Charles J. Russo, 'The Supreme Court Rejects Parental Reimbursement for Expert Witness Fees Under the IDEA: *Arlington Central School District Board of Education v Murphy', 213 Educ. L. Rep.* 333 (2006).

the attorneys' fees provision to the IDEA. Insofar as parents must now pay expert witnesses to obtain services that their children should otherwise have received, doing so would be a significant step in the direction of further safeguarding the rights of parents who are acting on behalf of their children. While the authors of this chapter believe that making such a change would be beneficial, it is simply hard to know whether it will occur. Moreover, given the current economic climate in the United States, it seems unlikely that this is a high priority for Congress, meaning that such a change is probably not going to happen any time soon.

Conclusion

In reflecting on how or why parents select the methods of dispute resolution that they do, clearly, mediation, resolution sessions, and due process hearings offer the advantage of being less expensive than litigation while providing shorter time frames within which disagreements are addressed. Still, once the parties have exhausted their administrative remedies, since parents can recover the legal fees if they prevail, litigation remains an attractive option if they remain dissatisfied with the alternative avenues that they have available. From the point of view of parents, to the extent that parents have this latter option, it is in their benefit to push disputes through the litigation process. By doing so, parents can more readily compel educators to comply with judicial orders while possibly setting precedent for later situations affecting them as well as other families in the future. By the same token, school boards often proceed to litigation, rather than compromise or negotiate settlement agreements with parents, out of concern for setting precedent whereby they will have to agree to provide more than is required by law to other parents in the future.

Studies suggest both that engaging parents in the education of their children will improve the effectiveness of the services that students receive (Nutting et al. 2006) and that there is a need to increase the reach of alternative models of dispute resolution (Mueller et al. 2008). There is also evidence that social class may be a factor in the route to redress that parents take in special education cases. Those from lower socio-economic backgrounds tend to use mediation more than middle class parents, who appear to prefer using more formal due process solutions (Reiman et al. 2007). In general, alternative dispute resolution appears to be growing in an attempt to avoid going to court, an activity that has almost become a sport to many Americans. This may continue, as there appears to be greater parental satisfaction with mediation than due process hearings (Reiman et al. 2007), although if mediation does not bring a satisfactory outcome the parents are likely to take a different option for any subsequent dispute (Schrag and Schrag 2004). A recent investigation on the effectiveness of alternative dispute resolution conceded that '[t]o date, however, there are no studies of school districts with high litigation rates that implemented system wide change. This line of inquiry is uncharted and will provide a starting point for further research' (Mueller et al. 2008). There is a great need for additional research not only on how to make alternative means of dispute resolution more effective but on how to assist parents to become better informed and more involved in the education of their children. One can only hope that the fruits of such inquiries can be employed to help reduce some of the conflict that arises when disagreements emerge over the placements of students with disabilities.

In sum, the shortcomings of the IDEA notwithstanding, if one compares the status of American students with disabilities before 1975 to the present, it is evident that their situations have improved dramatically. While, the only report of its kind, released by President's Commission on Excellence in Special Education, *A New Era: Revitalizing Special Education for Children and their Families*, in 2002, notes that parents range from generally pleased to some who are displeased with the IDEA, 'there are no studies comparing parents' opinions concerning special education' (Nutting et al. 2006, p. 55). Yet, since even good laws can be improved, and the IDEA certainly has areas in which improvement is merited, such as providing reimbursement for parents who rely on the assistance of expert witnesses to prevail in disputes against their school boards, it will be interesting to observe what the future brings.

References

Burgdorf, M.P. and Burgdorf, R. (1975), 'A History of Unequal Treatment: The Qualifications of Handicapped Persons as a 'Suspect Class' under the Equal Protection Clause', *Santa Clara Lawyer,* Vol. 15, 855–910.

Fitz, J.M. (2008), 'Improving Special Education Mediation', *International Review of Sociology*, Vol. 18, No. 3, 469–480.

Frank, J. (2003), 'The West London Mediation Project', in I.S. Gersch and A. Gersch (eds), *Resolving Disagreement in Special Educational Needs* (London: Routledge Falmer), pp. 113–123.

Henderson, K. (2008), *Optional IDEA Alternative Dispute Resolution* (Alexandria, VA: NASDSE, 2008).

Mueller, T.G., Singer, G.H.S. and Draper, L.M. (2008), 'Reducing Parental Dissatisfaction with Special Education in Two School Districts: Implementing Conflict Prevention and Alternative Dispute Resolution', *Journal of Educational and Psychological Consultation*, Vol. 18, 191–233.

Nespor, J. and Hicks, D. (2010), 'Wizards and Witches: Parent Advocates and Contentions in Special Education in the USA', *Journal of Education Policy*, Vol. 25, No. *3*, 309–334.

Nutting, B., Porfeli, E., Queen, A.J. and Algozzine, B. (2006), 'Parental Beliefs and Knowledge about Special Education and the Individuals with Disabilities Education Act', *Journal of Special Education Leadership, Vol. 19, No. 2,* 48–61.

Osborne, A.G. and Russo, C.J. (2009a), *Discipline of Students with Disabilities: Legal Issues* (Thousand Oaks, CA: Corwin Press).

Osborne, A.G. and Russo, C.J. (2009b), '*Forest Grove School District v T.A:* The Reimbursement Rights of Parents who Unilaterally Place Their Children with Disabilities in Private Schools without Having Had Them Receive Special Education From Public Agencies', *Education Law Reporter*, Vol. 250, No. 1, 1–17.

Osborne, A.G. and Russo, C.J. (2007), 'Resolution Sessions Under the IDEA: Are They Mandatory?', *Education Law Reporter*, Vol. 218, No. 1, 7–11.

Osborne, A.G. and Russo, C.J. (2006), 'The Supreme Court Rejects Parental Reimbursement for Expert Witness Fees Under the IDEA: *Arlington Central School District Board of Education v Murphy*', *Education Law Reporter,* Vol. 213, 333–348.

President's Commission on Excellence in Special Education (2002), *A New Era: Revitalizing Special Education for Children and their Families*. Available at http://www2.ed.gov/inits/commissionsboards/whspecialeducation/index.html

Ramirez, B.A. and Weintraub, F.J (eds), *Special Education in America: Its Legal and Governmental Foundations* (Reston, VA: The Council for Exceptional Children).

Reiman, J., Beck, L., Peter, M., Zeller, D., Moses, P. and Engiles, A. (2007), *Initial review of research literature on appropriate dispute resolution in special education* (Eugene, OR: Consortium for Appropriate Dispute Resolution in Special Education).

Russell, P. (2003), 'Mediation in Action: Messages from the United States', in I.S. Gersch and A. Gersch (eds), *Resolving Disagreement in Special Educational Needs* (London: Routledge Falmer), pp. 15–26.

Russo, C.J. (2007), 'The Rights of Non-Attorney Parents Under the IDEA: *Winkelman v Parma City School District*', *Education Law Reporter,* Vol. 221, No. 1, 1–19 (2007).

Russo, C.J. and Osborne, A.G. (2009), *Section 504 and the ADA* (Thousand Oaks, CA: Corwin Press).

Russo, C.J. and Osborne, A.G. (2008), *Essential Concepts and School-Based Cases in Special Education Law* (Thousand Oaks, CA: Corwin Press).

Russo C.J. and Osborne, A.G. (2006), 'The Supreme Court Clarifies the Burden of Proof in Special Education Due Process Hearings: *Schaffer ex rel. Schaffer v Weast*', *Education Law Reporter, Vol. 208, No. 2*, 705–717.

Russo, C.J., Osborne, A.G., Massucci, J.D. and Cattaro, G.M. (2009), *Non-Public Schools and the Law of Special Education* (Lanham, MD: Rowman & Littlefield Education).

Schrag, H. and Schrag J. (2003), *Dispute Resolution Procedures, Data Collection, and Caseloads* (National Center on Dispute Resolution in Special Education) online publication available at http://www. directionservice.org/cadre.pdf/Dispute%20Resolution%20Study.pdf [accessed 27 June 2011].

Schrag, J. and Schrag, H. (2004), *National Dispute Resolution Use and Effectiveness Study* (Eugene, OR: Consortium for appropriate dispute resolution in special education).

Scotch, R.K. (2001), From Good Will to Civil Rights: Transforming Federal Disability Policy (Philadelphia, PA: Temple University Press).

Zettel, J.J. and Ballard, J. (1982), 'Introduction: Bridging the Gap', in J. Ballard, B.A. Ramirez, and F.J. Weintraub (eds), Special Education in America: Its Legal and Governmental Foundations (Reston, VA: The Council for Exceptional Children), pp. 1–9.

Zirkel, P.A. and Gischlar, K.L. (2008), 'Due Process Hearings Under the IDEA: A Longitudinal Frequency Analysis', Journal of Special Education Leadership, Vol. 21, No. 1, 22–38.

Chapter 7
Resolving Disputes about Special Educational Needs: Cross-Border Comparisons and Reflections

Sheila Riddell and Neville Harris

Introduction

This book's initial chapters provided a conceptual overview of grievances, disputes and educational rights in the field of special educational needs, followed by discussion of methods of dispute resolution. Subsequently, the book analysed approaches to dispute resolution in special educational needs in four developed countries, England, Scotland, the Netherlands and the US. These countries were chosen deliberately in order to illustrate particular approaches to special educational needs policy and practice, with a focus on the dispute resolution methods available in each jurisdiction. This concluding chapter pulls together and offers some reflections on key themes developed in the various chapters. It begins with a brief overview highlighting and analysing the central characteristics of each system and then considers their underpinning models of procedural justice. It reflects on the extent to which the judicial and non-judicial dispute resolution methods are capable of safeguarding parents' and children's rights against a background of socio-economic diversity and inequality.

The special education systems and redress mechanisms operating within four jurisdictions

The special education system of each country was described in detail in the earlier chapters. It is clear that there are many similarities between them, pointing to the effects of globalisation in the educational arena. In each system, for example, discrimination against disabled children is prohibited, inclusive education is promoted, and the rights of disabled children and their parents are protected. Underlining the growing influence of trans-national bodies in educational governance, the UK, the Netherlands and the US are signatories to the United Nations Convention on the Rights of Persons with Disabilities (although only the UK has ratified), Article 24 of which promotes the inclusion of disabled children in mainstream schools and the need for reasonable adjustments to enable this to happen effectively. At the same time, reflecting each country's distinctive political, historical and social context, these broad policy commitments lead to somewhat different practices and outcomes.

The *United States* provides an example of a system which invests considerable resources in special education, with federal funding making up about 7 per cent of the total expenditure and the school district and the state providing the remainder. It has been argued that this funding regime, which allocates resources to individual children, has an inflationary effect on the proportion of children identified as having special educational needs (Bowers and Parrish 2000). The rights of children with special educational needs and those of their parents are protected by both education and disability discrimination legislation. As noted by Florian and Pullin (2000) and by Russo and Osborne in chapter 6 of this volume, over the past three decades federal and state statutes, regulations and legal judgments have played a major part in the development of special educational needs policy, strongly influenced by disability activism and the US's civil rights tradition. One of the key principles informing US special education is that a child with special needs should receive a free appropriate public education in the least restrictive environment. The majority of children are educated in mainstream schools, but about 3 per cent of all children are educated in special provision in the form of special classes in mainstream schools and separate special schools. Tightly prescribed multi-disciplinary assessment procedures are used to determine whether a child has special educational needs and medically-based categorisation systems, which vary by state, are used. About 11.5 per cent of all pupils in the US receive an 'individualised educational program', which has statutory status, entitling the pupil to regular reviews and stipulating the additional resources to be allocated. Individualised educational programmes used in the US therefore differ from the individual education plans used in England, Scotland and the Netherlands, which do not have statutory status. Legal disputes often concern the proposed placement or procedural matters, and if the case is found in favour of the parents, then they may be awarded costs to cover compensatory educational services. As explained by Russo and Osborne (in chapter 6), litigation is frequently used by American citizens to resolve civil disputes, and while increasingly efforts have been made to resolve disagreements through mediation, its use is far from the norm.

In *England*, the state education system, catering for 93 per cent of all children, is very diverse, including faith schools, selective schools and special schools. Only about 1 per cent of children are educated in separate special schools, but there is an increase in the number of special units attached to mainstream schools and facilities such as short stay schools (previously known as pupil referral units, although likely soon to revert to that name, under forthcoming legislation) catering for excluded children and others who are deemed difficult to include in mainstream schools. The presumption is that as far as possible all children will be educated in mainstream schools, although parents have the right to express a preference as to the school which they believe will best meet their child's needs in either the special or mainstream sector. Under education legislation, local authorities have a duty to assess and meet the needs of children who have greater difficulty in learning than their peers and are unlikely to make progress without additional help. Disability equality legislation prohibits discrimination, defined as unequal treatment of disabled children compared with non-disabled children for a reason relating to their disability or a failure to make reasonable adjustment. A statutory support plan (a statement of special educational needs) is provided for about 2.5 per cent of all children attending school in England, and a further 18 per cent of children are identified as having special educational needs requiring additional support by school staff (referred to as School Action) or by external professionals working alongside school staff (referred to as School Action Plus). At the time of writing, the government recently published a Green Paper (DfE 2011) suggesting that too many children were being identified as having special educational needs. It was proposed that the SEN statement be replaced by an Education, Health and Care Plan, presumably for children requiring multi-agency input. The two levels of support (that is, School Action and School Action Plus) would be replaced by one broad category. In the interests of reducing bureaucracy, it was proposed that guidance on the drafting of Individual Education Plans would be withdrawn, leaving schools and local authorities to make decisions on what type of plan to use for children who do not qualify for an Education, Health and Care Plan. Many of these proposals are still sketchy, including qualification criteria for the new statutory support plan. However, if implemented, then it is likely that, as in Scotland, a far smaller group of children would be issued with a statutory support plan, with possible knock-on consequences for eligibility to make a tribunal appeal.

Formal assessment is required for a statement of needs, but there are no hard and fast rules about how assessments should be conducted and no rigidly applied standards for the identification of particular conditions. As we saw in chapter 3, since 1995, parents have been able to appeal to a tribunal, and since 2002 it has been mandatory for local authorities to ensure the availability of independent mediation for those parents who want to use it. Indeed, before 2002 many local authorities provided access to mediation, even though they were not obliged to do so.

There are both similarities and differences in the special education systems operating north and south of the Border. In *Scotland*, until the mid-1990s, policies and practices were broadly aligned with those in England. However, whereas England established a tribunal and published a Code of Practice at this point, Scotland did not follow suit until a decade later, and was also slightly later in establishing the right to formal mediation, available from 2005. Furthermore, the definition of additional support needs is much broader than the definition of special educational needs in England. In Scotland, children are deemed to have additional support needs if they have greater difficulty in learning than their peers, including, at least theoretically, a wide range of social difficulties as well as disabilities and learning difficulties. Despite this expansive definition, Scotland formally identifies just over five per cent of children as having additional support needs, and fewer than 0.5 per cent have a statutory co-ordinated support plan (CSP). Criteria for the award of a CSP are very strict. A child must be assessed as having needs which are significant, enduring and require services from agencies outwith education. The types of cases which may be referred to the tribunal are also more restricted than is the case in England and the Scottish tribunal does not pay compensation or parents' legal costs. Patterns of school placement in Scotland are very similar to those in England, with a presumption of mainstreaming ensuring that almost all children are educated in inclusive settings with about one per cent being enrolled in special schools or units.

Special education in *the Netherlands* differs considerably from the systems of the three countries discussed above. Traditionally, there has been a large special school sector, and despite the official endorsement of inclusion in Dutch policy and legislation, about 2.5 per cent of children are still placed in separate special schools, more than twice the proportion in England and Scotland and also higher than the US. As in the US, rigid forms of medical and psychological assessment are used to allocate children to particular categories of disability or learning difficulty, and thence to a particular type of special school. Pijl (2010) notes that there are ongoing debates in the Netherlands about whether the school system is too segregated, and a number of measures have been introduced to try to increase parental rights to choose a mainstream school. For example, since 2003, personalised budgets have been available for children assessed as having special educational needs to pay for necessary adaptations in mainstream schools. These budgets are portable and may be used in either mainstream or special settings. However, mainstream schools are still often reluctant to accept children with special educational needs, and have the right to refuse admission on a number of grounds. For example, the school may argue that the child, because of their impairment, is unlikely to benefit from the type of education on offer, and the onus tends to be placed on the child to adapt to the curriculum and pedagogy of the school, rather than the other way round (Pijl 2010). As we saw in chapter 5, legal systems of redress in the Netherlands are either to a civil court if the case involves a private school or to an administrative court if the case involves a state school. The type of accessible and user-friendly tribunals which exist in England and Scotland are not available, reflected in the relatively low numbers of cases which reach either administrative or civil courts each year (only 50–100 cases). Non-judicial dispute settlement methods are also available, involving a degree of formality, although less formal mediation methods are used in some instances (depending on the nature of the case). However, these are also used rather sparsely, not exceeding the number of court cases per year.

Use and perceptions of different redress mechanisms

From the summary above, it is evident that all four countries provide access to judicial and non-judicial routes to redress. There has been little comparative work on the way in which redress mechanisms are viewed by parents on the one hand and public bodies on the other. However, the ESRC study, drawn on in chapters 3 and 4, facilitates the making of direct comparisons between England and Scotland with regard to the use of different systems of redress and local authority officers' and parents' perceptions of the strengths and weaknesses of each.

Looking at the dispute resolution models that have been introduced over the past decade and a half, it is evident that the English tribunal, underpinned by the discourse of legality or rights, has been used extensively, whereas the Scottish tribunal has been used relatively little. This is almost certainly as a result of the extremely high qualification criteria which were set by the Scottish Government in response to active lobbying against its inception by Scottish local authorities. Mediation, underpinned by a discourse of consumerism rather than rights, has been used very little in either country, despite the fact that it is regarded as a more satisfactory form of dispute resolution by local authority officers, particularly in Scotland. Despite this approval, it appears that local authorities north and south of the Border do not go out of their way to encourage parents to use mediation. Although parents of children with statutory support plans are informed routinely of the different routes of redress, parents of children with non-statutory individual education plans or other support plans often struggle to obtain this information, which may not be accessible on local authorities' websites. Local authority officers in both countries questioned the necessity and cost of independent mediation, since they believed that council staff were able to deal with most disputes without involving a third party. Council staff in both countries thought that tribunals were a more expensive and stressful way of resolving disputes compared with mediation. In Scotland, there was a strong view that tribunals had shattered the trust which had previously existed between parents and professionals and a tendency to believe that the balance of power had swung too far in the direction of parents. One officer in Scotland commented:

> Parental guidance might emphasise the fact that professional educationists are likely to know more about education and how it works than a lay person – and need not always be suspected of preferring the cheapest option. Parental advice might usefully discuss the possibility that 'taking the views of parents and pupils into account' does not mean the LA must do whatever they wish. (Local authority officer 13)

By way of contrast, parents who had used the tribunal in both England and Scotland regarded it quite positively, whilst recognising that participating in any sort of judicial process was bound to be stressful. They welcomed the fact that the tribunal reached a clear conclusion which they regarded as generally fair, although they were frustrated that local authorities did not always act on tribunal recommendations. Mediation, on the other hand, whilst generally supported by local authorities, was regarded much more sceptically by the minority of parents who used it. Those whose use of mediation led to a successful resolution of their disagreement were positive about it, but some tended to be frustrated by the fact that there was no means of enforcing the settlement reached via the mediator. Some parents using mediation believed that local authorities did not always take the process as seriously as they should, often fielding a representative who was not empowered to enter into negotiations with the parent that were really meaningful, in the sense that they had the authority to enter into an agreement on the authority's behalf. Parents' greater faith in the tribunal compared with mediation is reflected in the much greater use of judicial rather than non-judicial methods of dispute resolution. Their preference for a decisive appeal process, crucially combined with a lack of awareness and understanding of mediation and the likelihood that negotiation, if it has not already resolved the matter, is unlikely to succeed, ultimately accounts for the low take-up of mediation north and south of the Border. In the US, it also seems to be the case that parents whose case is not informally settled prefer to take court action, or perhaps invoke the quasi-judicial 'due process hearing', rather than engage in mediation to resolve disagreements in the field of special educational needs. In the Netherlands, as noted above, neither judicial nor non-judicial action is greatly used as a result of limited opportunities for parents to challenge public bodies' decisions and the existence of a culture which privileges professional and bureaucratic power over that of parents.

Parents' and children's rights

All developed countries seek to obtain better value for money in relation to educational expenditure, and engaging parents more closely as citizens and consumers is often seen as a means of achieving this goal. Harris (2005) and Dean (2002) draw a distinction between contractarian and solidaristic citizenship. Individual competition, associated with contractarian citizenship, uses consumer choice to improve services within a marketised system. Competitive individualism inevitably favours those who are better able to operate as critical consumers, but proponents of this approach believe that individuals seeking the best deal for themselves will bring about a general improvement in services for all. Solidaristic citizenship, by way of contrast, entails individuals working together to shape services in ways which promote equal outcomes and social justice and cohesion. Across all developed countries, efforts to promote parental engagement in education over the past 20 years have employed a blend of contractarian and solidaristic approaches to citizenship, with right-leaning governments tending to favour individualistic approaches and left-leaning governments favouring more collectivist approaches.

In the light of this promotion of consumerism and citizenship, concrete efforts have been made to ensure that parents are involved in education decision making in a range of areas including special educational needs. In addition, in line with the UN Convention on the Rights of the Child, educational policy documents produced in a range of developed countries promote the implementation of services which reflect children's choices. However, in practice there are few concrete measures which ensure children's active engagement. For example, in theory children should always be engaged in drawing up educational targets which feature in individual education plans, but research has found that this often does not happen because of time constraints and beliefs about children's capacities (Kane et al. 2003). This bias is evident in the special education redress systems in the four countries featured in this book, where the judicial and non-judicial systems are generally invoked by parents rather than children or young people and where parents almost exclusively hold procedural rights as decision challengers. Scotland is something of an exception, where young people aged 16–18 have the same right as parents to make a reference to the tribunal or request adjudication or mediation. However, this remains a largely hypothetical right since in practice it is parents, rather than young people, who seek redress.

In the hierarchy of power, it appears to be the case that children's rights are still subordinate to those of their parents and this raises questions about what can be done to provide children with greater rights and greater opportunities to exercise these rights. The Lamb Inquiry which examined parental confidence in the special educational needs system in England (Lamb 2009), recommended the implementation of a right of appeal to the tribunal for children and young people, such as is being introduced in Wales. However, experience in Scotland suggests that unless resources are invested in supporting children and young people, for example, by appointing children's advocacy workers, this right is likely to be little used. Questions also arise in relation to the particular circumstances under which children and young people might wish to bring cases to the tribunal independently of their parents. Perhaps the most obvious example here concerns children who are looked after by the local authority. It is clearly not possible for a local authority to take a case against itself to a tribunal, as discussed in chapter 1, and yet in Scotland, for example, children looked after by the local authority are much more likely than others to achieve very poor educational outcomes, have special educational needs and be excluded from school (Riddell 2009). Looked after children, then, might be regarded as a priority group by local authorities in terms of needing the provision of advocacy to help with the resolution of disagreements, including the use of tribunal or mediation. For some children with special educational needs, particularly those with severe cognitive impairments, it may be more important to devise imaginative ways of eliciting preferences in relation to modes of learning, rather than trying to help them participate in tribunals, which are likely to remain the terrain of adults.

Social disadvantage and access to justice

A major theme across all four countries concerns disproportionalities in the identification of certain types of special educational needs, particularly social, emotional and behavioural difficulties and learning difficulties/cognitive impairments amongst children from socially disadvantaged backgrounds. Harry (2007) and Donovan and Cross (2002) have noted the disproportional identification of mental retardation and emotional disturbance amongst African American boys and argue that this reflects both poverty at home and discriminatory attitudes amongst teachers. According to Harry, the social marginalisation of disadvantaged groups through placement in special education, often outside of mainstream classes, is not a problem which is unique to the US, but is common to, and in, many other societies. For example, in the Czech Republic, 50 per cent of Roma students are placed in mainstream schools, compared with 1.8% of non-Roma students (European Roma Rights Centre 2005). This pattern is also reflected in New South Wales, Australia, where Aboriginal students account for just 5 per cent of total school enrolments, but in some parts of the state constitute 40 per cent of enrolments in special schools (Graham et al. 2010).

Theoretically, children identified as having special educational needs should benefit from the additional resources allocated. However, Hills et al. (2010), drawing on analysis by Keslair and McNally (2009), show that the performance of children identified as having behavioural, social and emotional difficulties in England declines over time relative to that of their peers. Riddell et al. (2010) have demonstrated that children living in the most deprived areas of Scotland are more likely to be identified as having additional support needs than children living in more advantaged areas, but are proportionately less likely to have a statutory support plan which would enable their parents to make a reference to the tribunal. These discrepancies are particularly marked for children with social, emotional and behavioural difficulties. Across all four countries discussed in this book, and many others in the developed world, there are concerns that special education systems serve to further isolate pupils who are already socially marginalised. Furthermore, in line with notions of competitive individualism, redress systems may skew resources in the direction of those who are already relatively socially advantaged. Whether the actions of relatively advantaged parents in seeking legal redress helps to improve the situation for all children with special educational needs remains a moot point. Recognising these social inequalities, the Scottish Government has passed legislation to establish a national advocacy service for parents who wish to use judicial and non-judicial redress systems in Scotland. Similar needs for support have been identified in England by the Lamb Inquiry, but have not as yet been implemented. Clearly, researchers will need to explore the extent to which such services are successful in facilitating access to justice for socially disadvantaged parents, particularly where children with special educational needs face exclusion from school.

Balancing competing models of administrative justice in different countries

Returning to the theme of trade-offs between models of administrative justice within different countries, it is evident that the four countries featured here occupy different positions on a spectrum. The US system is highly legalistic, encouraging consumerist forms of parental power as drivers of an educational market. This policy approach has been emulated in England, where, since the mid-

1990s, parents have been able to challenge the decisions of the public authorities in the field of special educational needs via an independent appeal process. At the same time, the US has a system which might be described as bureaucratised professionalism, where school board officers and other professionals wield a great deal of power in the assessment of children's needs and decisions on resources and placement. Scotland has been slower than England in providing accessible routes to redress for parents, but legislation has put in place a tribunal which is broadly similar to that in England, but with greater restrictions on access. This has meant that professionalism and bureaucracy remain stronger in Scotland than in England, with less use of judicial and non-judicial approaches to dispute resolution. By way of contrast, the Netherlands has a system where bureaucracy and professionalism are extremely powerful, and parents and children appear to have weaker routes of redress. This seems to have produced a system where parents have fewer opportunities to challenge public bodies' decisions and the majority of children with special education needs continue to be educated in segregated settings. As noted by Zoontjens (chapter 5 in this volume), possibly because parents have such difficulty in challenging professional decisions, for most people in the Netherlands the special education system remains a 'terra incognita'.

The important question, of course, is what mix of policy models is most effective in delivering the best outcomes for children with special educational needs. It would appear that providing parents with accessible legal remedies to enable them to challenge decisions which they believe to be wrong is very important in increasing the profile of special educational needs and raising its share of the educational cake. The Cinderella status of special educational needs in the Netherlands, where parents have very limited rights, appears to support this argument. At the same time, allowing rampant individual competition, and encouraging a culture in which litigation is seen almost as a sport by many US citizens (see Russo and Osborne, chapter 6 in this volume), may have the effect of widening inequalities in access to special education resources. Whilst middle class parents may thrive in such a regime, exacting financial penalties from the state when they feel they have been badly served, less powerful groups may be further marginalised by a system which stigmatises and segregates. In England and Scotland, attempts have been made to devise a system where proportionate dispute resolution is used and a range of models of administrative justice are kept in play, so that parents' rights are balanced against the need for public bodies to maintain a role as arbiters in the fair distribution of resources. In the aftermath of the economic crisis, whose aftershocks continue to reverberate across the world, it will be even more crucial for countries to ensure that social justice goals are not forgotten, as competition for scarce resources increases.

Concluding comments

Throughout this book we have reflected on the use of mediation, and the broader role of negotiation/settlement, in the realisation of parents' rights. There is an increasing momentum towards settlement of disputes in relation to educational arrangements for individual children with special needs and disabilities through non-judicial means. Mediation may be highly effective when the problem relates to inter-personal communication, which may be resolved by encouraging individuals to reflect on their relationship with each other and how this may be improved in the future. On the one hand, when the dispute concerns resource allocation, the essentially 'private' aspect of mediation, and the more widely used mechanism of negotiation/settlement, can arguably lead to less assertive and knowledgeable parents achieving a worse settlement than they might have done through the more open judicial process. The risks here relate not only to individual outcomes, but also, from a collective societal viewpoint, to the fair allocation of public resources. On the other hand, although formal judicial processes may produce fairer and more transparent outcomes for the individuals who use them, they are more likely to be invoked by socially advantaged parents, with the risk that they too can accentuate inequality. These are real and persistent dilemmas which cannot be easily resolved. Nonetheless, there is clearly a need to encourage a better understanding of the salience of parents' social location amongst all those who are involved in working with children with special educational needs and their families or charged with ensuring equal access to justice for all those seeking to enforce their rights in this field.

Negotiation continues to play a dominant role in the resolution of disagreements concerning special educational needs, from the early stages of disagreement through to the final stages in a dispute that has entered the appeal process. Mediation is, however, seen as affording better safeguards for parents, procedurally speaking, than direct negotiation as it is a structured process which affords some guarantee of 'fair play'. Mediation is thus regarded as an acceptable means of realising an underlying belief that if the parties can be brought to a settlement it means that the ultimate objective of a dispute resolution process is served. As discussed in chapter 2, however, there are those such as Genn (2010), who question whether this provides a sufficient moral basis for the legitimacy that its proponents would attach to mediation. Moreover, dispute resolution in a public sphere must serve the ends, and operate in ways, that are consistent with the wider goals of administrative justice. Cane (2009, p. 215), for example, says that 'the ultimate concern of administrative justice is the acceptability and legitimacy of decisions by government departments affecting individual citizens' and that to that end 'facilities for the resolution of disputes and grievances about primary decision-making' afforded by tribunals and courts can be important. Yet there are other values that have currency, such as giving people choice of how to resolve their dispute, and ensuring that they are able to participate effectively in their own right and that the cost of dispute resolution is not disproportionate (however that may be defined). These are consistent with the consumerist and citizenship underpinnings of parental rights in the field of special educational needs, noted above, and in any event seem difficult to ignore, especially at a time when the sway of economic forces is so strong.

References

Adler, M. (2003), 'A socio-legal approach to administrative justice', *Law and Policy*, 25, (4), 323–352.

Bowers, T. and Parrish, P. (2000), 'Funding of special education in the United States and England and Wales', in McLaughlin, M.J. and Rouse, M. (eds), *Special Education and School Reform in the United States and Britain* (London: Routledge Falmer), pp. 167–195.

Cane, P. (2009), *Administrative Tribunals and Adjudication* (Oxford: Hart).

Clarke, J., Newman, J., Smith, N., Vidler, E. and Westmarland, L. (2007), *Creating Consumer-Citizens: Changing Identities in the Making of Public Services* (London, Sage).

Dean, H. (2002), *Welfare Rights and Social Policy* (Harlow: Prentice Hall).

DfE (Department for Education) (2011) *Support and Aspiration: A New Approach to Special Educational Needs and Disability A Consultation*, Cm 8027 (Norwich: The Stationery Office).

Donovan, M.S. and Cross, C.T. (eds) (2002), *Minority Students in Special Education and Gifted Education* (Washington D.C. National Academy of Sciences).

European Roma Rights Centre (2005), *The ERRC Legal Strategy to Challenge Racial Segregation and Discrimination in Czech Schools* http://tolerance.cz/english/sem2000/ecmi07.htm

Florian, L. and Pullin, D. (2000), 'Defining difference: a comparative perspective on legal and policy issues in education reform and special educational needs', in McLaughlin, M.J. and Rouse, M. (eds), *Special Education and School Reform in the United States and Britain* (London: Routledge Falmer), pp. 11–38.

Genn, H. (2010), *Judging Civil Justice* (Cambridge: Cambridge University Press).

Graham, L., Sweller, N. and Van Bergen, P. (2010), 'Detaining the usual suspects: charting the use of segregated settings in New South Wales government schools', *Contemporary Issues in Early Childhood*, 11, 3, 234–248.

Harris, N. (2005), 'Empowerment and state education: rights of choice and participation', *Modern Law Review*, 68, 6, 925–957.

Harry, B. (2007), 'The disproportionate placement of ethnic minorities in special education', in Florian, L. (ed.), *The SAGE Handbook of Special Education* (London: Sage Publications), pp. 67–84.

Hills, J., Brewer, M., Jenkins, S., Lister, R., Lupton, R., Machin, S., Mills, C., Modood, T., Rees, T. and Riddell, S. (2010), *An Anatomy of Economic Inequality in the UK: Report of the National Equality Panel* (London: LSE).

Kane, J., Riddell, S., Banks, P., Baynes, A., Dyson, A., Millward, A. and Wilson, A. (2003), 'Special educational needs and individualised educational programmes: issues of parent and pupil participation', *Scottish Educational Review*, Vol. 35, 1, 38–48.

Keslair, F. and McNally, S. (2009), *Special Educational Needs in England: Final Report for the National Equality Panel* (London: Centre for Economic Performance, London School of Economics).

Lamb, Sir B. (2009), *Lamb Inquiry, Special Educational Needs and Parental Confidence* (London: DCSF).

Pijl, S.J. (2010), 'Preparing teachers for inclusive education: some reflections from the Netherlands', *Journal of Research in Special Educational Needs*, 10, Issue Supplement s1, 197–201.

Riddell, S. (2003), 'Procedural Justice and Special Educational Needs Assessments in England and Scotland', *International Journal of Inclusive Education,* 7, 3, 201–23.

Riddell, S. (2009), 'Social justice, equality and inclusion in Scottish education', *Discourse: Studies in the Cultural Politics of Education*, 30, 3, 283–296.

Riddell, S., Stead, J., Weedon, E. and Wright, K. (2010), 'Additional support needs reform and social justice in Scotland', *International Studies in Sociology of Education*, 20, 3, 179–199.

Index

For Product Safety Concerns and Information please contact our EU representative GPSR@taylorandfrancis.com
Taylor & Francis Verlag GmbH, Kaufingerstraße 24, 80331 München, Germany

www.ingramcontent.com/pod-product-compliance
Ingram Content Group UK Ltd.
Pitfield, Milton Keynes, MK11 3LW, UK
UKHW021301190926
475701UK00009B/574
* 9 7 8 1 1 3 8 2 7 1 0 9 8 *